PROFESSIONAL JQUERY™

W9-DDY-823

PROFESSIONAL

jQuery™

Cesar Otero
Rob Larsen

John Wiley & Sons, Inc.

Professional jQuery™

Published by
John Wiley & Sons, Inc.
10475 Crosspoint Boulevard
Indianapolis, IN 46256
www.wiley.com

ISBN: 978-1-118-02668-7
ISBN: 978-1-118-22211-9 (ebk)
ISBN: 978-1-118-23592-8 (ebk)
ISBN: 978-1-118-26079-1 (ebk)

Manufactured in the United States of America

10 9 8 7 6 5 4 3 2 1

For general information on our other products and services please contact our Customer Care Department within the United States at (877) 762-2974, outside the United States at (317) 572-3993 or fax (317) 572-4002.

Wiley publishes in a variety of print and electronic formats and by print-on-demand. Some material included with standard print versions of this book may not be included in e-books or in print-on-demand. If this book refers to media such as a CD or DVD that is not included in the version you purchased, you may download this material at http://booksupport.wiley.com. For more information about Wiley products, visit www.wiley.com.

Library of Congress Control Number: 2012932975

To Kala.

—Cesar Otero

This book is dedicated to my wife, Jude, for her support throughout this project.

—Rob Larsen

CREDITS

EXECUTIVE EDITOR
Carol Long

PROJECT EDITOR
Ed Connor

TECHNICAL EDITOR
Andrew Montalenti

PRODUCTION EDITOR
Kathleen Wisor

COPY EDITOR
Kim Cofer

EDITORIAL MANAGER
Mary Beth Wakefield

FREELANCER EDITORIAL MANAGER
Rosemarie Graham

ASSOCIATE DIRECTOR OF MARKETING
David Mayhew

MARKETING MANAGER
Ashley Zurcher

BUSINESS MANAGER
Amy Knies

PRODUCTION MANAGER
Tim Tate

VICE PRESIDENT AND EXECUTIVE GROUP PUBLISHER
Richard Swadley

VICE PRESIDENT AND EXECUTIVE PUBLISHER
Neil Edde

ASSOCIATE PUBLISHER
Jim Minatel

PROJECT COORDINATOR, COVER
Katie Crocker

PROOFREADERS
Paul Sagan, Word One
Scott Klemp, Word One

INDEXER
Johnna VanHoose Dinse

COVER DESIGNER
LeAndra Young

COVER IMAGE
© iStock / Andrew Rich

ABOUT THE AUTHORS

 **CESAR OTERO** is a freelance web developer currently living in Mountain View, California. His technical interests include Python, Django, JavaScript, and jQuery. Cesar occasionally contributes articles to IBM's developer works. He holds a degree in electrical engineering from the Inter American University of Puerto Rico.

 **ROB LARSEN** has more than 12 years' experience as a front-end engineer and team leader, building websites and applications for some of the world's biggest brands. He is currently a Senior Specialist, Platform at Sapient Global Markets.

Prior to his time at Sapient, Rob spent time at Isobar, The Brand Experience, Cramer, and as an independent consultant. Over the course of his career, Rob has solved unique problems for clients like Adidas, Motorola, Philips, Reebok, Gillette, Boston's Museum of Science, State Street Corporation, and Harvard Kennedy School.

Rob is an active writer and speaker on web technology with a special focus on emerging standards like HTML5, CSS3, and the ongoing evolution of the JavaScript programming language. He's also active in the open-source community, helping to bridge the gap between the front lines of web development and the people actively working on the tools that drive the web.

ABOUT THE TECHNICAL EDITOR

 **ANDREW MONTALENTI** is a technologist with over a decade of experience in software engineering, and over eight years of experience in web application development. He is cofounder and CTO at Parse.ly, a tech startup that provides insights to the web's best publishers. He is also the founder and CEO of Aleph Point, a boutique consulting firm that specializes in large-scale text analysis, information retrieval, and UI design, with a focus on Python, Grails, and JavaScript web programming. He specializes in the rapid development of prototypes. Prior to becoming an entrepreneur, he was a technical lead and project manager for a small, super-bright team within a top-tier investment bank.

ACKNOWLEDGMENTS

MANY THANKS to Andrew Montalenti for taking on the technical editing, and, of course, the editors at Wiley, Carol Long and Edward Connor. A special thanks to Lynn Haller: without her, this project wouldn't have come together. Also, PJ Cabrera for both helping me kickstart my writing career and introducing me to jQuery.

Thanks to the Hacker Dojo for providing such an amazing coworking space, and to the dojo members who contributed input.

I'm also grateful to my friends and family for their support and input, most notably Paul Wayland, Alejandro Valsega, and Valerie Voigt.

—CESAR OTERO

I'D LIKE TO THANK the folks at Wiley for giving me this opportunity and especially Carol Long and Edward Connor for helping me hit the ground running. I'd be crazy not to mention our copy editor, Kim Cofer, and Andrew Montalenti, our technical editor. Without them, we'd be working without a spotter. Knowing they're there to catch us when we stumble makes this a lot easier. I'd also like to thank Renée Midrack and Lynn Haller from Studio B for steering me towards the opportunity in the first place.

I definitely want to thank the jQuery team and community for being generally phenomenal. Here's a big high five to all the great front-end engineers I've worked with at Cramer, Isobar, and Sapient — thanks for pushing me to be a better programmer, manager, and colleague. From Sapient, I need to specifically thank Jarlath Forde, Joe Morgan, and Alvin Crespo for direct support on the book.

—ROB LARSEN

CONTENTS

INTRODUCTION

OVER THE PAST SEVERAL YEARS JAVASCRIPT has undergone a remarkable transformation. Where once it was a "toy" language relegated to secondary status it's now one of the most important programming languages in the world. With the ongoing importance of Ajax-based development and the rise of full-featured JavaScript libraries, the stigma surrounding JavaScript has all but vanished. As easily the most popular and beginner-friendly library, jQuery is responsible for the lion's share of that progress.

jQuery is more than just a beginner's choice; however, it's in use at some of the largest organizations in the world, adding interactivity to billions of page views every month. Amazon, IBM, Twitter, NBC, Best Buy and Dell are just a few of the companies using jQuery in production.

With a web-scale footprint it should come as no surprise that jQuery is evolving at web speed. 2011 saw no less than three major releases and the community surrounding jQuery continues to blossom as developers the world over contribute bug fixes, plugins and work on related projects like jQuery UI and QUnit. This flurry of activity ensures that jQuery presents a full-featured option for any developer looking to do world-class JavaScript development.

This is true no matter what programming philosophy or technique is followed: jQuery is prominently featured in the front end of Java/Spring, PHP, .NET, Ruby on Rails, and Python/Django stacks all over the Web.

If you have experience with HTML, CSS, and JavaScript, then this book is for you. This book will expand your jQuery knowledge by focusing on the core library with the benefit of strong core JavaScript expertise coloring the lessons. The first few chapters will help you to set up a development environment, and reviews important JavaScript concepts. Chapters 3 to 7 examine the jQuery core concepts. The second half of the book focuses on applying jQuery in the real world, detailing jQuery UI, plugin development, templates, unit testing, best practices, and JavaScript design patterns applied with jQuery.

Hopefully, this book will give you the hardcore jQuery chops you'll need to solve whatever problems the Web throws at you.

WHO THIS BOOK IS FOR

This book is aimed at three groups of readers:

- ➤ Experienced server-side web application developers looking to move more heavily into the client side using the world's most popular front-end library

- ➤ Experienced JavaScript programmers looking to ramp up quickly on jQuery

- ➤ Novice to intermediate jQuery developers looking to expand their jQuery knowledge into more advanced topics

This book is not aimed at beginners. For beginners looking to start from the basics of HMTL, CSS, and JavaScript/jQuery development, *Beginning JavaScript and CSS Development with jQuery (Wrox Programmer to Programmer)* by Richard York is a more appropriate choice.

WHAT THIS BOOK COVERS

Professional jQuery provides a developer-level introduction to jQuery as well as providing an in-depth look at more advanced features.

Starting with the first part, the book offers an in-depth introduction to jQuery fundamentals, selecting elements, manipulating to the DOM, and binding and reacting to browser events.

Building on that solid foundation the book will outline more advanced topics, including plugin development, unit testing with JavaScript and other advanced features of the library.

The book focuses on features available as of jQuery 1.7.1, but tries to make note of feature support in older versions of the library wherever relevant.

HOW THIS BOOK IS STRUCTURED

This book is divided into two parts, jQuery Fundamentals and Applied jQuery. jQuery Fundamentals introduces the core concepts and Applied jQuery focuses on more advanced subjects.

Part I — jQuery Fundamentals consists of the following chapters:

1. **Getting Started** — This chapter sets up an environment for developing and debugging jQuery and JavaScript code and defines the code standards that will be used throughout the book. It also talks about ways to package JavaScript for production and sets up code.

2. **JavaScript Primer** — This chapter goes through the basics of the JavaScript programming language to firm up the foundation upon which the rest of the book is built. jQuery is a JavaScript library after all, and many of the best features spring from clever application of core JavaScript techniques.

3. **The jQuery Core** — Introduces the basic functions that make up the library. It illuminates usages of the core jQuery functions and then introduces many of the utility functions that you'll use to perform a variety of tasks.

4. **DOM Element Selection and Manipulation** — This chapter dives into one of the core features of jQuery, the ability to select and manipulate HTML elements.

5. **Event Handling** — Introduces another key feature of jQuery, the cross-browser ability to bind and manage browser events.

6. **HTML Forms, Data, and Ajax** — Explores one of the biggest revolutions in web development of the past 10 years — Ajax.

7. **Animations and Effects** — Explores some of the shortcuts that jQuery offers for animating components in your web applications such as moving, fading, toggling, and resizing elements.

Part II — Applied jQuery covers the following topics:

8. **jQuery UI Part I: Making Things Look Slick** — Introduces jQuery UI. jQuery UI is an associated user interface library for jQuery that contains widgets, effects, animations, and interactions.

9. **jQuery UI Part II: Mouse Interactions** — Explores additional jQuery UI features including moving, sorting, resizing, and selecting elements with the mouse.

10. **Writing Effective jQuery Code** — Teaches a variety of techniques, best practices, and patterns that you can apply to your code immediately to make it more efficient, maintainable, and clear.

11. **jQuery Templates** — Focuses on the jQuery Template plugin. jQuery templates are a standard way of marrying data and markup snippets.

12. **Writing jQuery Plugins** — Focuses on authoring jQuery plugins. Being able to extend the power of jQuery with custom methods is a fundamental skill for a top jQuery developer.

13. **Advanced Asynchronous Programming with jQuery Deferred** — Introduces the jQuery Deferred object. `$.Deferred`, introduced in version 1.5, is a chainable utility object that provides fine-tuned control over the way callback functions are handled.

14. **Unit Testing with QUnit** — Introduces the general concept of unit testing and goes into detail with the specific unit testing framework created and used by the jQuery project itself, QUnit.

WHAT YOU NEED TO USE THIS BOOK

jQuery supports the following web browsers. You'll need one of them to run the samples provided with the book:

➤ Firefox 3.6, Current – 1 version

➤ Internet Explorer 6+

➤ Safari 5.0.x

➤ Opera Current – 1 version

➤ Chrome Current – 1 version

CONVENTIONS

To help you get the most from the text and keep track of what's happening, we've used a number of conventions throughout the book.

Boxes with a warning icon like this one hold important, not-to-be-forgotten information that is directly relevant to the surrounding text.

 The pencil icon indicates notes, tips, hints, tricks, and asides to the current discussion.

As for styles in the text:

➤ We *highlight* new terms and important words when we introduce them.

➤ We show keyboard strokes like this: Ctrl+A.

➤ We show file names, URLs, and code within the text like so: `persistence.properties`.

➤ We present code in two different ways:

```
We use a monofont type with no highlighting for most code examples.
```

```
We use bold to emphasize code that is particularly important in the present context
or to show changes from a previous code snippet.
```

SOURCE CODE

As you work through the examples in this book, you may choose either to type in all the code manually, or to use the source code files that accompany the book. All the source code used in this book is available for download at www.wrox.com. When at the site, simply locate the book's title (use the Search box or one of the title lists) and click the Download Code link on the book's detail page to obtain all the source code for the book. Code that is included on the website is highlighted by the following icon:

**Available for
download on
Wrox.com**

Listings include the filename in the title. If it is just a code snippet, you'll find the filename in a code note such as this:

Code snippet filename

 Because many books have similar titles, you may find it easiest to search by ISBN; this book's ISBN is 978-1-118-02668-7.

Once you download the code, just decompress it with your favorite compression tool. Alternately, you can go to the main Wrox code download page at www.wrox.com/dynamic/books/download. aspx to see the code available for this book and all other Wrox books.

ERRATA

We make every effort to ensure that there are no errors in the text or in the code. However, no one is perfect, and mistakes do occur. If you find an error in one of our books, like a spelling mistake or faulty piece of code, we would be very grateful for your feedback. By sending in errata, you may save another reader hours of frustration, and at the same time, you will be helping us provide even higher quality information.

To find the errata page for this book, go to www.wrox.com and locate the title using the Search box or one of the title lists. Then, on the book details page, click the Book Errata link. On this page, you can view all errata that has been submitted for this book and posted by Wrox editors. A complete book list, including links to each book's errata, is also available at www.wrox.com/misc-pages/ booklist.shtml.

If you don't spot "your" error on the Book Errata page, go to www.wrox.com/contact/techsupport .shtml and complete the form there to send us the error you have found. We'll check the information and, if appropriate, post a message to the book's errata page and fix the problem in subsequent editions of the book.

P2P.WROX.COM

For author and peer discussion, join the P2P forums at p2p.wrox.com. The forums are a Web-based system for you to post messages relating to Wrox books and related technologies and interact with other readers and technology users. The forums offer a subscription feature to e-mail you topics of interest of your choosing when new posts are made to the forums. Wrox authors, editors, other industry experts, and your fellow readers are present on these forums.

At http://p2p.wrox.com, you will find a number of different forums that will help you, not only as you read this book, but also as you develop your own applications. To join the forums, just follow these steps:

1. Go to p2p.wrox.com and click the Register link.

2. Read the terms of use and click Agree.

3. Complete the required information to join, as well as any optional information you wish to provide, and click Submit.

4. You will receive an e-mail with information describing how to verify your account and complete the joining process.

You can read messages in the forums without joining P2P, but in order to post your own messages, you must join.

Once you join, you can post new messages and respond to messages other users post. You can read messages at any time on the Web. If you would like to have new messages from a particular forum e-mailed to you, click the Subscribe to this Forum icon by the forum name in the forum listing.

For more information about how to use the Wrox P2P, be sure to read the P2P FAQs for answers to questions about how the forum software works, as well as many common questions specific to P2P and Wrox books. To read the FAQs, click the FAQ link on any P2P page.

PART I
jQuery Fundamentals

- ▶ **CHAPTER 1:** Getting Started

- ▶ **CHAPTER 2:** JavaScript Primer

- ▶ **CHAPTER 3:** The jQuery Core

- ▶ **CHAPTER 4:** DOM Elements Selection and Manipulation

- ▶ **CHAPTER 5:** Event Handling

- ▶ **CHAPTER 6:** HTML Forms, Data, and Ajax

- ▶ **CHAPTER 7:** Animations and Effects

Getting Started

WHAT'S IN THIS CHAPTER?

➤ What jQuery is Good At

➤ The jQuery "Hello World" Code Conventions and Development Tools

You probably spend more time in front of a computer than with your significant other. Hence, having a nice comfortable seat, a fast computer, and software that accelerates development is essential.

Starting with the basics, we'll review requirements, different ways to obtain jQuery, and how to run it on both client and server, and set up some conventions for the rest of the book, using Google's JavaScript standards.

In this chapter you set up your work environment for developing and debugging jQuery and JavaScript code. A major portion of development time goes into debugging, so a good debugger isn't really an option. After reviewing Firebug, Chrome, and IE debuggers a portion of this chapter covers debugging JSON, tools for inspecting HTTP headers, and the JSLint code quality tool.

You learn to package your `.js` files for production use, explore tools, and establish some coding conventions.

WHAT JQUERY IS GOOD AT

Without a doubt, one of the strong points of using jQuery is how it diminishes many cross-browser concerns. Without it, writing cross-browser-compatible JavaScript code is a tedious, and unnecessary, exercise. It's difficult not to marvel at how much time is saved getting things running in both IE and Firefox with jQuery. The core is also excellent at traversing the DOM tree and selecting elements. It's also very lightweight, with the production version standing at 29 kb, which is minified and compressed. That's a lot of kick for a small file. When debugging and testing, you're better off using the uncompressed development version, which is 212 kb.

jQuery is also good at handling fairly complex JavaScript code with relatively little code. This was one of my initial attractions to the framework. For a newbie trying to learn the "ropes" with Ajax, jQuery lowers the learning curve. Understanding what's going on under the hood is important, but as a first step, using `$.ajax()` isn't a bad start.

An active user community means active support. Googling jQuery returns about 36.8 million results at the time of this writing. New official and third-party plugins come out every day, extending its core functionality. With so many projects dependent upon jQuery, it's easy to find help online (and really cool print books too).

With that said, it might be overkill in some cases. Remember that including the jQuery library has some overhead, even if it's small, and if you're only using the selectors to get an element by its ID, then the built-in JavaScript capability of the browser is enough. But, if you plan to build a feature-rich, dynamic Ajax web application, jQuery is the way to go.

HARDWARE AND BROWSER REQUIREMENTS

Your requirements for running jQuery are very light: a computer, smart phone, or device capable of running a modern browser. The browser requirements are fairly liberal as well. The official site lists the following browsers that are supported as well:

➤ Firefox 2.0+

➤ Internet Explorer 6+

➤ Safari 3+

➤ Opera 10.6+

➤ Chrome 8+

The following browsers are known to give problems:

➤ Mozilla Firefox 1.0.x

➤ Internet Explorer 1.0–5.x

➤ Safari 1.0–2.0.1

➤ Opera 1.0–9.x

➤ Konqueror

Quirksmode has a great page detailing the CSS compatibilities of different browsers, including CSS3. To find out more visit `www.quirksmode.org/css/contents.html`.

OBTAINING JQUERY AND JQUERY UI

Besides the links found on `jquery.com` for downloading the production and development versions, you have a few other options for obtaining or linking to the jQuery libraries. You can link to several content delivery networks (CDNs) in your applications such as Google, Microsoft, and the jQuery CDN that are mentioned on the official jQuery website.

The following code illustrates obtaining jQuery from the various available CDNs. Simply add a script tag, point it at the proper URL and you're ready to go.

```
<script src="https://googleapis.com/ajax/libs/jquery/1.7.1/jquery.min.js"></script>

<script src="http://ajax.aspnetcdn.com/ajax/jQuery/jquery-1.7.1.min.js"></script>

<script src="http://code.jquery.com/jquery-1.7.1.min.js"></script>
```

Code snippet is from cdns.txt

A Git repository also hosts a "Work in Progress," or WIP, build. This is a constantly revised development version, which is not meant for production. The WIP build is generated every minute. To use this bleeding-edge version you can directly link from `http://code.jquery.com/jquery-git.js` or you can clone the Git repository to build jQuery from scratch. The following code shows the Git command used to clone the latest version of the library.

```
$ git clone https://github.com/jquery/jquery.git jquery-build
```

In order to build, you'll need GNU to make 3.8+ and Node.js .2+. After cloning the repo, change into the jQuery directory and execute the `make` command. This will generate a complete minified version of jQuery, and run through JSLint (more on JSLint later). If you don't want this, run `make jquery` instead of `make`.

"HELLO WORLD" EXAMPLE

No programming text is complete without the ubiquitous "Hello World" program:

```
<html>
    <head>
        <script
         src=" https://ajax.googleapis.com/ajax/libs/jquery/1.5.1/jquery.min.js">
        </script>
        <script
            jQuery(document).ready(function(){
                alert('Hello World');
            });
        </script>
    </head>
    <body>
    </body>
</html>
```

Code snippet is from hello-world.txt

In a nutshell, a minified version of jQuery is loaded from an online CDN over the Web. The jQuery function is called with the document object passed in as a parameter. This creates a jQuery wrapper object which has a `ready()` method whose only argument is a function. This function is invoked when the browser has finished converting the HTML on the page into the document object model (or DOM). At that moment, your function displays an alert, "Hello World." There's much more going on here than meets the eye and if you don't understand yet, don't worry. Chapter 2 revisits JavaScript, and most importantly, JavaScript's way of managing functions. There you'll understand the reason for the anonymous function. In Chapters 3 and 4, you see the concepts behind the jQuery wrapper, and using selectors to get elements from the DOM. Then you'll have a better idea of what `jQuery(document)` means. Finally, in Chapter 5 you get acquainted with event handling, such as the aforementioned `.ready()`. So, although the code written for this example is rather brief, it's rather dense and will be unpacked later.

JAVASCRIPT CONVENTIONS USED IN THIS BOOK

Throughout this book, we'll stick to a small subset of the *Google JavaScript Style Guide* found at `http://google-styleguide.com/svn/trunk/javascriptguide.xml` and the *jQuery Core Style Guidelines* found at `http://docs.jquery.com/jQuery_Core_Style_Guidelines`. The Google JavaScript Style Guide specifies the following:

➤ Declarations of variables always use `var`, except when intentionally creating a global variable.

➤ Always use semicolons. This is important for minifying code.

➤ Constants are uppercase, with each word separated by an underscore.

➤ Functions, variables, and method names all use camel case notation with the first letter lowercase.

➤ Classes and enum names also use camel case notation but with the first letter uppercase.

The big exception to any of these rules is when an example demonstrates how not to do something.

The jQuery team also published a set of conventions for development of the core library. The documentation mentions the following:

➤ **Spacing code:** Abundantly use spacing, using tabs to indent code. Don't use white spaces at the end of lines and empty lines should not have spaces either. This example illustrates the preferred spacing.

```
if ( test === "test string" ) {
    methodCall( "see", "our", "spacing" );
}
```

➤ **Using comments:** For multiple-line comments use `/* */` and for single-line comments use `//`, with an empty line above the comment. The single-line comment precedes the comment that it refers to, and should be the only thing on the line.

```
// my comment
var x = 'blah';

var x = 'blah'; // bad
```

➤ **Equality:** Always use identity (===) comparison over simple quality (==). The jQuery team makes the exception of using simple equality when testing for null. As the guidelines say, "It's actually quite useful to do == null or != null as it will pass (or fail) if the value is either null or undefined."

➤ **Block presentation:** Always use braces for control constructs (if/else/for/while/try), and distribute over multiple lines. Don't use the one liner ifs without braces. Braces should always be placed on the same line as else/else if/catch. It's also suggested to avoid replacing if/else statements with ternary operators. Here are some examples:

```
// bad
if( stuffHappens ) alert('blaaaah');

// good
if( stuffHappens ) {
    alert('blaaaah');
}

// also good
if( option ) {
    // code here
} else {
    // code here
}
```

➤ **Function call format:** Include extra spaces around function call arguments with the exception of when a function call is nested, a function call is empty, or object literals and arrays are passed:

```
// These are OK
f( arg );
f( g(arg) );
f();
f({ });
f([ ]);
```

➤ **Arrays and objects:** No extra spacing is preferred for empty object and array literals, but do use a space after commas and colons:

```
var a  = {};
var b = [];
var c = [ 1, 2, 3 ];
```

➤ **Assigning variables/objects:** Always use a semicolon at the end of assignments with an endline afterwards. As noted by the Google Style Guide, semicolons should always be used.

➤ **Type checks:** Table 1-1 demonstrates what strings to use when doing a type check.

TABLE 1-1: Type Checks

OBJECT	TYPE CHECK EXPRESSION
String	typeof object === "string"
Number	typeof object === "number"
Boolean	typeof object === "boolean"
Object	typeof object === "object"
Element	object.nodeType
null	object === null
null or undefined	object == null

Table 1-2 illustrates objects that are type checked using the jQuery API.

TABLE 1-2: Type Checks Using the jQuery API

OBJECT	JQUERY METHOD TO USE FOR TYPE CHECKING
Plain Object	jQuery.isPlainObject(object)
Function	jQuery.isFunction(object)
Array	jQuery.isArray(object)

Table 1-3 illustrates methods for type checking `undefined`.

TABLE 1-3: Checking **undefined**

OBJECTS	
Global Variables	typeof variable === "undefined"
Local Variables	variable === undefined
Properties	object.prop === undefined

➤ **RegExp:** Create regular expressions (RegExp) with `.text()` `.exec()`.

➤ **Strings:** Double quotes are preferred to single quotes.

The docs also mention validations with JSLint. JSLint is covered in the next section on Development Tools.

There are differences between the Google JavaScript Style Guide and jQuery's Style Guide. For example, the Google JavaScript Style Guide suggests the use of single quotes, whereas the jQuery team uses double quotes as a standard. For this book, we stick to the jQuery team's suggestion.

DEVELOPMENT TOOLS

You have several tools at your disposal for developing JavaScript and jQuery, other than the traditional editor/browser setup. If your style of development is more command-line-oriented, you have jconsole and Rhino. jconsole is a web application that enables you to interactively enter JavaScript code. It comes with a few additional functions such as `print()`, `load()`, and `clear()`. Multiple line entries are allowed by pressing Ctrl+Enter after each line. Pressing Enter executes the current code in the text area. jconsole also maintains a history of entered commands, which is accessed by pressing the up or down arrows to use the previous and next entered commands. Figure 1-1 shows jconsole in action.

FIGURE 1-1

To load jQuery into jconsole use the `load()` function with a CDN URL. For example:

```
load('https://ajax.googleapis.com/ajax/libs/jquery/1.5.1/jquery.min.js');
$(document).click(function(){ alert('It worked!'); });
```

jconsole also has a tab autocompletion feature, and the ability to dynamically change the execution context by entering the `scope()` function. For quickly testing small bits of code, jconsole really is priceless.

You probably picked up this book for using jQuery in a browser environment, but it's also possible to use jQuery on the server. Mozilla Rhino is a JavaScript interpreter implemented in Java. It's commonly used to embed JavaScript into Java applications. It features a JavaScript shell, debugger, and compiler. Along with the framework Envjs, also written by the jQuery creator John Resig, it's possible to use jQuery in a server environment. Envjs is a portable JavaScript implementation of a "headless browser," or browser that lacks a user interface that provides a scripting environment. It's possible to get the same effect with other host environments, such as Google V8, but I'll stick to Rhino for this example.

Table 1-4 lists the dependencies for getting up and running with jQuery and Rhino.

TABLE 1-4: Dependencies for Running jQuery with Rhino

DEPENDENCY	FUNCTIONALITY
Rhino	Command-line JavaScript interpreter
JLine (optional, but useful)	Java console input library, readline-like functionality
Envjs	"Headless browser," scripting environment

To get readline-like functionality, run Rhino with the JLine library. This way you can access the history of commands by pressing the up arrow, and edit entered characters with left and right arrow keys. The following code block shows how to get started with JLine.

```
java -cp js.jar:jline.jar jline.ConsoleRunner \
org.mozilla.javascript.tools.shell.Main -opt -1
```

The following session demonstrates how to get jQuery running with Rhino. Lines with `js>` indicate input.

```
js> load('env.rhino.1.2.js');
[  Envjs/1.6 (Rhino; U; Linux i386 2.6.24-25-generic; en-US; rv:1.7.0.rc2)
Resig/20070309
PilotFish/1.2.13  ]
js> window.location = "http://localhost"
http://localhost
js> load('jquery.js');
js> jQuery

function (selector, context) {
    return new jQuery.fn.init(selector, context);
}
```

Back in the regular browser world, Firefox also has plugins for simplifying your life as a developer. One of the most popular is Firebug, a debugging tool for web development. Firebug enables live editing of HTML and CSS, debugging, and monitoring of web applications. Figure 1-2 shows the Firebug interface.

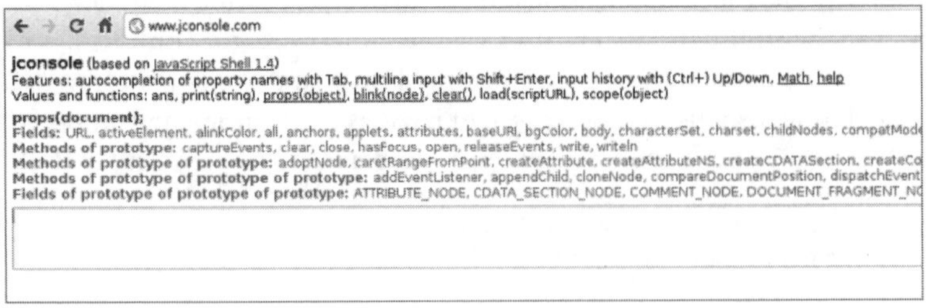

FIGURE 1-2

To install Firebug, go to Tools ⇨ Add Ons on the menu bar, click Get Add Ons on the resulting dialog, and search for Firebug. Click Add to Firefox. After installing, you'll notice a bug icon at the bottom right of the window. Click it to open the Firebug explorer.

You'll notice Firebug includes six tabs: Console, HTML, CSS, Script, DOM, and .NET. Each tab contains features to simplify your life as a web developer.

The Console tab provides an output interface for viewing warning and error messages, logs, debugging information, general info, and XmlHttp Request and response objects.

Firebug loads into the global namespace an object called console. Use this object to log console messages of the inner workings of your application. The console object contains several methods, which you can check out at `http://getfirebug.com/wiki/index.php/Console_API`. Table 1-5 lists a small subset of the methods contained by the console object with descriptions provided by the Firebug Wiki.

TABLE 1-5: Some Console Object Methods

METHOD	DESCRIPTION
`console.log(object[, object, ...])`	Writes a message to the console.
`console.debug(object[, object, ...])`	Writes a message to the console, including a hyperlink to the line where it was called.
`console.info(object[, object, ...])`	Writes a message to the console with the visual "info" icon and color coding and a hyperlink to the line where it was called.
`console.warn(object[, object, ...])`	Writes a message to the console with the visual "warning" icon and color coding and a hyperlink to the line where it was called.
`console.error(object[, object, ...])`	Writes a message to the console with the visual "error" icon and color coding and a hyperlink to the line where it was called.
`console.assert(expression[, object, ...])`	Tests that an expression is true. If not, it will write a message to the console and throw an exception.
`console.clear()`	Clears the console.

The profiler is used for performance analysis of your application. Profiling is as simple as clicking a button. Load your page, click the Profile button under the Console tab, use your application for a while, and click the Profile button again to generate a report.

The HTML tab enables you to peruse the DOM and edit HTML code "on the fly." The tags are displayed in a tree widget, which expands to show the children of each node. The CSS tab also enables editing of styles and layout, while neatly displaying the values of each cascading style sheet.

Perhaps one of Firebug's most useful features is the interactive command line, which allows execution of JavaScript code in the context of the web page you're developing. There's no need to manually load jQuery and other dependencies. The console also has command completion. The Script tab also has the ability to add/remove breakpoints, view stack traces, and watch variable values over time.

It's also possible to use Firebug with other browsers via Firebug Lite. To do so, include in your HTML file a script tag that links to the .js file online:

```
<script src="https://getfirebug.com/firebug-lite.js"></script>
```

Along with Firebug, Live HTTP Headers, another Firefox plugin, gives a nice rounded view of the data flowing in and about your application. The "Live" means that the HTTP header information is displayed in real time.

To install, follow the same procedure you used for Firebug. After installing, you can access Live HTTP Headers from the menu bar by selecting Tools ⇨ Live HTTP Headers. A dialog displays the get requests with all kinds of useful debug information such as server type, encoding type, cookies, host, and so on. The replay feature enables you to edit request headers and resend a URL, great for debugging Ajax.

When trying to load JSON data directly from Firefox, the default behavior of the browser is to give you a Download File dialog. Using the JSONView extension Firefox will interpret and display JSON data in a nice legible manner. Furthermore, the nodes are collapsible, similar to when Firefox interprets XML data directly. For example, say you have the following .json file:

```
{
  "users": {
    "user": [{
        "name":"Tom",
        "email":"tom@bigcorp.com",
        "role":"admin"
    },
    {
        "name":"Nick",
        "email":"nick@bigcorp.com",
        "role":"employee"
    },
    {
        "name":"Lynn",
        "email":"lynn@bigcorp.com",
        "role":"manager"
    },
    {
        "name":"Carol",
        "email":"carol@bigcorp.com",
        "role":"manager"
    }]
  }
}
```

With JSONView, the output should look similar to the following code snippet. The minus sign indicates a collapsible node, and a plus sign indicates an already collapsed node. The last two records are collapsed.

```
{
  - users: {
    - user: [
        - {
            name: "Tom",
            email: "tom@bigcorp.com",
            role: "admin"
          },
        - {
            name: "Nick",
            email: "nick@bigcorp.com",
            role: "admin"
              },
          + { ... },
          + { ... }
        ]
      }
}name: "Lynn"email: "lynn@bigcorp.com"
role: "manager"
```

Google Chrome also offers a top-notch development environment. A set of developer tools comes by default with Chrome. These are in active development, so the feature set is constantly evolving and improving. The Chrome Developer Tools come with all the same goodies as Firebug: an interactive command line, element inspector, the ability to add/remove breakpoints, and so on. To access the developer tools press Shift+Ctrl+I.

Figure 1-3 shows the Chrome Developer Tools.

FIGURE 1-3

Microsoft, never one to be left behind, includes its own set of development tools with Internet Explorer, although not as complete as Firefox's plugins and extensions. They're called the F12 Developer Tools, which is a handy reminder of the key needed to access them. The F12 Developer Tools are quite similar to Chrome's Inspector and Firebug's. Figure 1-4 shows Internet Explorer's F12.

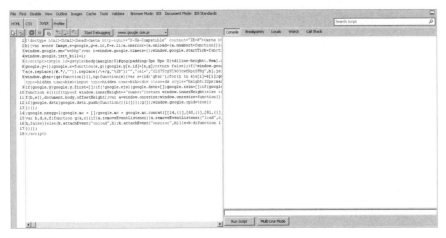

FIGURE 1-4

Another essential tool is JSLint, the "JavaScript code quality tool," which checks and validates code. Douglas Crockford explains it best: "JSLint takes a JavaScript source and scans it. If it finds a problem, it returns a message describing the problem and an approximate location within the source." Just like jconsole, there's a convenient web application for validating your JavaScript code; see www.jslint.com. Optionally, clone the source from Github at https://github.com/douglascrockford/JSLint.git. In the source code you'll find fulljslint.js, which you can run outside of a web browser. Using Mozilla Rhino, you can use a short script for validating JavaScript/jQuery code from a command line.

```
load('JSLint/fulljslint.js');
var src = readFile(arguments[0]);
var passes = JSLINT(src);
print(passes ? 'Passes Lint Validation' : 'Failed Validation');
```

The functions load(), readFile(), and print() are Rhino-specific functions. The load() function takes the input string pointing to the fulljslint.js file, loads the code into memory, and executes it giving you access to the JSLINT() function. The readFile() function obtains the first parameter passed in from the command line, using the arguments array, and reads the source into a string. The JSLINT() function then validates the content of the src variable, and returns a Boolean object signaling whether or not the string validated. With a ternary operator a message is then printed to the console depending on whether the file read passed validation. Open a terminal, and try validating a simple JavaScript file:

```
$ rhino runLint.js test.js
Passes Lint Validation
```

If the above seems like too much work, you can also take a look at the project, jslint4java at http://code.google.com/p/jslint4java/, which simplifies the command to the single line seen in the following code snippet.

```
$ java -jar jslint4java-1.4.jar test.js
```

In addition to JSLint, there's an alternative code quality tool that's gaining popularity, JSHint `www.jshint.com/`. Originally forked from JSLint in order to create a more configurable version of JSLint that didn't enforce one particular coding style, JSHint has grown into a project of its own, with its own goals and ideals. If you find yourself running up against specific, non-configurable rules in JSLint or merely want to try out an alternative then JSHint might be a good option for you.

Finally, after finishing development of any modules or plugins, and validating using JSLint, you'll probably want to minify your `.js` files for production. Several options are available on the market, but I'll just discuss a few. Some popular open source options are the YUI Compressor, the Google Closure Compiler, UglifyJS, and JSMin. YUI Compressor offers the additional ability to minify CSS alongside your JS. While it is convenient to have one-stop shopping for all of your minification needs, the two dominant choices right now are UglifyJS, a NodeJS-based utility, and Google's Closure Compiler. Both are in use at major JavaScript performance-obsessed projects. UglifyJS is the minifier of choice for the jQuery project itself and the Java-based Closure Compiler is the minification choice for HTML5 Boilerplate `http://html5boilerplate.com`. Both can be run from the command line, which allows you to automate this minification process alongside any JSLint tests you may also be running. The HTML5 Boilerplate project offers a full-featured Ant build script which does both minification and JSLint or JSHint tests (and more).

If you're interested in getting your hands dirty, the following code samples show how easy it is to run both UglifyJS and Closure Compiler from the command line.

Assuming you're running NodeJS, installing UglifyJS is as simple as the following:

```
npm install -g uglify-js
```

Running it is as simple as calling UglifyJS, setting the -o (output) flag, and setting an output filename and passing in the input filename to be mininfied:

```
uglifyjs -o app.min.js app.js
```

Using Closure Compiler is also very simple. Simply download the latest jar from `http://closure-compiler.googlecode.com/files/compiler-latest.zip`, unzip it and then run the following from the command line. It follows a similar pattern with an input file and an output file provided as command line arguments.

```
java -jar compiler.jar --js app.js --js_output_file app.min.js
```

If you aren't a guru, or don't understand how to use a command line, don't sweat it. There are the web-based applications to get the same results.

DEBUGGING JAVASCRIPT AND JQUERY

It's time to use the tools discussed in this chapter, especially Firebug (or the Chrome developer tools) and JSLint—they'll catch many errors for you. Rather than using alert calls with variables and objects, place breakpoints and inspect the values of each object/variable as they are manipulated by your scripts. Also, make liberal use of the real-time editing.

Separating markup from functionality is the way of modern web development, for many reasons. One reason for keeping your JavaScript/jQuery code in an external `.js` file is that it helps the debugger correctly match the error with the actual line number, not to mention it keeps your code unobtrusive.

Make your projects test driven. Later in the book, I describe how to use QUnit to add unit tests to your projects. As you probably already know, although jQuery handles most cross-browser concerns, it's still necessary to test in different browsers and environments, including portable devices like iPhones. Having a full test suite will make it easier to detect and squash cross-browser bugs.

For small bits of code, like one-liners, use console applications like jconsole and Rhino to make sure you're getting the expected results.

Make sure of the obvious. The most experienced programmer may miss something obvious. Who hasn't added a script tag for including jQuery, only to find out much later, to great dismay, that the path was mistyped? The debuggers will let you know quickly if the $ variable is undefined.

Being aware of browser-specific issues and their particular behaviors is important. That trailing comma in an object literal is just *priceless* after you've developed in a browser like Firefox or Safari for hours, only to have your beautifully scripted project explode in IE.

One point we mention time and again in this book is the necessity to really grok JavaScript. The learning curve for jQuery is low; it's a wonderful framework for beginners to create dazzling JavaScript effects. However, advanced users doing full development shouldn't treat it as a black box. It embraces and extends JavaScript, and thus requires JavaScript understanding.

Of course, there are all the other regular tips as well. For example, make sure your HTML and XML are well formed, use version control tools like Mercurial or Git, and call on the Google or Stack overflow gods when you're really stuck.

USING THE FIREQUERY PLUGIN

There's another Firefox plugin for your jQuery repertoire: the FireQuery plugin, which enhances Firebug for better handling of jQuery. Features include:

➤ Elements and handlers dynamically added by jQuery at run time can be visually inspected in the console.

➤ Elements that are members of a jQuery "collection" are highlighted in the window on a mouseover event.

➤ jQuery-specific expressions are recognized and presented in the Firebug console.

One of its more interesting features is the "jQuerify" button, which dynamically loads jQuery into any web page viewed by the browser. This is very useful if you're running tests with jconsole, because it cuts out the step of loading jQuery from a CDN using the `load()` command in the console.

After you install FireQuery, you can check that everything is working correctly by visiting the test page at `http://firequery.binaryage.com/test/index.html`. Figure 1-5 shows a successful install of FireQuery.

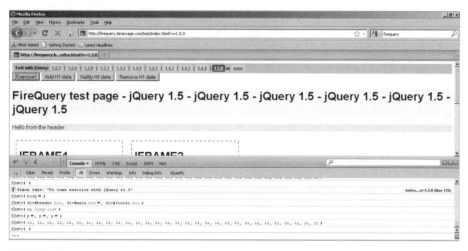

FIGURE 1-5

SUMMARY

In this chapter you explored a couple of different options for obtaining, building, and running jQuery. Not only that, but you know now how to run JavaScript code from the server, instead of just the traditional browser client. After you've learned to develop your own jQuery plugins, you can use the techniques in this chapter to minify and prepare your code for deployment to a larger audience. You've also sipped a taste of the many debugging tools out there.

In the following chapter you go full blast into coding, and put all these tools to use, but our focus is more toward general JavaScript before getting back to jQuery-focused code.

2

JavaScript Primer

WHAT'S IN THIS CHAPTER?

➤   Understanding JavaScript Primitives

➤   Using Variables, Functions, and Objects

➤   JavaScript Scope, Closures, and Execution Context

It's easy to forget that jQuery is a JavaScript framework; after working with it for an appreciable amount of time, jQuery seems and feels almost like its own language. Inside the jQuery source, examples are abound of how to apply great JavaScript techniques. However, to truly master jQuery, you must master JavaScript. JavaScript is a very powerful and expressive language. All the major browsers support it, it's the driving force in modern web applications utilizing Ajax, and now it's made a major debut on the mobile web platform.

JavaScript inherits some names and naming conventions from the Java language, but that's about it. In contrast to Java, JavaScript is a dynamically typed, object-oriented scripting language that runs in a host environment, usually a web browser. It contains no classes, and uses prototypes for inheritance. It also has functional programming features; closures, functions as first-class objects, anonymous functions, and higher order functions. In reality, JavaScript is closer to a language like Lisp than it is to Java.

This chapter revisits a subset of JavaScript syntax necessary for understanding how jQuery works, its core, and how to better apply it to your projects. It begins with a brief review of data types and object-oriented programming, and then delves into functional programming with JavaScript. The end of the chapter lists some pitfalls in the language that you need to watch out for. Whenever you have a doubt about what's going on with JavaScript, use this chapter as a reference. Also, while you're running through this chapter feel free to test out the examples using jconsole or Rhino.

UNDERSTANDING NUMBERS

Like any other programming language, JavaScript manipulates values such as numbers or text. The kinds of values a language can work with are its data types. JavaScript supports the basic data types of number and string. All numbers are 64-bit double-precision, and range from −5e-324 to 1.7976931348623157e308. In other words, there's no difference between integers and floating-point numbers; they are both just numbers. The following example uses the `typeof` operator to demonstrate:

```
> typeof 1;
number
> typeof 1.5;
number
```

Code snippet is from typeof.txt

All JavaScript numbers are represented in binary as IEEE-754 Doubles. That also means you should apply some caution when doing arithmetic. For example, if you are summing two number values that, in your mind, represent a currency operation, you may get very unexpected results, as shown in the following code:

```
> .1 + .2
0.30000000000000004
```

Code snippet is from unexpected-addition.txt

Unfortunately, JavaScript has no built-in decimal type. The language does offer two methods on `Number`, `toPrecision`, and `toFixed`, which will format a number using a fixed number of decimal places. The following code shows both in action.

```
>var num = 1234.12345123;
>num.toFixed(2);
1234.12

var num2 = 1234.12345123 ;
num2.toPrecision(8);
1234.1234
```

Code snippet is from decimal.txt

If you use a number, or obtain a result, outside of the 64-bit range, JavaScript returns a special number called Infinity, or -Infinity. Division by zero returns Infinity. There is one more special value, NaN, meaning "Not a Number" which is a "toxic value" that is often the source of bugs.

NaNs occur when attempting to cast an invalid string object to a number. It has a viral nature; in other words, performing an operation between numbers and a NaN returns a NaN. You can test if a variable is a NaN by using the built-in `isNaN()` function.

```
> 10*1+100 - 1 - Nan
NaN

>var x = NaN;
>isNaN(x);
true
```

Code snippet is from isNaN.txt

JavaScript supports Octal (base 8) and Hexadecimal (base 16) numbers as well. Octal literals are prefixed with a 0 (zero), and Hexadecimal numbers are prefixed with an x.

JavaScript has a built-in `Math` object for common math operations. For example, you can use the `Math.round()` method to get a two decimal point accuracy.

```
Math.round((.1+.2)*100)/100
0.3
```

Code snippet is from math-round.txt

Making good use of the built-in objects can save time and effort.

WORKING WITH STRINGS

Strings are a series of zero or more 16-bit unicode characters enclosed by either single quotes or double quotes. I emphasize unicode because of its importance in internationalization. There is no special data type for characters. Strings are also (immutable) objects, and hence have methods and properties as well.

```
>"Test String".indexOf("S")
5
>"Test String".charAt("5")
S
```

Code snippet is from stringMethods.txt

Later on, you'll see how you can augment the built-in `String` object to your benefit.

UNDERSTANDING BOOLEANS

The Boolean type represents true and false values. In the appropriate context, such as inside an `if` statement, any value is converted to Boolean to test for "truthiness." Empty strings, NaNs, null, undefined, the number zero (0), and the keyword `false` evaluate as false in a test; any other values resolve to true.

```
if(''){
    console.log('something happens');
} else {
    console.log('nothing happens');
}
nothing happens
```

Code snippet is from basic-boolean.txt

There are also Boolean operations: the logical and (&&), or (||), and not (!). These are useful for validating required fields in inputs, a very common task.

```
function validate(){
    var name_input = 'Jimmy';
    var age_input;
    return name_input && age_input;
}

if(validate()){
    console.log('pass');
} else {
    console.log('fail');
}

// outputs fail
```

Code snippet is from boolean-operations.txt

NaN by definition means *Not a Number*. Try the following:

```
>typeof NaN
Number
```

Code snippet is from typeofNaN.txt

See any irony? This is just one of the many strange behaviors of the typeof operator.

COMPARISON TYPES

JavaScript has the equality (==) and identity (===) operators. The == is dangerous, because it does type coercion to make comparisons. For example:

```
> 1 == "1";
True
```

Code snippet is from simple-comparison.txt

More than likely, this isn't what you want. Hence, the === operator will return true if both the left-hand side and right-hand side really are identical.

```
> 1 === "1";
False
```

Code snippet is from strict-comparison.txt

There's also the equivalent != and !==. Always use === and !==.

A BRIEF NOTE ABOUT DATES

The built-in Date object is created using the new operator and the Date() constructor function (more on prototypes and constructors later), and is used for date and time data, as you would suspect. Creating a new Date object without any parameters results in a Date object of the current date and time.

```
> var thisMoment = new Date();
> console.log(thisMoment);
Sun Jan 30 2011 21:37:19 GMT-0400 (AST)

> thisMoment.getFullYear();
2011
```

Code snippet is from date.txt

Although Date is a convenient object, and it's certainly useful to know it's there, I highly recommend using the open source Date.js library for doing date/time arithmetic found at www.datejs.com.

REVIEWING MISCELLANEOUS TYPES

Declaring a variable without giving it a value, or accessing a nonexistent object property, results in a type called undefined. Null is a built-in object, and indicates there is no value. Both convert to a false when doing comparison, but it's best to avoid undefined. In many JavaScript interpreters, undefined is re-assignable, resulting in hackish code like the following:

```
undefined = true;
if(undefined){
    console.log('tricked you!');
}

// output: tricked you!
```

Code snippet is from undefined-equals-true.txt

See www.gibdon.com/2006/05/javascript-difference-between-null-and.html for a full explanation of the differences between null and undefined.

The following is a list of the different types found in JavaScript. Regular expressions, or `RegEx`, are beyond the scope of this tutorial.

➤   Number

➤   String

➤   Boolean

➤   Object

➤   Function

➤   Array

➤   Date

➤   RegEx

➤   Null

➤   Undefined

Some additional built-in error types are useful with `try/catch` statements. Creating an error object is usually done in conjunction with `throw`.

```
try{
    throw new Error('Something really bad happened');
} catch(e){
    console.log(e.name + ": " + e.message);
}

// Error: Something really bad happened
```

Code snippet is from try-catch.txt

The following list displays the different error types.

➤   Error

➤   EvalError

➤   RangeError

➤   ReferenceError

➤   SyntaxError

➤   TypeError

➤   URIError

REVISITING VARIABLES

Variables are declared by either assignment (`implicit`) or using the keyword `var` (`explicit`). If you declare a variable using `var`, it becomes permanent and cannot be deleted. You can declare a variable as many times as you desire without causing any errors. Uninitialized variables contain the special value `undefined`.

```
i = 0; // implicit declaration
var i = 0; // explicit declaration
var x; // undefined
```

Code snippet is from variable-declaration.txt

Scope refers to the visibility of a variable or object. Globals are visible anywhere in your application, whereas locals are visible only in the function in which they're declared.

Implicitly declared variables always have global scope, even if declared inside a function body. To avoid problems, it's suggested that you always use `var` when declaring variables. Douglas Crockford, the creator of JSLint, also suggests that you declare all your variables at the top of a given scope, to avoid redefinition problems. If you declare the same variable outside a function and inside, the local variable supersedes the outer variable, or hides it.

```
function where(){
   var v1 = "local scope";
   v2 = "global scope";
}

where();

console.log( v2 );
console.log( v1 );

// result
global scope
ReferenceError: v1 is not defined
```

Code snippet is from global-scope.txt

Variable names must start with a character letter, underscore, or dollar sign followed by zero or more alphanumeric characters, underscores, or dollar signs. Keywords cannot be used as a variable name.

UNDERSTANDING OBJECTS

Objects are collections of properties, each property having a name and value. Properties can contain any type except for `undefined`, and are assignable even after the object is created. Arrays, functions, and regular expressions are all objects. Numbers, strings, and Booleans are also objects, but they are immutable. You can instantiate objects in a couple ways. One is to use the `new` keyword:

```
var myObject = new Object();
```

Code snippet is from new-object.txt

The `new` keyword invokes a constructor function, or more commonly constructor. The constructor initializes the newly created object. The following code snippet shows a constructor for an object called `Zombie`, which initializes its property name and then instantiates a `Zombie` object using `new`. The `this` keyword refers to the current object, and it cannot be assigned a value, although you can save its value in another variable.

```
// constructor
function Zombie( name ){
    this.name = name;
}
var smallZombie = new Zombie( "Booger" );
```

Code snippet is from this.txt

A more convenient way to instantiate a new object is to use object literals; in this manner objects are more like hashes or associative arrays from other languages.

```
var myObject = {};

var objectWithProperties = {
    "property1": "a string value",
    "myObjectAsProperty": myObject
};
```

Code snippet is from object-literal.txt

Avoid using a trailing comma on the last value of your list of properties. It's interpreted inconsistently across browsers. You can access an object's properties by using either square brackets or the dot operator. The following code snippet shows both cases:

```
objectWithProperties['property1']
"a string value"
objectWithProperties.property1
"a string value"
```

Code snippet is from property-lookups.txt

Using the former case allows you to use keywords for properties (not that I recommend that); the latter doesn't. On the other hand, using the dot method is shorter. JSLint will encourage you to use the dot syntax when appropriate. Because properties can be objects, you can nest objects at an arbitrary level.

```
var species = {
    'mammals' :  {
      'biped': {
          'monkey' : 'George' ,
          'human' : 'Tim'
      }
    }
}

console.log(species.mammals.biped.human);
```

Code snippet is from nested-objects.txt

JavaScript is a dynamic language, so to update a property just reassign its value. To remove a property from an object, use the `delete` operator. There's no danger in deleting a nonexistent property. To access the properties of an object you can use the `for...in` loop as shown in the following code snippet:

```
var obj = {
    'property1' : 1,
    'property2' : 2
}

var i;

for( i in obj ){
    console.log( i );
}

property1
property2
```

Code snippet is from for-in.txt

JavaScript uses prototypal inheritance; in other words, objects inherit directly from objects, and they create other objects. More concisely, an object inherits the properties of another object. There are no classes, a big difference as compared to languages like Java or C#. The prototype is a model for other objects.

This may sound difficult, but in practice, it's much simpler than class/object-based inheritance. A built-in object, `Object.prototype`, is inherited by all other objects, and is at the top of the inheritance hierarchy. Each object in an inheritance tree is linked by the `prototype` property.

Property retrieval occurs through delegation. Upon attempting to retrieve a nonexistent property, JavaScript looks for the property from the prototype object. If it still fails to find the property, it runs up the prototype tree looking for the property, until it reaches the primordial `Object` `.prototype`. After that, if it still can't find the property in question, the interpreter just gives up and returns an `undefined`.

Functions that are properties of objects are called methods, which are either added to an object by assignment to the prototype object, or directly. Methods always receive a free argument, bound in the function scope as `this`, which refers to the object the method was invoked from. The following code snippet shows an example of prototype-based inheritance. Behind the scenes, a `Monster` `.prototype` object is created.

```
function Monster( type ){
    this.type = type;
}

Monster.prototype.getType = function(){
    return this.type;
}

function Zombie( name ){
    this.name = name;
```

```
  }

  Zombie.prototype = new Monster();

  Zombie.prototype.eatPeople = function(){
    console.log( 'tastes like chicken' );
  }
```

A reference is a pointer to the location of an object instance. Objects are reference types and because all objects are passed by reference, changing a property bound to a prototype changes the prototypes of all other objects based on that prototype, as demonstrated in the following code:

```
> smallZombie.eatPeople();
Tastes like chicken
> delete Zombie.prototype.eatPeople;
true
> smallZombie.eatPeople();
TypeError: Object #<a Zombie> has no method 'eatPeople'
```

When creating new objects, watch out for how you initialize them. The following code shows two variables that refer to the same object, although you might think you're taking a shortcut:

```
// obj1 and obj2 reference the same object
var obj1 = obj2= {};

// obj1 and obj2 refer to different objects
var obj1 = {},
obj2 = {};
```

Objects are self-aware, or in other words, know their own properties. To test for the existence of a property, use the `hasOwnProperty()` method, which returns a `boolean` value.

Global variables, as any programmer will tell you, should be avoided. There are a few ways to avoid cluttering the global namespace; one way is to use a single global variable that serves as the top-level object for all the methods and properties of your program or framework. By convention, namespaces use all capital letters, but beware that constants are usually written in caps as well. You learn much more about using objects for code organization in Chapter 10.

```
ZOMBIE_GENERATOR = {};
ZOMBIE_GENERATOR.Zombies = {
  smallZombie : 'Booger',
  largeZombie : 'Bruce'
}
```

Now your Zombies won't clash with any other variables in the global namespace. The other way to minimize clutter is using closures, which you'll explore in a bit.

USING FUNCTIONS

Douglas Crockford, in his book *JavaScript: the Good Parts* calls, functions the "best thing about JavaScript." He's right. Once you truly understand them you'll be certain to agree. The flexibility and power of JavaScript functions can't be understated.

This is *especially* true when working with jQuery, a library that fully leverages the expressive power of JavaScript functions.

Basically defined, a function is a block that encapsulates a series of JavaScript statements. Functions can accept and return values. The following code sample shows a simple function statement that explicitly returns the value of a calculation.

```
function calc( x ){
    return x*2;
}
console.log( calc( 10 ) )
20
```

Code snippet is from simple-function.txt

If a function doesn't return a specific value, it returns `undefined`. The following code sample shows a function statement that omits a return value. It still performs its operations, adjusting the value of the variable x, but returns `undefined` when the return value is examined in the console.

```
var x = 2;

function calc(  ){
    x = x*2;
}

console.log( x )
4

console.log ( calc() );
undefined
```

Code snippet is from undefined-value.txt

This is where things get interesting. Unlike languages like C# and Java, however, JavaScript functions first-class objects. This means that JavaScript functions can be handled like any other JavaScript object. Functions can be assigned to a variable or stored in another data structure (such as an array or object); they can be passed as an argument to another function; they can be the return value of another function and can take the form of an anonymous function: a function not bound to an identifier at all. The following code shows a function expression assigned to a variable.

```
var calc = function(x){
   return x*2;
}

calc( 5 );
10
```

Code snippet is from function-variable-assignment.txt

Using parentheses with the function name will pass the result of the executed function rather than the reference to the function.

```
var calc = function(x){
   return x*2;
}

var calcValue = calc( 5 );

console.log( calcValue );
10
```

Code snippet is from function-variable-result.txt

For a jQuery developer, two other features of first-class functions are especially important. The first is the ability to pass functions as arguments to other functions. The second is the anonymous function. Combine these and you have one of the hallmarks of fluent jQuery code. jQuery wouldn't be jQuery without the ability to pass function expressions into other functions on the fly. This will become especially clear when you learn about event handling in Chapter 5. Beyond events, jQuery is *full* of methods that accept function arguments.

The following code shows example of both of these important features. The function `reporter` accepts a function as an argument and logs the return value of the executed function argument. Additionally, two of the examples feature anonymous functions. The first is an anonymous function that contains no statements at all, but, as you've just learned, still returns undefined. The second is an anonymous function that returns the string "a simple string."

```
function reporter( fn ){
   console.log( "the return value of your function is "+ fn() );
}

reporter( function(){} );
the return value of your function is undefined

reporter( function(){ return "a simple string" } );
the return value of your function is a simple string

function calc() {
```

```
    return 4 * 2
}

reporter( calc );
the return value of your function is 8
```

Code snippet is from function-arguments.txt

One especially important variation on the anonymous function is the "immediately-invoked function expression" (IIFE) or "Self-executing anonymous function." Why two names? Read Ben Alman's blog post for a well-thought out discussion of the name for this very common pattern: http://benalman.com/news/2010/11/immediately-invoked-function-expression/. Whatever you decide to call it, this pattern is defined as a function expression wrapped in parentheses, and then immediately invoked. The simple trick of wrapping the function expression in parentheses forces the JavaScript engine to recognize the function(){} block as a function expression and not the beginning of a function statement. The following code sample illustrates this pattern with a simple example that accepts two values and simply adds them together.

Available for download on Wrox.com

```
(function( x,y ){
    console.log( x+y );
})( 5,6 );
11
```

Code snippet is from iife.txt

Because it's immediately invoked, this pattern is used to ensure that the execution context of the code block is as expected. This is best illustrated in one of the most important uses of this pattern. By passing in arguments to the function at execution you can "trap" variables in the *closure* created by the function. A closure is a function that "closes over" variables from the current execution context inside the body of a function. This is extremely powerful and you'll see several real-world uses of this in Chapter 12, when you learn about some advanced jQuery plugin patterns. For now, the following code sample will illustrate a basic usage of this pattern. It will also introduce another interesting feature of JavaScript functions, the ability for a function to return another function.

In the sample, the IIFE is set to a variable, message. message returns another function that simply logs a message about the value of x. The interesting part is that when we pass in an initial value of x as an argument to the function, we capture that value within the closure created at the time of function execution. No matter what happens to x in the outer scope, the closure remembers the value of x from the time of the function's execution.

Available for download on Wrox.com

```
var x = 42;
console.log( x );
var message = (function( x ){
    return function() {
        console.log( "x is " + x );
    }
})( x );
message();
```

```
x = 12;
console.log( x );
message();
```

Code snippet is from captured-variables.txt

Even with just this simple introduction you should begin to see the power of JavaScript functions. In the sections that follow in this chapter and the chapters that follow you'll learn even more about the power of functions.

UNDERSTANDING EXECUTION CONTEXT

Execution context is the object within which your code is executing. Access to context occurs through the `this` keyword, which refers to the object it resides within. In the current version of the language, if your code doesn't reside in a custom object or function, it will then belong to the global context.

As a note, in future versions of the language, including "strict mode" a special subset of the language defined the 5th edition of the JavaScript standard available in a small subset of browsers, functions defined without specific context are bound to `undefined` as their `this` value.

The `eval` and `setTimeout` functions also have their own separate execution context.

```
> console.log(this);
[object DOMWindow]
```

Code snippet is from this-value.txt

When execution of a function or method begins, JavaScript creates a new execution context and enters into that function's execution context. When a function finishes executing and returns, control is relinquished back to the original execution context, and the current context is set up for garbage collection except in the case of a closure where the context persists.

WORKING WITH SCOPE AND CLOSURES

When discussing scope it's important to consider where a variable is defined as well as its lifetime. Where is the variable accessible? In the case of JavaScript, scope is maintained at the function level, not the block level. Hence, variables defined with the keyword `var` and parameters are visible only inside the function in question.

A nested function has access to its outer function's variables, except for `this` and arguments. The mechanism through which a nested function continues to keep the references of its outer function even after the outer function finishes execution is called closure. Closures also help to reduce namespace pollution.

Each time an enclosed function is called, a new scope is created, although the code doesn't change. The following code shows this behavior.

```
function getFunction(value){
  return function(value){
    return value;
  }
}

var a = getFunction(),
    b = getFunction(),
    c = getFunction();

console.log(a(0));
0

console.log(b(1));
1

console.log(c(2));
2

console.log(a === b);
false
```

Code snippet is from more-closures.txt

When defining a standalone function (not bound to any object), this is bound to the global namespace. As a direct result, when creating an inner function within a method, the inner function's this variable is bound to the global namespace, not the method. To circumvent this situation, the enclosing method's this variable is assigned to an intermediate variable called that, by convention.

```
obj = {};

obj.method = function(){
  var that = this;
  this.counter = 0;

  var count = function(){
    that.counter += 1;
    console.log(that.counter);
  }

  count();
  count();
  console.log(this.counter);
}

obj.method();
1
2
2
```

Code snippet is from this-that.txt

UNDERSTANDING ACCESS LEVELS

There's no official syntax for access levels in JavaScript, like the private or protected keywords provided in Java. By default, all members in an object are publicly accessible. But it's possible to get the same effect of private and privileged properties. To achieve the effect of private methods and properties, use closures.

```
function TimeMachine(){
    // private members
    var destination = 'October 5, 1955';

    // public members
    this.getDestination= function(){
        return destination;
    };
}

var delorean = new TimeMachine();
console.log(delorean.getDestination());
// October 5, 1955
> console.log(deloreon.destination);
// undefined
```

Code snippet is from access-levels.txt

The method `getDestination` is a privileged method because it has access to private members of the `TimeMachine`. Meanwhile, the variable, destination, is "private" and its value is only accessible through the privileged method.

APPLYING MODULES

Just like the private and privileged access levels, JavaScript has no built-in syntax for packages. The module pattern is an easy and popular way to create self-contained, modularized code. To create a module, declare a namespace, bind an immediate function to it, and define any private and privileged members. Let's rewrite the `TimeMachine` object.

```
// create namespace object
TIMEMACHINE = {};

TIMEMACHINE. createDelorean = (function(){

  // private
  var destination = '';
  var model = '';
  var fuel = '';

  // public access methods
  return {
    // setters
    setDestination: function(dest){
     this.destination = dest;
```

```
            },

        setModel: function(model){
         this.model = model;
        },

        setFuel: function(fuel){
         this.fuel = fuel;
        },

        // getters
        getDestination: function(){
           return this.destination;
        },

        getModel: function(){
         return this.model;
        },

        getFuel: function(){
         return this.fuel;
        },
        // misc members
        toString : function(){
           console.log( this.getModel() + ' - Fuel Type: ' +
                   this.getFuel() + '  -  Headed: ' + this.getDestination());
        }

        // init procedures go here

    };
())；

var myTimeMachine = TIMEMACHINE. createDelorean;
myTimeMachine.setModel('1985 Delorean');
myTimeMachine.setFuel('plutonium');
myTimeMachine.setDestination('October 5, 1955');
myTimeMachine.toString();

1985 Delorean - Fuel Type: plutonium - Headed: October 5, 1955
```

Code snippet is from module.txt

This module has a factory function that returns an object with your public/private API.

You'll learn more about modules and using them with jQuery in Chapter 10.

USING JAVASCRIPT ARRAYS

Arrays are a special kind of object that works as an ordered collection of values, called elements. Each element has an index, or numeric position, within the array. You can mix and match different kinds of elements in an array. They don't all have to be of the same type. Arrays, just like objects and functions, can also be nested arbitrarily.

As with regular objects, there are two ways to create an array. The first is using the `Array()` constructor:

```
var array1 = new Array(); // empty array
array1[0]  = 1;           // add a number to index 0
array1[1]  = 'a string';  // add a string to index 1
```

Code snippet is from array-constructor.txt

The second and much more common method for creating an array is using an array literal, which consists of brackets enclosing zero or more comma-separated values.

```
var niceArray = [1,2,3];
```

Code snippet is from array-literal.txt

Mixing array literals with object literals provides very powerful construct, and forms the basis for JavaScript Object Notation (JSON,) a popular data exchange format with implementations across many languages beyond JavaScript.

```
var myData = {
   'root' : {
      'numbers' : [1, 2, 3],
      'letters' : ['a', 'b', 'c'],
      'mirepoix' : ['tomatoes', 'carrots', 'potatoes']
   }
}
```

Code snippet is from json.txt

Arrays contain a `length` property, which is always equal to the number of elements in the array minus one. Adding new elements to an array changes its `length` property as well. To remove elements from an array use the `delete` operator.

```
>var list = [1, '2', 'blah', {}];
>delete list[0]
>console.log(list);
,2,blah,[object Object]

>console.log(list.length);
4
```

Code snippet is from delete-operator.txt

Deleting an element does not change the length of the array, it just leaves a hole in the array.

AUGMENTING TYPES

JavaScript allows the facility for binding methods and other properties to built-in types, such as strings, numbers, and arrays. `Strings`, just like any other object, have prototypes. You can also augment `String` with convenience methods. For example, `String` has no method for converting the string `"false"` or `"true"` to a `Boolean`. You can add this capability as the following code demonstrates:

```
String.prototype.boolean = function() {
    return "true" == this;
};

var t = 'true'.boolean();
var f = 'false'.boolean();

console.log(t);
console.log(f);

true
false
```

Code snippet is from string-boolean.txt

Admittedly, it's annoying to have to redundantly type `prototype` every time you want to add a method. Douglas Crockford has a neat bit of code for getting around this, which augments the `Function.prototype` with a method called, `method` (please pardon the redundancy.) This is shown in the following code sample.

```
Function.prototype.method = function(name, func){
    this.prototype[name] = func;
    return this;
};
```

Code snippet is from method-method.txt

Now you can rewrite the `boolean` method for strings:

```
String.method('boolean', function(){
    return "true" == this;
});

> "true".boolean();
True
```

Code snippet is from newBoolean.txt

This technique is useful for writing a library of utility methods and including it in your projects.

APPLYING JS BEST PRACTICES

This is a short list of things to do, and not to do, when developing JavaScript:

➤ Use `parseInt()` to convert a string to an integer, but make sure to always give the base. Better yet, use the unary + operator to convert a string to a number.

```
Good: parseInt("010", 10); // we know it's base ten and not octal
Better: + "010" // simple and efficient
```

Code snippet is from cool-conversions.txt

➤ Use the identity === operator to compare two values. This avoids unwanted type coercion.

➤ Don't leave a trailing comma in an object definition literal, for example:

```
var o = {
    "p1" : 1,
    "p2" : 2, // very bad!
}
```

Code snippet is from trailing-comma.txt

➤ The `eval()` function allows you to take a string and execute it as JavaScript code. Limit use of `eval()`; it opens up your code to all kinds of nasty security issues.

➤ End your statements with a semicolon. This is particularly pertinent when minifying code.

➤ Avoid global variables! Always declare variables using the keyword `var`. Wrap pieces of code inside anonymous functions to avoid name clashes, and use modules.

➤ Use capital letters with a function meant to be used as a constructor with `new`, but don't capitalize the first letter of any other function.

➤ Don't use the `with` statement. I didn't explain what the `with` statement is, because you shouldn't use it.

➤ Create functions inside of loops sparingly. It's extremely inefficient.

PUTTING IT ALL TOGETHER

With the background you now possess on JavaScript, you can grasp a good deal about jQuery without even reading the docs. For example:

```
$('#submit_button_id').click(function(){
    $.ajax({
    'url':'/place2post.php',
    'type':'post',
    'success': function(){
```

```
        // code here
    }
  });
});
```

Code snippet is from put-it-all-together.txt

Here you see many of the topics mentioned in this chapter: an object literal used to send a list of parameters, anonymous functions, or the single dollar sign ($) as a valid identifier. If you didn't already know, $ is an alias for the jQuery core object. It's safe to assume, without looking at a line of code, that internally jQuery is using closures to hide data.

SUMMARY

In this chapter you've had a taste of the dynamic and expressive nature of JavaScript. You've seen a brief review of its data types, expressions, and object-oriented behavior, but most importantly, its functional nature. You can explore each of these topics in far more depth, but you now have a much stronger footing for using jQuery. After reading and really understanding this chapter, you can even open up the jQuery source code and you'll notice that it's not as alien looking as you might have expected before.

NOTE

All code in this chapter is tested using jconsole. Hence, there may be some additional commands available such as print() and clear(), which aren't implemented in browsers.

3

The jQuery Core

WHAT'S IN THIS CHAPTER?

➤ jQuery Utility Functions

➤ Unobtrusive JavaScript the Structure of the jQuery Framework

➤ Understanding the DOM and Events

With a good grasp of JavaScript, you're now ready to tackle the jQuery core. As you know, it has a small footprint, and rather than a mishmash of functionality it has a coherent base. It provides the capacity to easily select elements, separating the behavior of the document from its structure, as well as the ability to manipulate the DOM on the fly.

In this chapter, you learn about basics of using the jQuery core, about wrapper objects, and briefly take a look under the hood. You'll find it useful to have some IDE with the ability to collapse blocks of code when perusing through the jQuery source. You'll also revisit DOM elements and how jQuery handles events.

UNDERSTANDING THE STRUCTURE OF A JQUERY SCRIPT

Some mainstream languages (which shall go unnamed) contain a monolithic "standard library," which really isn't so standard. Rather than using a standard library with a common denominator set of tools, several additional modules are added. This results in unnecessarily large downloads, wasted resources, and functionality that you may never use. On the other hand, the creators of jQuery very thoughtfully kept out these kinds of "add on" modules, and kept the jQuery core small and compact. It is, however, extensible through the plugin system, which is covered in Chapter 12.

The jQuery core function, sometimes also referred to as a factory object, is referenced as either *jQuery()* or, more commonly, by its alias *$()*. If you recall from the JavaScript primer, this is a completely valid name for a variable. In this case, the variable has the type of "function." This function accepts either a selector string, a string of raw HTML, a DOM element, an existing jQuery object, or no argument at all. The function returns a jQuery object which also has several methods attached to it, for example, $.ajax() or $.each(). More on these later.

Typically, your scripts will follow the pattern shown in the following code snippet. Remember to include the jQuery JavaScript file before any other dependent code.

```
<!DOCTYPE html>
<html>
  <head>
    <script src="jquery.js"></script>
    <script >
… jquery code here
    </script>
  </head>
  <body>
<!--
tags here, no embedded javascript here
-->
  </body>
</html>
```

The doctype declaration, as always, is placed at the beginning of the HTML file, even before the html tag, to indicate the document definition type (DTD). In this book, you will always use the HTML 5 doctype, which is very simply:

```
<!DOCTYPE html>
```

Most of the time when you use jQuery, you'll follow the pattern of selecting a DOM element, or set of DOM elements, performing some operation or manipulation on the selected element(s). Select and manipulate, rinse and repeat. The basic call to jQuery is

```
$(selector);
```

where selector is a string-enclosed expression for matching DOM elements. The selector format is the same used with CSS, so you can carry over your existing knowledge of CSS to jQuery. For example, # matches elements by their id attribute and . matches by CSS classes. For example, to get a div with the ID feed use the following:

```
$("div#feed");
```

The next chapter covers selectors in-depth.

When using the jQuery object to either select elements or create new elements, it returns what's known as a wrapper object. It's called a wrapper object because you "wrap" jQuery functionality around a collection of DOM elements. A wrapper object is array-like, meaning you can index it with square brackets or check the number of elements using its .length property. I'll use the .length property often to verify that a selector matched a set of elements. It's easy to check out the .length property of a jQuery wrapper using the Firebug console.

When you call a jQuery method, such as `.addClass()`, it applies the method to all of the selected elements. There's no need to iterate over the collection with a loop.

We've mentioned that the jQuery object contains several methods. Table 3-1 shows a sampling of just some of them.

TABLE 3-1: jQuery Methods

METHOD	CATEGORY	DESCRIPTION
`.ready()`	Events	Specifies a function to run when the DOM is fully loaded.
`.click()`	Events	Sets click event handlers on the set of matched elements.
`.ajax()`	Ajax	jQuery's Ajax utility.
`.addClass()`	CSS	Adds a CSS class to the set of matched elements.
`.removeClass()`	CSS	Removes a CSS class from the set of matched elements.
`.attr()`	Attributes	Gets or sets the value of the specified attribute.
`.html()`	Attributes, DOM Insertion	Gets or sets the HTML content of the first matched element.
`.type()`	Utility	Determines the internal JavaScript [[Class]] of an object.

jQuery is eco-friendly; it doesn't pollute the namespace with globals except for *jQuery* and *$*. Although the *$* alias might be used in other libraries, it's highly unlikely that any other library uses *jQuery* as a variable.

Utility Functions

If you recall, functions are also objects. Hence, a function may have properties and its own methods. The jQuery object has several useful methods conveniently called *utility methods*. Methods exist for enhancing operations for arrays, objects, functions, and even data manipulation.

Objects

The plain-old JavaScript way of checking the type of an object is using the `typeof()operator`, which is sometimes inconsistent. In some instances `typeof()` returns an incorrect or unexpected value. Take for example `typeof(null)` — it returns `object` instead of `null`. Luckily, jQuery has a custom `.type()` method for these situations:

```
$.type(null); // returns null
$.type([]); // returns array
```

The `.isEmptyObject()` method is used to test whether an object contains any properties, including inherited properties, independent of object type:

```
$.isEmptyObject(""); // returns true
$.isEmptyObject({}); // returns true

var mailman = {};
mailman.letters = 100;
$.isEmptyObject(mailman); // returns false
```

There's a similar `.isPlainObject()` method. It also tests whether an object contains any properties, but must be of an *Object* instance. So an empty string will return false in this case:

```
$.isPlainObject(""); // false
$.isPlainObject({}); // true
$.isPlainObject(new Object); // true
```

You mention, "OK, that's great, but what else can I do with objects?" Glad you asked. You can also merge two or more objects with the `.extend()` method. More specifically, `.extend()` combines the properties of one or more objects into a target object. In the next example, `obj1` receives the properties of `obj2` and `obj3`:

```
var obj1 = {"1":"property 1"};
var obj2 = {"2":"property 2"};
var obj3 = {"3":"property 3"};
$.extend(obj1, obj2, obj3);
console.log(obj1["3"]); // displays property 3
```

An interesting note about `.extend()` is that you can use it to clone JavaScript objects (this is different from the `$.clone()` method):

```
var clonedObject = $.extend({}, anObject);
```

`$.extend()` accepts an additional first argument for doing a deep merge of objects, in other words, a recursive copy. You can also use this to do a deep clone of objects as well:

```
var clonedObject = $.extend(true, {}, anObject);
```

Functions

jQuery has two utility methods for functions: `.isFunction()` and `.noop()`. As its name implies, `.isFunction()` tests whether an object is also a function. Make sure not to use parentheses in the function name. In the next example, `.isFunction()` is passed to itself. Because it is itself a function, it must return true.

```
$.isFunction({}); // false
$.isFunction($.isFunction); // true
$.isFunction($.isFunction()); // false, because of parenthesis
```

The `.noop()` method is a stub function; it doesn't perform any operation. But, it's still useful for moments when you'd like to pass an empty function as an argument, e.g., to install a new event that does nothing by default.

Array Operations

Similar to `.isObject()` and `.isFunction()`, you also have an `.isArray()` at your disposal. Besides checking whether an object is an array, you can turn an array-like object to a true array using `.makeArray()`. By converting an array-like object to an array, you lose its methods and properties. The following illustrates a simple usage of `makeArray` which converts a cloned version of jQuery into a standard Array.

```
// clone jQuery object
var clonedjq = $.extend(true, {}, $);
//returns "object"
$.type(clonedjq);

// convert to JS array
var jqArray = $.makeArray(clonedjq);

// returns "array"
$.type(jqArray);
```

jQuery also provides an additional convenience method for combining arrays called `.merge()`, which takes the elements from a second array and appends them to the elements of a first array, preserving the order of the elements of the two arrays:

```
var spooks = ["wraiths", "vampires", "lichs"];
var nums = [1,2,3];
var mergedArrays = $.merge(spooks, nums);
alert(mergedArrays); // displays: wraiths, vampires, lichs, 1, 2, 3
```

The next two methods are useful for working with the elements of an array. `.inArray()` checks for the existence of a value (*in the array no less*) and returns the index of the value if found. If the value isn't in the array, –1 is returned. The `$.unique()` removes duplicate elements from an array of DOM elements. This following snippet demonstrates both methods:

Available for download on Wrox.com

```
<!DOCTYPE html>
<html>
  <head>
  </head>
  <body>
    <p></p>
    <p></p>
    <p></p>
    <p class="duplicate"></p>
    <p class="duplicate"></p>
    <p class="duplicate"></p>
    <p></p>
    <script
        src="http://ajax.googleapis.com/ajax/libs/jquery/1.7.1/jquery.min.js">
```

```
    </script>
    <script>
      $(document).ready(function(){
          // select all paragraph elements
          var paragraphs = $( "p" );

          //returns 7
          console.log( paragraphs.length );

          //turn it into an array

          paragraphs = $.makeArray( paragraphs );

          //get elements of class duplicate and immediately convert them to an array
          var dupes = $.makeArray($( ".duplicate" ))

          //concat them into our paragraphs array
          paragraphs = paragraphs.concat( dupes );

          //returns 10
          console.log( paragraphs.length );

          //get rid of the dupes
          paragraphs = $.unique( paragraphs );

          //returns 7
          console.log( paragraphs.length );

           var index = $.inArray("6", paragraphs);
          console.log(index); // returns -1
      });
    </script>

  </body>
</html>
```

Code snippet is from in-array-and-unique.tx

Using a jQuery tag selector, you get all of the paragraph elements, then using .makeArray() you convert to a plain-old JavaScript array. You then use a jQuery class selector to get all elements of class "duplicate" and add them into our original paragraphs array. With that action, paragraphs now contain duplicate elements. Its total length is 10. Then using .unique() you get the set of paragraph elements without the duplicates. Its total length is now 7. Finally, you check for "6" in the list of paragraphs, which of course returns –1.

You can iterate through an array using an old-fashioned for loop, but as you've probably predicted, jQuery has an alternate method called .each(). This will work with objects, array-like objects, and arrays. $.each() is zero-based and accepts two arguments: the collection to iterate over and a callback function. The callback function accepts the arguments: the index currently operated on and the element value. The following code illustrates using $.each() to iterate over the members of a simple array:

```
<!DOCTYPE html>
<html>
  <head>
    <script type="text/javascript" src="jquery.js"></script>
    <script type="text/javascript">
      $.ready(function(){
          var numArray = [1,2,3,4];
          $.each(numArray, function(index, value){
              value = value * 2;
              console.log("index is:"+index+" new value is:"+value);
          });
      });
    </script>
  </head>
  <body>
  </body>
</html>
```

Code snippet is from each.txt

The last jQuery utility method for working with arrays you'll check out is .map(), which has a similar syntax to .each(), accepting an array or array-like object as its first argument and a callback function. The callback function — according to the jQuery docs, is a "...function to process each item against" — accepts one of the array elements and its current index.

```
<!DOCTYPE html>
<html>
  <head>
    <script type="text/javascript" src="jquery.js"></script>
    <script type="text/javascript">
      $.ready(function(){
          var numArray = [42,1024,486,109821];
          console.log(numArray);
          var newArray = $.map(numArray, function(value, index){
            return Math.sqrt(value).toFixed(4);
          });
          //logs ["6.4807", "32.0000", "22.0454", "331.3925"]
          console.log(newArray);
      });
    </script>
  </head>
  <body>
  </body>
</html>
```

Code snippet is from map.txt

Data Structures

A queue is a "First In, First Out" data structure, meaning elements are added to the back and removed from the front. In jQuery, you can use $.queue() to maintain a list of functions. The default function queue is `fx`, the standard effects queue. In the fx context the power of queues is very clear. The following code sample illustrates a simplified animation queue. Our `animation` div slides up and then, when it's finished, the next animation in the queue, the `fadeIn`, runs.

```
$('#animation').slideUp().fadeIn();
```

The `$.queue` supports the operations push and pop. To remove all functions from a queue, use `.clearQueue()`. Using the corresponding method `.dequeue()` you can remove an item from a queue and execute it. The following code sample shows a simplified example of a manual usage queue and dequeue. A second animation is added to the queue, and then is pulled off the stack and executed with `dequeue`.

```
<!DOCTYPE html>
<html>
<head>
    <script type='text/javascript' src='http://code.jquery.com/jquery-1.7.1.js'></script>
    <style type='text/css'>
      #animation {
          width:200px;
          height:200px;
          background:#ccc;
      }
      </style>

      <script type='text/javascript'>
        $.ready (function(){
        $("#animation").show("slow");
        $("#animation").queue(function () {
            $(this).animate({width:'+=400'},1000);
            $(this).dequeue();
          });
            });
      </script>
      </head>
      <body>
      <div id ="animation" style="display:none"></div>
    </body>
</html>
```

Code snippet is from queue-and-dequeue.txt

Strings

There is just one utility method for working with strings: `.trim()`. JavaScript already contains a powerful mechanism for working with strings via its regular expressions, but its string objects don't contain a built-in `.trim()` method. As the following code example illustrates, trimming removes the trailing and leading whitespaces from a string.

```
var phrase1 = "        1. Either this wallpaper goes          ";
var phrase2 = " or I go.                                      ";

// Last words of Oscar Wilde
```

```
var quote = $.trim(phrase1) + " " + $.trim(phrase2);
console.log(quote);
//logs 1. Either this wallpaper goes or I go.
```

Data

Ajax is a major part of the modern Web. The ability to wire data from client to server and back again, without a full page refresh, has resulted in a serious usability boon for modern web applications. Two of the most common data exchange formats are XML and JSON (JavaScript Object Notation). jQuery has the ability to parse both formats locally and over a URL with the .parseXML() and .parseJSON() methods. You learn about those later when you explore Ajax.

Arbitrary data can be attached to HTML element storage/retrieval. The utility method .data() is used for this purpose. .data() will be covered in detail in Chapter 6.

Other Useful Utility Methods

These last few utility methods don't fit into any of the other categories: .contains(), .isWindow(), .isXMLDoc(), .now(), .support(), and .globalEval(). This section tackles each one.

Checking for Subnodes

The method .contains() checks to see if a DOM node is a child, or subnode, of another node. It expects two arguments — the possible container and the contained node:

```
$.contains($("head")[0], $("title")[0]); //
```

The jQuery wrapper is array-like, so to get the reference to the actual element, you'll need to use the square brackets to retrieve the element references. The title tag is always a child of the head tag, and hence returns true.

Checking for Windows

Consider the situation were you have an iframe. In one of your operations you may want to distinguish between that iframe and the browser window. To do this use the .isWindow() method:

```
<!DOCTYPE html>
<html>
  <head>
    <script type="text/javascript" src="jquery.js"></script>
    <script type="text/javascript">
      $.ready(function(){
          var inlineFrame = $("#frame")[0];
          $.isWindow(inlineFrame); // returns false
          $.isWindow(window);      // returns true
      });
    </script>
  </head>
  <body>
    <iframe id="frame" src="externalPage.html"></iframe>
  </body>
</html>
```

Code snippet is from isWindow.txt

Determining the Current Time

For checking the current time, use the `$.now()` shortcut, as its name implies. It's a shortcut for `(new Date).getTime()`, and obviously it's much easier to just write `$.now()`.

Detecting Browser Features

You've probably heard that it's better to detect browser features rather than detect browsers. Using the `.support()` method you can detect what features a browser supports. This function deprecates `$.browser` from earlier versions of jQuery. A good example of its use: if `($.support.ajax) { }` to check if a browser supports Ajax requests (aka XMLHttpRequest object creation).

Evaluation in the Global Context

The last utility method we'll look at is `.globalEval()`. You may recall the `eval()` expression, used to execute arbitrary JavaScript code:

```
// create a variable x, and initialize it to 0 after all DOM elements are loaded
$(function(){
    eval("var x = 0;");
});
```

The execution context of `eval` is not global, but rather local. You may want the execution context for statements you're evaluating to exist globally, for example when loading external JavaScript files. This is where `.globalEval()` comes into play:

```
// now in global context
$(function(){
    $.globalEval("var x = 0;");
});
```

Table 3-2 summarizes all of the utility methods discussed.

TABLE 3-2: Summary of Utility Methods

METHOD	CATEGORY	DESCRIPTION
`$.type()`	Utilities	Determine the internal JavaScript [[Class]] of an object.
`$.isEmptyObject()`	Utilities	Check to see if an object is empty (contains no properties).
`$.isPlainObject()`	Utilities	Check to see if an object is a plain object (created using "{}" or "new Object").
`$.extend()`	Utilities	Merge the contents of two or more objects together into the first object.
`$.isFunction()`	Utilities	Determine if the argument passed is a JavaScript function object.

METHOD	CATEGORY	DESCRIPTION
`$.noop()`	Utilities	An empty function.
`$.inArray()`	Utilities	Search for a specified value within an array and return its index (or -1 if not found).
`$.isArray()`	Utilities	Determine whether the argument is an array.
`$.makeArray()`	Utilities	Convert an array-like object into a true JavaScript array.
`$.merge()`	Utilities	Merge the contents of two arrays together into the first array.
`$.map()`	Utilities	Pass each element in the current matched set through a function, producing a new jQuery object containing the return values.
`$.each()`	Utilities	A generic iterator function, which can be used to seamlessly iterate over both objects and arrays. Arrays and array-like objects with a length property (such as a function's arguments object) are iterated by numeric index, from 0 to length -1. Other objects are iterated via their named properties.
`$.unique()`	Utilities	Sort an array of DOM elements, in place, with the duplicates removed. Note that this only works on arrays of DOM elements, not strings or numbers.
`$.queue()`	Data, Utilities	Show the queue of functions to be executed on the matched element.
`$.clearQueue()`	Custom, Data, Utilities	Remove from the queue all items that have not yet been run.
`$.dequeue()`	Data, Utilities	Execute the next function on the queue for the matched element.
`$.trim()`	Utilities	Remove the whitespace from the beginning and end of a string.
`$.grep()`	Utilities	Find the elements of an array which satisfy a filter function. The original array is not affected.
`$.contains()`	Utilities	Check to see if a DOM element is within another DOM element.
`$.data()`	Data, Utilities	Store arbitrary data associated with the specified element. Returns the value that was set.
`$.parseXML()`	Utilities	Parse a string into an XML document.

continues

TABLE 3-2 *(continued)*

METHOD	CATEGORY	DESCRIPTION
`$.parseJSON()`	Utilities	Take a well-formed JSON string and return the resulting JavaScript object.
`$.isWindow()`	Utilities	Determine whether the argument is a window.
`$.isXMLDoc()`	Utilities	Check to see if a DOM node is within an XML document (or is an XML document).
`$.now()`	Utilities	Return a number representing the current time.
`$.support()`	Properties of the Global jQuery Object, Utilities	A collection of properties that represent the presence of different browser features or bugs.
`$.globalEval()`	Utilities	Execute some JavaScript code globally.

USING JAVASCRIPT UNOBTRUSIVELY

In the dark days of JavaScript, code like the following was common:

```html
<!DOCTYPE html>
<html>
  <head>
    <script type="text/javascript">
      function showStuff(){
        var content = document.getElementById("content");
        content.style.display = "block";o com
      }

      function changeBGColor(elem){
        elem.style.backgroundColor = "green";
      }
    </script>
  </head>
  <body>
    <ul id="content" onLoad="javascript:showStuff();" style="display:none;">
      <li onClick="javascript: changeBGColor(this);">Item 1</li>
      <li onClick="javascript: changeBGColor(this);">Item 2</li>
      <li onClick="javascript: changeBGColor(this);">Item 3</li>
      <li onClick="javascript: changeBGColor(this);">Item 4</li>
    </ul>
  </body>
</html>
```

Code snippet is from dark-days.txt

You might have cringed at the sight of an embedded CSS style in one of the tags. It's a common tenet of standards-based web development that presentation information, in the form of CSS styles, should be separated from the content and structure of the page, represented by the HTML. To do this with the preceding example, the styles should be placed in an external CSS file. The improved example should look more like this:

Available for
download on
Wrox.com

```
<!DOCTYPE html>
<html>
  <head>
    <style type="text/css" src="myCss.css"></style>
    <script type="text/javascript">
      function showStuff(){
        var content = document.getElementById("content");
        content.style.display = "block";
      }

      function changeBGColor(elem){
        elem.style.backgroundColor = "green";
      }
    </script>
  </head>
  <body>
    <ul id="content" onLoad="javascript:showStuff();" class="contentClass">
      <li onClick="javascript: changeBGColor(this);">Item 1</li>
      <li onClick="javascript: changeBGColor(this);">Item 2</li>
      <li onClick="javascript: changeBGColor(this);">Item 3</li>
      <li onClick="javascript: changeBGColor(this);">Item 4</li>
    </ul>
  </body>
</html>
```

Code snippet is from separation-of-content-and-style.txt

What's true for the markup (HTML) and style (CSS) is also true for the behavior (JavaScript). Code representing the behavior of the page should also be removed from the page. Inline event handlers, and inline JavaScript should be avoided wherever possible. This is called unobtrusive JavaScript. The following code sample shows the preceding example rewritten to fully separate style, content and behavior.

Available for
download on
Wrox.com

```
<!DOCTYPE html>
<html>
  <head>
    <style type="text/css" src="myCss.css"></style>
    <script>

      (function(document){
          document.onload = function(){
              content.style.display = "block";
          }

          var listItems = document.getElementsByTagName("li");
          for(i = 0; i < listItems.length; i++){
```

```
                    listItems[i].onclick = function{
                        listItems[i].style.backgroundColor = "green";
                    }
                }
            })(document);

        </script>
    </head>
    <body>
        <ul id="content" class="contentClass">
            <li>Item 1</li>
            <li>Item 2</li>
            <li>Item 3</li>
            <li>Item 4</li>
        </ul>
    </body>
</html>
```

That's much better on the eyes — the HTML is semantic and the JavaScript unobtrusive. The markup is exactly that, markup not behavior. But, the JavaScript is fairly verbose. This is where jQuery makes life much easier:

```
<!DOCTYPE html>
<html>
    <head>
        <style type="text/css" src="myCss.css"></style>
        <script src="jquery.js"></script>
        <script>
            $(document).ready(function(){
                $("#content").show();
                $("li").click(function(this){
                    this.css("backgroundColor","green");
                });
            });
        </script>
    </head>
    <body>
        <ul id="content" class="contentClass">
            <li>Item 1</li>
            <li>Item 2</li>
            <li>Item 3</li>
            <li>Item 4</li>
        </ul>
    </body>
</html>
```

Immediately, you'll notice that the JavaScript code shrank from 11 lines to 7; not bad. The document DOM element is passed into the jQuery function. jQuery wraps it, then applies to the returned wrapper a .ready() method.

The .ready() method registers a handler, which executes code after all of the DOM elements have been loaded, but not necessarily all assets (like images or Flash files) and accepts a function as an argument. For example, the following code sample shows a functionToExecute(), which is passed to .ready() While this pattern works technically, it has the unwanted side effect of adding to the namespace a function that is executed only once.

```
function functionToExecute(){
    // do stuff here
}
$(document).ready(functionToExecute);
```

This is a perfect place to use an anonymous function instead.

```
$(document).ready(function(){
   // do stuff here
});
```

In the previous example, after the DOM is loaded, the content unordered list is made visible, and then all of the list items in the document are given an onClick event handler, which changes the background color to green using the .css() method.

The .ready() method (or event) used in this example can also take the form

```
$(function(){
   // on ready code goes here
});
```

which is functionally equivalent, but more abbreviated. For the remainder of this book, we'll use the latter form.

Finally, the JavaScript code is moved to a separate file called unobtrusive.js:

Available for download on Wrox.com

```
<!DOCTYPE html>
<html>
  <head>
    <style type="text/css" src="myCss.css"></style>
    <script type="text/javascript" src="jquery.js"></script>
    <script type="text/javascript" src="unobtrusive.js"></script>
  </head>
  <body>
    <ul id="content" class="contentClass">
      <li>Item 1</li>
      <li>Item 2</li>
      <li>Item 3</li>
      <li>Item 4</li>
    </ul>
  </body>
</html>
```

Code snippet is from full-separation.txt

With this approach, the artist can do his/her job without affecting the markup of the page, and the programmer can do his/her job without conflicting with the artist's changes.

This is a good moment to explain chaining, an often used feature of jQuery. Consider the following code:

```
<!DOCTYPE html>
<html>
  <head>
    <style type="text/css">
      .class1 {
          color: "white";
          background-color: "black";
          width:200px;
          height:100px;
      }

      .class2 {
          color: "yellow";
          background-color: "red";
          width:100px;
          height:200px;
      }

    </style>
    <script type="text/javascript" src="jquery.js"></script>
    <script type="text/javascript">
      $(function(){
          $("#myDiv").addClass("class1");
          $("p#blah").removeClass("class1");
          $("p#blah").addClass("class1");
      });
    </script>
  </head>
  <body>
    <div id="myDiv">
      <p id="lorem">Lorem Ipsum</p>
      <p id="blah">blah blah blah</p>
    </div>
  </body>
</html>
```

Code snippet is from no-chaining.txt

Here you have three calls to the jQuery function; each selects an element from the DOM and performs some operation like adding or removing a CSS class to an element. There's not actually anything wrong with this, but there is a more efficient method. A call to the jQuery function with a selector argument returns an instance of a jQuery object with a collection of selected DOM elements wrapped.

Several jQuery methods also return wrapped objects. For example:

```
$('body').find('div');
```

Because `.find()` returns another wrapper object, you can do another successive method invocation like so:

```
$('body').find('div').addClass('cssClass');
```

This is called *chaining* and it's not unusual to see long jQuery method chains. Besides readability, this also has a performance advantage over instantiating a new jQuery object, searching through the DOM, and then applying a method. Here's the rewritten example using chaining instead of separate instances:

```html
<!DOCTYPE html>
<html>
  <head>
    <style type="text/css">
      .class1 {
        color: "white";
        background-color: "black";
        width:200px;
        height:100px;
      }
      .class2 {
        color: "yellow";
        background-color: "red";
        width:100px;
        height:200px;
      }

    </style>
    <script type="text/javascript" src="jquery.js"></script>
    <script type="text/javascript">
      $(function(){
          $("#myDiv")
           .addClass("class1")
           .find("p#blah")
           .removeClass("class1")
           .addClass("class1");
      });
    </script>
  </head>
  <body>
    <div id="myDiv">
      <p id="lorem">Lorem Ipsum</p>
      <p id="blah">blah blah blah</p>
    </div>
  </body>
</html>
```

Code snippet is from chaining.txt

Using Cody Lindley's terminology, any jQuery method that returns another wrapper object is denoted as a "constructive" method because it can continue a chain, whereas any method that doesn't return a wrapper (like `.text()` or `.html()`) is denoted a "destructive" method.

Writing Less Verbose JavaScript with jQuery

JavaScript, although a very powerful language in its own right, is sometimes verbose. JavaScript frameworks like jQuery offer numerous shortcuts for reducing the amount of code needed to accomplish common web development tasks. You've already seen a few:

JAVASCRIPT WAY

```
window.onload = function() {
    var elements = document.getElementsByTagName("div");
    for(var = 0; i < elements.length; i++){
        elements[i].style.color = green;
    }
});
```

JQUERY WAY

```
$(function(){
    $("div").each(function(index, value){
        $( this ).css( "color" , "green" )
    });
});
```

The code feels more concise and abbreviated, and although the difference between the number of lines of code isn't big overall, you wrote much less. It quickly becomes a habit to use the `$(function(){…});` instead of `window.onLoad()`.

Of course, there are other, deeper benefits to using a library like jQuery. Shorter code is nice, but adding powerful features in a cross-browser way is even better. In this specific example, jQuery grants you the ability to, in a cross-browser way, set multiple callbacks for the onLoad event. Without a cross-browser solution only one callback could be set for events which meant that you could accidentally overwrite methods if you weren't careful.

As an aside, this problem was originally solved by the community centering on a series of blog posts by the influential JavaScript developer Dean Edwards: `http://dean.edwards.name/weblog/2005/09/busted/` and `http://dean.edwards.name/weblog/2006/06/again/`. One name that appears as an important contributor to the completed solution was none other than the creator of jQuery, John Resig.

THE JQUERY FRAMEWORK STRUCTURE

Because jQuery is a well-written modular framework, it's easy to treat it as a black box. But, it's instructive to look at the underlying code, and see how the nuts and bolts go together. If you're interested, as of jQuery 1.3, the selector engine is now based on a separate project by John Resig, called sizzle, and offers several performance enhancements over the previous method for selecting elements. See `http://sizzlejs.com` for more.

If you recall from Chapter 2, a self-invoking anonymous function looks like this:

```
(function(arguments){
  // do something
})();
```

jQuery is also a self-executing anonymous function, which accepts two arguments — the `window` object and `undefined`:

```
(function( window, undefined)
  {…} // definition of core
) (window);
```

The `window` object is passed in as a small performance boost. For any call to the global `window` object inside the jQuery function definition, instead of looking up the definition of the window in the global context, it looks inside the local context avoiding one step in the lookup. It's small, but does represent an improvement.

At first, it might seem a little baffling to pass in `undefined`, but there is a good reason. The `undefined` built-in type is assignable. So, conceivably, someone on your development team could do something like `undefined = true;` and then your comparisons won't work as expected. (Paul Irish has a special term for team members like this; see his video on "10 Things I Learned from the jQuery Source" at `http://paulirish.com/2010/10-things-i-learned-from-the-jquery-source/`.)

Looking further down in the code, you can see how the utility methods are added to the jQuery function:

```
…
jQuery.extend({
      noConflict: function( deep ){
        …
      isFunction: function( obj ){
        …
      isArray: Array.isArray || function( obj ){
    …
```

The jQuery function is `.extend()`-ed with an object literal, with key-value pairs of method names to method definitions, as you can see from the previous snippet taken from jQuery source. Looking through the method definitions you can see exactly how the comparisons are done, and what each method expects.

Our favorite lesson from looking at the source is how the `$.ready()` works. There isn't an `.onReady()` event in the DOM. Again, looking at the source code is instructive:

```
// The DOM ready check for Internet Explorer
function doScrollCheck() {
      if ( jQuery.isReady ) {
            return;
      }
}

      try {
            // If IE is used, use the trick by Diego Perini
            // http://javascript.nwbox.com/IEContentLoaded/
            document.documentElement.doScroll("left");
      } catch(e) {
            setTimeout( doScrollCheck, 1 );
```

```
        return;
    }

    // and execute any waiting functions
    jQuery.ready();
}

// Expose jQuery to the global object
return jQuery;
…
```

`.ready()` executes when all of the DOM elements are loaded, but not necessarily all parts of the page, such as images or Flash files. At this point, it's nice to have the capacity to manipulate the DOM at once. The JavaScript method `.doScroll()` throws an exception when you try to run it and the DOM isn't loaded. The call to `doScroll()` is wrapped around a try/catch statement. When an exception occurs (while the DOM elements are loading), the `doScrollCheck()` method calls itself recursively, until the DOM is fully loaded. At that point, `doScroll` stops causing an exception, and jQuery then executes the code bound to `.ready()`.

This section is very small, and doesn't really do justice to all of the powerful coding techniques used in jQuery. But, we highly recommend that you look through it, and apply the ideas to your own projects.

UNDERSTANDING THE DOM AND EVENTS

Both HTML and XML are hierarchical tree structures of tags (or elements). The window contains a document; documents contain an HTML element, which in turn contains a child header and body element, and so forth. The best definition of the DOM is the one specified by the W3C:

> *"The Document Object Model is a platform- and language-neutral interface that will allow programs and scripts to dynamically access and update the content, structure and style of documents. The document can be further processed and the results of that processing can be incorporated back into the presented page."*

Most of the cross-browser concerns pertaining to variations in the DOM are silently taken care of for you in jQuery. You don't need to worry (much) about the differences in the DOM redundant between the Gecko-friendly browsers, IE, Safari, and Opera.

USING JQUERY WITH OTHER JAVASCRIPT LIBRARIES

From time to time you may want to include in your program other JavaScript frameworks or libraries with your code. If those frameworks use the dollar sign as a variable, this will cause conflicts. But, because jQuery plays nice with others, it has a method for avoiding these conflicts. To do so, use the `$.noConflict();` method after loading the libraries that may conflict. This has the effect of reverting the dollar sign to its previous value. After invoking `.noConflict()`, use jQuery instead of `$` to refer to the jQuery core. The following code demonstrates an example:

```
<html>
 <head>
    <script src="conflictingFramework.js"></script>
    <script src="jquery.js"></script>
    <script>
      jQuery.noConflict();

      jQuery("<p>I am a paragraph</p>").appendTo(body);

      // $ references conflictingFramework.js, not jQuery
      $.blahMethodFromOtherLibrary();
    </script>
 </head>
 <body>
 </body>
</html>
```

Opening up the hood, you can see the actual definition of `$.noConflict()`:

```
...
noConflict: function( deep ) {
    window.$ = _$;

    if ( deep ) {
        window.jQuery = _jQuery;
    }

    return jQuery;
},
...
```

As you can see, it's very short. jQuery maintains an internal reference to the value of `$` — after `$.noConflict` is called, the value of `$` is restored to its previous value, which is the value of the conflicting library.

SUMMARY

In review, you're now familiar with the structure and syntax of jQuery-based JavaScript programs, taking view of how jQuery makes use of the pattern of unobtrusive JavaScript separating behavior from markup. Without fear or reserve, you've also taken a very basic tour of the jQuery core. Choosing not to treat jQuery as a black box gives you an advantage over many other web developers. Studying the core also teaches several JavaScript techniques that you can apply in your own projects.

Now that you've had some exposure to the basics, you can delve into one of the most powerful features of jQuery — its very complete selector mechanism — in the following chapter.

NOTES

http://jqfundamentals.com/book/index.html#example-3.13

http://paulirish.com/2010/10-things-i-learned-from-the-jquery-source/

http://ejohn.org/blog/ultra-chaining-with-jquery/

http://perfectionkills.com/instanceof-considered-harmful-or-how-to-write-a-robust-isarray/

http://stackoverflow.com/questions/5773723/difference-between-jquery-isplainob-ject-and-jquery-isemptyobject/5773738#5773738

http://stackoverflow.com/questions/122102/what-is-the-most-efficient-way-to-clone-a-javascript-object

http://nfriedly.com/techblog/2009/06/advancedjavascript-objects-arrays-and-array-like-objects/

http://en.wikipedia.org/wiki/Queue

http://www.bitstorm.org/weblog/2011-2/How_to_use_the_jQuery_queue_function.html

http://www.myinkblog.com/2009/09/11/sizzle-a-look-at-jquerys-new-css-selector-engine/

http://www.youtube.com/watch?v=ijpD8ePLBds

http://webhole.net/2009/11/28/how-to-read-json-with-javascript/

http://ajax.sys-con.com/node/676031

http://www.w3.org/DOM/#what

http://www.quirksmode.org/dom/intro.html

DOM Element Selection and Manipulation

WHAT'S IN THIS CHAPTER?

➤ The Power of jQuery Selectors

➤ Doing DOM Traversal

➤ Accessing and Modifying HTML Elements

Previously, you got your feet wet learning about the jQuery core, and getting a bird's-eye view of how it works. In this chapter, you delve more into selectors, and manipulating elements retrieved by jQuery selectors.

Paraphrasing the Apple iPhone's phrase, "There's a selector for that" should be the jQuery motto. A necessity for web application development is the common pattern of selecting a DOM element, and then performing some operation on the selected element. With jQuery's selector engine, this is a snap. If you've ever used CSS selectors, you will feel right at home using jQuery selectors. The syntax used by jQuery is a combination of CSS1-3 and XPath selectors.

This chapter takes you in depth into the many different ways to retrieve elements, control the context within which you select elements, and how to generate new HTML code on the fly. You'll also check out the many shortcuts for manipulating the DOM.

To interactively experiment with the various selectors, use the interactive jQuery tester found at www.woods.iki.fi/interactive-jquery-tester.html. To try out the interactive tester, enter the selector pattern inside the text input at the top, and the HTML code in the text area on the bottom right. Upon changing the selector pattern, the matched elements are highlighted in the text area on the bottom left.

THE POWER OF JQUERY SELECTORS

Probably at some point, every JavaScript developer tries something similar to this. You want to find all of the table rows that have a CSS class of "highlighted," and you'd like to change it to a class of "normal":

```
var tr = document.getElementByTagName("tr");
for ( var = i; i < tr.length; i++ ) {
    if ( tr[i].class === 'highlighted' ) {
        tr[i].class = 'normal';
    }
}
```

It works, but it's verbose. The jQuery way is much more concise:

```
$("tr.highlighted").removeClass("highlighted").addClass("normal");
```

No loop, no `if` statement, no intermediate variables needed, and condensed from six lines of code to one, but still readable; not bad at all. Here you're using a few different jQuery concepts: the selector, chaining, and utility methods. The important point to note is that jQuery selectors greatly reduce the amount of code needed to get an array of DOM elements.

Selecting Elements

jQuery provides a myriad of ways to select DOM elements: you can select elements by attributes, element type, element position, CSS class, or a combination of these. The syntax for selecting elements is as follows:

```
$(selector,[context])
```

or

```
jQuery(selector, [context])
```

To select elements by tag name, use the tag name in the selector. For example, `$("div")` retrieves all of the `div`s in a document. Running the previous example in a "jQuerified" jconsole, you can see the returned object in the Firebug window.

In the next example, the same `div` selector expression is used, with three empty `div`s in the body. With the `length` property, you can verify that the selector returns three elements using a console.log.

```
<!DOCTYPE html>
<html>
  <head>
    <script src="http://code.jquery.com/jquery-1.7.1.js">
    </script>

    <script>

      $(document).ready(function(){
```

```
            var wrappedElements = $("div");
            console.log(wrappedElements.length);
        });

    </script>
  </head>
  <body>
    <div id="1"></div>
    <div id="2"></div>
    <div id="3"></div>
  </body>
</html>
```

Code snippet is from tag-selector.txt

Another way to select elements is by their ID attribute. For example, `$("div#elementId")` selects all `div`s with an ID of `elementId`. In general, the format for selecting by ID is the element name, followed by a hash (#), and the ID to match against. The following code example illustrates this with a code sample that selects an element with the ID of `myList`.

```
<!DOCTYPE html>
<html>
  <head>
    <script src="http://code.jquery.com/jquery-1.7.1.js">
    </script>

    <script>

      $(document).ready(function(){
          var wrappedElements = $("ul#myList");
          console.log(wrappedElements.length);
      });

    </script>
  <body>
    <div id="main">
      <ul id="myList">
        <li>foo</li>
        <li>bar</li>
      </ul>
    </div>
  </body>
</html>
```

Code snippet is from id-selector.txt

You can also get all of the elements in the DOM using the all selector (*) as demonstrated in the next snippet. The resulting length is 9 elements.

```
<!DOCTYPE html>
<html>
  <head>
    <script src="http://code.jquery.com/jquery-1.7.1.js">
```

```
    </script>
    <script>
      $(document).ready(function(){
          var allElements = $("*");
          console.log(allElements.length);
      });
    </script>
  <body>
    <div id="main">
        <ul id="myList">
          <li>foo</li>
          <li>bar</li>
        </ul>
    </div>
  </body>
</html>
```

Code snippet is from all-selector.txt

By default, when selecting elements, jQuery searches through the entire DOM tree. At times, you may want to search through a subtree of the DOM. You can accomplish this by passing an optional second parameter to the jQuery function to give the selection a *context*. For example, say you have a series of links you'd like to retrieve from just a single div in the DOM. You could do the following:

```
$("a","js_links#div");
```

Selecting by CSS Styles

In a similar fashion to CSS, if you want to select elements by class, use a dot (.). For example:

```
$("p.highlighted");
```

Up to now, you've selected elements using the format `$("element#id")`, `$("element.class")`, or something similar. It's not actually necessary to precede any of these selectors with an element name followed by the filter. It's just as valid to rewrite the previous examples like this:

```
$("#stuffId")
$(".myCssClass")
```

Because characters such as hash (#) have special meaning, if you want to use them in selection expressions, you'll need to backslash escape those characters. The following list of characters all contain special meanings inside of selectors, and should be backslash escaped if you want to match against them:

```
# ; & , . + * ~ ' : "  ! ^ $ [] ( ) = > | /
```

For example, if you use the dollar sign as a naming convention for IDs in your HTML documents, you'd write an ID selector like this:

```
<!DOCTYPE html>
<html>
  <head>
    <script src="http://code.jquery.com/jquery-1.7.1.js">
    </script>
    <script>
      var n = $"#\\$specialId").length;
      console.log(n);
    </script>
  </head>
  <body>
    <div id="$specialId">T-Rex</div>
  </body>
</html>
```

Code snippet is from escaped-selectors.txt

The last two basic selectors in this section are the multiple selector and descendant selector. The descendant selector, which takes the form `$("ancestor descendant")`, returns a wrapper object with the descendants of a specified ancestor. For example:

```
$("form input")
```

returns a wrapper with all of the inputs that are children of a form.

By no means are you limited to passing only a single selector expression. You can also combine different kinds of selectors, with a comma-delimited list of selectors:

```
$("div#gallery, div#userInfo, form");
```

Table 4-1 summarizes the basic selector types.

TABLE 4-1: Basic Selectors

SELECTOR	DESCRIPTION
*	All selector
.	Class selector
"Element"	Element selector
#	ID selector
"select1, select2," etc.	Multiple selector

Selecting by Attributes

jQuery allows for an extraordinary amount of flexibility for selecting elements according to their attributes. First, and most obvious, is selecting an attribute that matches an exact string pattern:

```
$("[attributeName='string2match']")
```

or

```
$("[attributeName='string2match']")
```

But, there are also attribute selectors reminiscent of regexes, so you can match using part of a string as well; for example, the attribute starts and ends selectors. The attribute starts selector selects all elements that begin with a specified string. Likewise, the attribute ends selector selects all those elements that end with a particular string:

```
$("[attributeName^='value']"); // attribute starts
$("[attributeName $='value']"); // attribute ends
```

Let's say that you have several input elements with IDs that begin with the string "user": The following code sample illustrates using a regular expression to select all elements that have IDs that include the string "user" at the beginning of the ID.

Available for download on Wrox.com

```
<!DOCTYPE html>
<html>
  <head>
    <script src="http://code.jquery.com/jquery-1.7.1.js">
    </script>

    <script>

      var userInfo = $("[id^='user']").length;
      console.log(n);

    </script>
  </head>
  <body>
    <form>
      <input id="userName" type="text" />
      <input id="userId" type="text" />
      <input id="userPhone" type="text" />
    </form>
  </body>
</html>
```

Code snippet is from attribute-starts-selector.txt

In contrast to the attribute selectors that match, you also have attribute selectors that don't match. The following example shows an example of a selector that does matches against IDs that do *not* equal "cheese."

```html
<!DOCTYPE html>
<html>
  <head>
    <script src="http://code.jquery.com/jquery-1.7.1.js">
    </script>

    <script>

      var userInfo = $("[id!='cheese']").length;
      console.logconsole.log(n);

    </script>
  </head>
  <body>
    <div id="eggs"></div>
    <div id="ham"></div>
    <div id="cheese"></div>
  </body>
</html>
```

Code snippet is from negative-selector.txt

You can also select by a string that exists anywhere in the attribute value, using *=:

```
$("[attributeName*='value']");
```

So, for example, say you have a document with a set of divs, each with an ID attribute, and you'd like to get the subset of divs that contain the string 'zombie', which may appear at the beginning or end of the ID value. The following code illustrates selecting any ID that contains "zombie" anywhere in the ID attribute value:

```html
<!DOCTYPE html>
<html>
  <head>
    <script src="http://code.jquery.com/jquery-1.7.1.js">
    </script>

    <script>

      var userInfo = $("[id*='zombie']").length;
      console.log(n);

    </script>
  </head>
  <body>
    <div id="greenzombie"></div>
    <div id="zombieman"></div>
    <div id="madscientist"></div>
  </body>
</html>
```

Code snippet is from anywhere-selector.txt

As you can see you can select elements with exact matches on the attribute values, matches on the beginning and end of the attribute value, matching by a string an attribute value doesn't contain, and a string appearing anywhere in the attribute value. Is there more? Yep. There's also the attribute contains word selector, where each word is space delimited. This small snippet shows the syntax for using an attribute contains selector.

```
$("[attributeName~='value']");
```

This is useful for extracting words from an input box (among many other uses I haven't considered). For example the following code searches through the DOM for elements with an ID that contains the word "zombie."

```
<!DOCTYPE html>
<html>
  <head>
    <script src="http://code.jquery.com/jquery-1.7.1.js">
    </script>

    <script>

      var userInfo = $("[id~='zombie']").length;
      console.log(n);

    </script>
  </head>
  <body>
    <div id="greenzombie"></div>
    <div id="zombie man"></div>
    <div id="mad scientist"></div>
  </body>
</html>
```

Code snippet is from attribute-contains.txt

And just like the basic selectors, you use multiple attribute selectors as well for more complicated situations. The next example has four forms: two containing form data for admin users and two containing form data for regular users. All four contain three text inputs, `userName`, `employeeId`, and `age`. All of the form names follow the convention `userType/User/OfficeNumber`. To get the desired form, `adminUserOffice1`, a multiple attribute selector is used, `$("form[name$='Office1'] form[name^=admin]")`, which can also be written as `$("[name$='Office1'][name^=admin]")`. You can also use a single matching string, like `$("[name='adminUserOffice1']")`. This example is here for demonstration purposes.

```
<!DOCTYPE html>
<html>
  <head>
    <script src="http://code.jquery.com/jquery-1.7.1.js">
    </script>

    <script>

      $(function(){
```

```
            var n = $("form[name$='Office1']form[name^=admin]").length;
            console.log(n);
        });

    </script>
  </head>
  <body>
    <form name="adminUserOffice1" method="post" action="sendUserData.php">
      <input type="text" id="userName"></input>
      <input type="text" id="employeeId"></input>
      <input type="text" id="age"></input>
    </form>
    <form name="adminUserOffice2" method="post" action="sendUserData.php">
      <input type="text" id="userName"></input>
      <input type="text" id="employeeId"></input>
      <input type="text" id="age"></input>
    </form>
    <form name="regularUserOffice1" method="post" action="sendUserData.php">
      <input type="text" id="userName"></input>
      <input type="text" id="employeeId"></input>
      <input type="text" id="age"></input>
    </form>
    <form name="regularUserOffice2" method="post" action="sendUserData.php">
      <input type="text" id="userName"></input>
      <input type="text" id="employeeId"></input>
      <input type="text" id="age"></input>
    </form>
  </body>
</html>
```

Code snippet is from multiple-attribute-selectors.txt

Table 4-2 summarizes the different kinds of attribute selectors.

TABLE 4-2: CSS Attribute Selectors

ATTRIBUTE SELECTOR	DESCRIPTION
elem[attr]	Select elements that match attribute attr.
elem[attr=val]	Select elements that contain an attribute attr that match value val.
elem[attr^=val]	Select elements that contain attribute attr and that begin with value val.
elem[attr|=val]	Select elements with attribute values that either begin with val, or are equal to val.
elem[attr$=val]	Select elements that contain attribute attr and that end with value val.
elem[attr!=val]	Select elements that don't contain an attribute attr with value val.

continues

TABLE 4-2 *(continued)*

ATTRIBUTE SELECTOR	DESCRIPTION
elem[attr~=val]	Select elements that contain an attribute attr with a value that contains the word val. Words are space delimited.
elem[attr*=val]	Selects elements that have the specified attribute attr with a value containing the a given substring val.

Selecting by Position

Elements can also be selected by their relation to other elements (child/parent relationships), or by hierarchical position in a document. Some examples might include selecting the first or last items in a list, or the even rows in a table. Suppose you have an ordered list like the one in the following code snippet. It presents an ordered list of "fowl." The JavaScript that follows illustrates several variations on jQuery's selectors by position. They resolve as follows:

- ➤ li:even returns the even numbered members of the matched set.
- ➤ li:odd returns the even numbered members of the matched set.
- ➤ li:first returns the first element of the matched set.
- ➤ li:last returns the last element of the matched set.
- ➤ li:eq(3) returns the 4th element in the matched set.
- ➤ li:gt(2) returns all elements of index greater than 2 in the matched set.
- ➤ li:lt(3) returns all elements of index less than 3 in the matched set.

Note that all position selectors start their count at zero except for the nth-child filter, which starts at 1, which we'll explain in the section on "Filtering by Relationships."

```
<ol id="fowl">
  <li>Turkey</li>  <!-- 0 -->
  <li>Chicken</li> <!-- 1 -->
  <li>Parrot</li>  <!-- 2 -->
  <li>Pigeon</li>  <!-- 3 -->
  <li>Hawk</li>    <!-- 4 -->
</ol>
$("li:even")  // returns turkey, parrot, and hawk
$("li:odd")   // returns chicken and pigeon
$("li:first") // returns turkey
$("li:last")  // returns hawk
$("li:eq(3)") // returns pigeon
$("li:gt(2)") // returns pigeon and hawk
$("li:lt(3)") // returns parrot, chicken, turkey.
```

Using Filter Selectors

Notice that the previous set of selectors all begin with a colon (:). This class of selectors is known as *filters*, because they filter a base selector. Just to add more to the jQuery filter mayhem, there are filters specifically for form elements, such as `:button` or `:input`, a filter for detecting if an element is in a state of animation, and other goodies. The jQuery docs classify the filter selectors into basic, visibility, content, child, and form. We talk about the `:animated` filter in Chapter 7.

Selection Using Basic Filters

Table 4-3 lists the basic filters available in jQuery. They all follow the same usage pattern as seen in the previous example.

TABLE 4-3: Basic Filters

TYPE	DESCRIPTION
`:animated`	Selects elements that are animated
`:eq()`	Selects elements that equal
`:even`	Selects even elements
`:first`	Selects the first element
`:gt()`	Selects elements greater than a value
`:header`	Selects all elements that are headers, like h1, h2, h3 and so on.
`:last`	Selects the last element
`:lt()`	Selects elements less than
`:not()`	Selects elements that don't equal a value
`:odd`	Selects the odd elements

Filtering Forms

As you well know, validating, parsing, and submitting form data is an everyday part of a web developer's life. So jQuery, of course, contains filters that make it trivially easy to select form elements. When we mention form elements, we're referring specifically to elements that belong to an HTML form used for submitting data to a server like button, input, or text area.

Available for download on Wrox.com

```
<!DOCTYPE html>
<html>
  <head>
    <script src="http://code.jquery.com/jquery-1.7.1.js">
    </script>

    <script>

      $(function(){
        var n = $(':input').length;
```

```
          console.log(n);
       });

    </script>
  </head>
  <body>
    <form name="" method="post">
      <input type="text" />
      <input type="hidden" />
      <input type="password" />
      <input type="radio" />
      <input type="reset" />
      <input type="submit" />
      <input type="image" />
      <input type="file" />
      <input type="checkbox" />
      <input type="reset" />
      <input type="button" value="hit me"/>
      <button>Hit me too</button>
      <select>
        <option>floor 1</option>
        <option>floor 2</option>
      </select>

      <textarea></textarea>

    </form>
  </body>
</html>
```

Code snippet is from filtering-forms.txt

The `:input` selector gets all form controls including `select`, `textarea`, and `button`. There are also more specific filters for individual controls like `:button`, `:password`, and `:text`. As you've probably noticed, there's a great amount of flexibility for how you select elements, and more than one way to get the same results. The following code snippet shows a few different ways to get all of the elements in the same form.

```
<!DOCTYPE html>
<html>
  <head>
    <script src="http://code.jquery.com/jquery-1.7.1.js">
    </script>

    <script>

      $(function(){
        var n1 = $("input").length;
        var n2 = $(":input").length;
        var n3 = $("form > *").length;
        var n4 = $(":text").length;
        var n5 = $("input[type='text']").length;
        console.log(n1 + ","+ n2 +","+ n3 + "," + n4 + "," + n5);
```

```
      });

    </script>
  </head>
  <body>
    <form name="" method="post">
      <input type="text" />
      <input type="text" />
      <input type="text" />
    </form>
  </body>
</html>
```

Code snippet is from multiple-form-filters.txt

If there had been a text area or button element, $("form > *") and $(":input") would've returned those elements as well. Table 4-4 summarizes all of the different form filters.

TABLE 4-4: Form Filters

FILTER	DESCRIPTION
:button	Selects all button elements and elements of type button.
:checkbox	Selects all elements of type checkbox.
:checked	Matches all elements that are checked.
:disabled	Selects all elements that are disabled.
:enabled	Selects all elements that are enabled.
:file	Selects all elements of type file.
:image	Selects all elements of type image.
:input	Selects all input, text area, select and button elements.
:password	Selects all elements of type password.
:radio	Selects all elements of type radio.
:reset	Selects all elements of type reset.
:selected	Selects all elements that are selected.
:submit	Selects all elements of type submit.
:text	Selects all elements of type text.

Filtering by Visibility

jQuery determines whether an element is visible depending on the properties offsetWidth and offsetHeight of an element. If both are zero, the element is considered hidden. If an element's visibility is toggled directly changing its styling from `display:block;` to `display:none;` jQuery will detect those as visible/invisible, respectively. Use the `:hidden` and `:visible` filters to match each type. The next example demonstrates usage of the visible and hidden filters.

Available for download on Wrox.com

```html
<!DOCTYPE html>
<html>
  <head>
    <script src="http://code.jquery.com/jquery-1.7.1.js">
    </script>

    <script>

      $(function(){
        var numInv = $(":text:hidden").length;
        var numVis = $(":text:visible").length;
        console.log(numInv);
        console.log(numVis);
      });

    </script>
  </head>
  <body>
    <form name="" method="post">
      <input type="text" name="text1" style="display:none;"/>
      <input type="text" name="text2" style="offsetWidth:0; offsetHeight:0;"/>
      <input type="text" name="text3" style="display:block;/>
    </form>
  </body>
</html>
```

Code snippet is from visibility-filters.txt

TABLE 4-5: Visibility Filters

TYPE	DESCRIPTION
`:hidden` Selector	Selects all elements that are hidden.
`:visible` Selector	Selects all elements that are visible.

Filtering by Content

Sometimes you may want to select according to what an element does (or doesn't) contain; for example, some text. Using the `:contains()` filter you can select an element that contains a matching text directly inside the element, inside of a descendant, or even a combination of both. The following code sample illustrates a use of contains. It selects all paragraphs that contain the text string "jenny" and stores them in a variable `jennies`.

Available for download on Wrox.com

```html
<!DOCTYPE html>
<html>
  <head>
    <script src="http://code.jquery.com/jquery-1.7.1.js">
```

```
        </script>

        <script>

          $(function(){
            var jennies = $("p:contains('jenny')").length;
            console.log(jennies); // returns 2
          });
        </script>
      </head>
      <body>
        <p>jenny smith</p>
        <p>jennyjones</p>
        <p>jim bob</p>
      </body>
    </html>
```

Code snippet is from content-filter.txt

A related selector, `:has()`, returns elements that contain at least one element that matches the specified selector. This allows you to select elements that have a descendent selector of a certain type amongst any of its children. You're not limited to those with a matching direct child. The following code sample illustrates using `:has()` to select a div that contains a paragraph as one of its many children out of all the divs on a page.

```
<!DOCTYPE html>
<html>
  <head>
    <script src="http://code.jquery.com/jquery-1.7.1.js">
    </script>

    <script>

$(function() {
    var hasDemo = $("div:has('p')").attr("id");
    console.log(hasDemo); // returns 'yay'
});

</script>
  </head>
  <body>
<div id="yay">
  <ul>
    <li>
      <p>The glorious paragraph</p>
      <p>Another, glorious paragraph</p>
      <p>The best paragraph yet</p>
    </li>
  </ul>
</div>
<div id="nay">
  <ul>
    <li> No paragraphs here. </li>
```

```
      </ul>
   </div>
   </body>
   </html>
```

If you want to select an element that doesn't contain anything, you can use the `:empty()` selector. This selector returns all elements that contain no children. This includes text.

```
<!DOCTYPE html>
<html>
   <head>
      <script src="http://code.jquery.com/jquery-1.7.1.js">
      </script>

      <script>

         $(function(){
            var nothing = $("p:empty").length;
            console.log(nothing) //returns 1
         });
      </script>
   </head>
   <body>
      <div>
         <p></p>
         <p>something here</p>
      </div>
   </body>
</html>
```

The opposite of `:empty()` is `:parent()`. It selects elements that have children, The following code shows an example of using `:parent()` selecting a single div with children and logging the div's ID.

```
<!DOCTYPE html>
<html>
   <head>
      <script src="http://code.jquery.com/jquery-1.7.1.js">
      </script>

      <script>

         $(function(){
            var parentDemo = $("div:parent");
            console.log(parentDemo.attr("id")) //returns proudParent
         });
      </script>
   </head>
   <body>
      <div id="empty"></div>
      <div id="proudParent">
```

```
      <ul>
        <li> Children! </li>
      </ul>
    </div>
  </body>
</html>
```

Code snippet is from parent-selector.txt

It's important to note that `:parent()` will select elements that contain child text nodes. This can include text nodes with just whitespace text as is illustrated in the following code sample. `#empty` isn't really empty. It contains a space, so it will match as a `:parent()`.

```
<!DOCTYPE html>
<html>
  <head>
    <script src="http://code.jquery.com/jquery-1.7.1.js">
    </script>

    <script>
      $(function(){
        var parents = $("div:parent").length;
        console.log(parents) //returns 2
      });
    </script>
  </head>
  <body>
<div id="empty">
</div>
<div id="proudParent">
  <ul>
    <li> Children! </li>
  </ul>
</div>
  </body>
</html>
```

Code snippet is from whitespace-parent.txt

Table 4-6 lists jQuery's available content filters.

TABLE 4-6: Content Filters

TYPE	DESCRIPTION
`:contains()`	Selects all elements that contain the specified text.
`:empty`	Removes all child nodes of the set of matched elements from the DOM.
`:has()`	Select elements which contain at least one element that matches the specified selector.
`:parent`	Selects all elements that are the parent of another element, including text nodes.

Filtering by Relationships

The following code snippet demonstrates the use of filter selectors that match according to specific relationships, for example :first-child or :only-child.

```
<!DOCTYPE html>
<html>
  <head>
    <script src="http://code.jquery.com/jquery-1.7.1.js">
    </script>

    <script>
 $(function(){
        console.log( $("div span:first-child") )
//[span#turkey, span#bear, span#martian]
        console.log( $("div span:last-child")   )
//[span#hawk, span#horse, span#martian]
        console.log( $("div span:only-child")   )
//[span#martian]
        console.log( $("div span:nth-child(2)") )
//[span#chicken, span#rabbit]
        console.log( $("div span:nth-child(2n+1)") )
//[span#turkey, span#parrot, span#hawk, span#bear, span#fox, span#horse, span#martian]
        console.log( $("div span:nth-child(even)") )
//[span#chicken, span#pigeon, span#rabbit, span#monkey]
        });
    </script>
  </head>
  <body>
    <div>
      <span id="turkey">Turkey</span>
      <span id="chicken">Chicken</span>
      <span id="parrot">Parrot</span>
      <span id="pigeon">Pigeon</span>
      <span id="hawk">Hawk</span>
    </div>
    <div>
      <span id="bear">bear</span>
      <span id="rabbit">rabbit</span>
      <span id="fox">fox</span>
      <span id="monkey">monkey</span>
      <span id="horse">horse</span>
    </div>
    <div>
      <span id="martian">martian</span>
    </div>
  </body>
</html>
```

Code snippet is from relationship-filter.txt

Table 4-7 summarizes the position selectors of this section.

TABLE 4-7: Child Filters

SELECTOR	DESCRIPTION
:first-child	Selects all elements that are the first child of their parent.
:last-child	Selects all elements that are the last child of their parent.
:nth-child()	Selects all elements that are the nth-child of their parent.
:only-child	Selects all elements that are the only child of their parent.

Custom User Selectors

If the current built-in selectors aren't enough, you can extend jQuery with your own custom-made selectors. To do so, you must extend the core jQuery object. The following code snippet creates a custom selector that selects elements with a green background:

Available for
download on
Wrox.com

```
<!DOCTYPE html>
<html>
  <head>
    <script src="http://code.jquery.com/jquery-1.7.1.js">
    </script>

    <script>

    $(function(){
        // Define custom filter by extending $.expr[":"]
        $.expr[":"].greenbg = function(element) {
          return $(element).css("background-color") === "green";
        };
        var n = $(":greenbg").length;
        console.log("There are " + n + " green divs");
    });
    </script>
  </head>
  <body>
    <div style="width:10; height:10; background-color:green;"></div>
    <div style="width:10; height:10; background-color:black;"></div>
    <div style="width:10; height:10; background-color:blue;"></div>
  </body>
</html>
```

Code snippet is from custom-filters.txt

The capacity to create your own ad-hoc selectors is a welcome feature, because you're not limited to the built-in selector domain.

DOING DOM TRAVERSAL

By now, we hope you're convinced that the jQuery selectors offer a diverse set of options for creating a wrapper object with elements selected from the DOM. The next set of tools you'll need in your arsenal will allow you to manage your wrapped set. Handling tasks such as getting element references, getting another wrapper object with a subset of the original, or generally just traversing the DOM are all handled with ease by jQuery.

Using the `.find()` method you can retrieve descendants from an already wrapped set of elements in a manner similar to selecting using the jQuery function. The `.find()` method also accepts a selector string. The net effect of using `.find()` is like updating the current wrapper set you're operating on. In contrast to the jQuery function, the selector expression is required.

```html
<!DOCTYPE html>
<html>
  <head>
    <script src="http://code.jquery.com/jquery-1.7.1.js">
    </script>

    <script>

      $(function(){
          var wrapper = $("ul");
          console.log("selected list count:" + wrapper.length);

          var newWrapper = wrapper.find("#techBooks");

          console.log("selected list count:" + newWrapper.length);
        });
    </script>
  </head>
  <body>
    <ul id="groceries">
     <li>Eggs</li>
     <li>Bacon</li>
     <li>Ham</li>
    </ul>
    <ul id="books">
     <li>
       <ul id="techBooks">
         <li>Pro jQuery</li>
         <li>JavaScript 101</li>
       </ul>
       <ul id="mathBooks">
         <li>Calculus for the Gods</li>
         <li>Intro to Finite State Machines</li>
       </ul>
     </li>
     <li>How to Win at Jeopardy</li>
     <li>How To Cook</li>
    </ul>
  </body>
</html>
```

Code snippet is from find.txt

In this example, the first console.log displays 4, whereas the second displays 1. The `.find()` method works for getting all of the descendants, but if you want to get only the first level of descendants use `.children()` instead.

jQuery also gives you several shortcuts for accessing special cases of a wrapped element set. It's very common to want to retrieve the first and last elements of a wrapped set, and jQuery has precisely those shortcuts as the following code example demonstrates:

```html
<!DOCTYPE html>
<html>
  <head>
    <script src="http://code.jquery.com/jquery-1.7.1.js">
    </script>

    <script>
      $(function(){
          var listElements = $("li");
          var firstEl = listElements.first();
          var lastEl = listElements.last();

          console.log("firstEl value:" + firstEl.html());
          console.log("firstEl length:" + firstEl.length);

          console.log("lastEl value:" + lastEl.html());
          console.log("firstEl length:" + firstEl.length);
      });
    </script>
  </head>
  <body>
    <ul>
     <li>eggs</li>
     <li>bacon</li>
     <li>ham</li>
    </ul>
  </body>
</html>
```

Code snippet is from children.txt

Here you have an unordered list with three items: eggs, bacon, and ham. Using the jQuery function, all of the list items are selected, and then using the methods `.first()` and `.last()`, the corresponding wrapped elements are retrieved. To verify this, two console.logs are called displaying the length of each wrapper, which should be 1. You've probably noticed a call to the method `.html()`, which retrieves the content from each list item. More on this later.

You can, of course, specify a particular element to retrieve using the `.eq()` method. Like `.first()` and `.last()`, `.eq()` returns a wrapped object.

```html
<!DOCTYPE html>
<html>
  <head>
    <script src="http://code.jquery.com/jquery-1.7.1.js">
```

```
    </script>

    <script>
      $(function(){
          var listElements = $("li");
          var secondEl = listElements.eq(1);
          var fourthEl = listElements.eq(3);

          console.log(secondEl.html()  + " and " + fourthEl.html());
      });
    </script>
  </head>
  <body>
    <ul>
     <li>eggs</li>
     <li>bacon</li>
     <li>ham</li>
     <li>cheese</li>
     <li>juice</li>
     <li>sausage</li>
    </ul>
  </body>
</html>
```

Code snippet is from eq.txt

The console.log will show "bacon and cheese."

Sometimes you may want to directly get a DOM node. For such cases you can use the `.get()` method, which accepts an index as its argument. `get` is zero-based, meaning that it begins its index count at zero, not one. The following code illustrates using `.get()` to access the underlying DOM element of members of the matched set.

> *There is another `.get()` method for Ajax requests. The two are distinguished by usage. The Ajax method is called directly off of the jQuery function (`$.get()`) and the `.get()` method being discussed here acts on a matched set generated by a jQuery selection (`$( selector ).get( x )`).*

Available for
download on
Wrox.com

```
<!DOCTYPE html>
<html>
  <head>
    <script src="http://code.jquery.com/jquery-1.7.1.js">
    </script>

    <script>
      $(function(){
          var listElements = $("li");
          var secondEl = listElements.get(2);
```

```
            var fourthEl = listElements.get(3);

            console.log(secondEl.innerHTML  + " and " + fourthEl.innerHTML);
            //"ham and cheese"
        });
      </script>
    </head>
    <body>
<ul>
      <li>eggs</li>
      <li>bacon</li>
      <li>ham</li>
      <li>cheese</li>
      <li>juice</li>
      <li>sausage</li>
     </ul>
    </body>
  </html>
```

Code snippet is from get.txt

The method `.get()` accepts an index value and returns a DOM node; it's possible to also perform the inverse operation with the method `.index()`. This method accepts a DOM element, and returns its index value. Just like `.get()`, `.index()` is zero-based.

```
<!DOCTYPE html>
<html>
   <head>
     <script src="http://code.jquery.com/jquery-1.7.1.js">
     </script>

     <script>
       $(function(){
           var item2 = document.getElementById("item2");


           console.log($("li").index(item2));
        });
     </script>
   </head>
   <body>
    <ul>
     <li id="item0">eggs</li>
     <li id="item1">bacon</li>
     <li id="item2">ham</li>
     <li id="item3">cheese</li>
     <li id="item4">juice</li>
     <li id="item5">sausage</li>
    </ul>
   </body>
  </html>
```

Code snippet is from index.txt

Not only can you pass a DOM element, but also a jQuery wrapper object. If the wrapper object passed in as an argument contains more than one element, then `.index()` returns the index of the first match.

A third type of argument that `.index()` accepts is a selector string. Again, if more than one element is returned, the zero-based index of the first match is returned. Both `.get()` and `.index()` are considered destructive because they break a jQuery chain. A chain is broken when the method invoked doesn't return a jQuery wrapper object, and hence the chain can't continue.

It's useful to think of a chain as if it were a stack, where each item on the stack is a set of elements. Upon calling a method, such as `.filter()` or `.find()`, a new element set is pushed onto the stack. At times you might want to revert back to the original wrapper object. This is accomplished with the `.end()` method as the following example shows:

```html
<!DOCTYPE html>
<html>
  <head>
    <script src="http://code.jquery.com/jquery-1.7.1.js">
    </script>

    <script>
      $(function(){
          var listElements = $("li");

          listElements
              .filter(":gt(3)")
              .css("color", "green")
            .end()
              .filter(":lt(3)")
              .css("color", "red")
            .end();
          console.log( listElements.length );
      });
    </script>
  </head>
  <body>
    <ul>
      <li>eggs</li>
      <li>bacon</li>
      <li>ham</li>
      <li>cheese</li>
      <li>juice</li>
      <li>sausage</li>
    </ul>
  </body>
</html>
```

Code snippet is from end.txt

Using `.filter()`, you get the last two list items from the original wrapper, `listElements`, and then using `.css()` you modify the text color to green. But, because you want to change every element with an index value less than 3 to red, a call is made to `.end()` returning the currently operated wrapper to the original set of list items. Notice the additional indentions made in the chain in order to make the code more readable.

Up to now, all the examples in this chapter have used the .length property to return the number of elements selected, but you can also use the .size() method as well. There is a performance disadvantage to using a method call instead of the length property, but if you prefer the method call for visual consistency with the rest of your code it's there.

Occasionally you'll need to convert the set of matched elements to a plain JavaScript Array. jQuery provides a method to do just that, called .toArray(). The following code sample illustrates this plainly named method in action. A list of names is selected using jQuery. It's converted into a native Array and the Array method reverse() is used to swap the order of the items. Looping through the new version of the array and logging the names illustrates the successful result.

```html
<!DOCTYPE html>
<html>
<head>
   <script src="http://code.jquery.com/jquery-1.7.1.js">
   </script>

   <script >
     $(function(){
       var winners = $( "#winners li" ).toArray();
       winners = winners.reverse();
      for ( var i = 0, test = winners.length; i < test; i++) {
        console.log(winners[i].innerHTML);
        /*logs
        Nicolas Frantz
        Mark Cavendish
        André Darrigade
        Lance Armstrong
        André Leducq
        Bernard Hinault
        Eddy Merckx
        */
      }
    });
   </script>
</head>
<body>
   <ol id="winners" ><li>Eddy Merckx</li>
     <li>Bernard Hinault</li>
     <li>André Leducq</li>
     <li>Lance Armstrong</li>
     <li>André Darrigade</li>
     <li>Mark Cavendish</li>
     <li>Nicolas Frantz</li>
</ol>

</body>
</html>
```

Code snippet is from toArray.txt

Finally, there's one more selection method to look at before moving onto modifying elements. `.andSelf()` is the kind of method that you don't always need, but when you do need it it's invaluable. As you learned when looking at `.end()` jQuery maintains a stack that keeps track of changes to the matched set of elements. When a method that traverses the DOM like `.filter()` or `.find()` is called the new matched set is pushed onto the stack. If you need to manipulate the previous set of matched elements as well, `.andSelf()` will come to the rescue. The following code sample illustrates using `.andSelf()` to add a div back onto the stack after doing a `.find()` manipulates the stack. The new set of matched elements matches the order of the elements in the DOM.

```html
<!DOCTYPE html>
<html>
<head>
    <script src='http://code.jquery.com/jquery-1.7.1.js'>
</script>

    <script >
    $(function(){
        console.log( $("div") );
    // [ div ]
        console.log( $( "div" ).find("p") );
    // [ p ,p, p ]
        console.log( $( "div" ).find("p").andSelf() );
    // [ div, p, p, p ]
    });
    </script>
</head>
<body>
  <div>
    <p>Paragraph</p>
    <p>Paragraph</p>
    <p>Paragraph</p>
  </div>
</body>
</html>
```

Code snippet is from andSelf.txt

ACCESSING AND MODIFYING ELEMENTS, ATTRIBUTES, AND CONTENT

Now that you've seen the myriad ways jQuery can select elements, you probably will want to do something with these retrieved elements such as getting/setting text, attributes, or even HTML content. jQuery provides several convenient methods for achieving all of this.

Working with Content

One of the most glorious features of JavaScript is the ability to update text on web pages on the fly, instead of waiting for a page reload. With jQuery, it's easy to not only change the contents of a node, but to retrieve them as well. Consider the case where you'd like to get the contents of a paragraph element of an HTML page. One manner to accomplish this is with the .text() method. But beware, the .text() method combines the text of all the elements in a selected set.

```
<!DOCTYPE html>
<html>
  <head>
    <script src="http://code.jquery.com/jquery-1.7.1.js">
    </script>

    <script type="text/javascript">
      $(function(){
          var content = $("p").text();
          console.log(content);
      });
    </script>
  </head>
  <body>
    <p>Where's </p>
    <p>The </p>
    <p>Beef?</p>
  </body>
</html>
```

Code snippet is from text.txt

This example displays "Where's the beef?" in the console. That's all fine and great, but what about updating the contents? You use the same method, .text(), but instead of an argument list, feed it a string argument containing the new text you'd like to insert. In this next example, after page load, the paragraph element doesn't display the text "blah" but rather "The trees are green."

```
<!DOCTYPE html>
<html>
  <head>
    <script src="http://code.jquery.com/jquery-1.7.1.js">
    </script>

    <script>
      $(function(){
          $("p").text("The trees are green.");
      });
    </script>
  </head>
  <body>
    <p>Blah</p>
  </body>
</html>
```

Code snippet is from text-setter.txt

The second way to get and set content is using the .html() method. Again, just like .text(), .html() gets or sets a value depending on whether you feed it an argument. So, what's the difference between .text() and .html()? .text() works with both XML and HTML documents; .html() doesn't. Also, .text() gets the text contents of all descendants, whereas .html() retrieves only the first element matched.

The following example both gets and sets HTML content of a div tag:

```html
<!DOCTYPE html>
<html>
  <head>
    <script src="http://code.jquery.com/jquery-1.7.1.js">
    </script>

    <script>
      $(function(){
          var content = $("div").html();
          console.log(content);
          $("div").html("<p style='color:red;'>RED</p>");
      });
    </script>
  </head>
  <body>
    <div>
      <ul>
      </ul>
    </div>
  </body>
</html>
```

Code snippet is from html.txt

Upon loading this example, you'll find the following in the console:

```html
<ul>
  <li>one</li>
  <li>two</li>
  <li>three</li>
</ul>
```

and after pressing Enter, the div content is updated to a paragraph element with the text RED. The CSS style in this example is hard-coded, but this really isn't the best way to accomplish the same effect. It's better to use the .css() method discussed in the next chapter.

Finally, both .text() and .html() also accept a function as a parameter for setting content. This allows for dynamic creation of content, instead of just static text.

```html
<!DOCTYPE html>
<html>
  <head>
    <script src="http://code.jquery.com/jquery-1.7.1.js">
    </script>

    <script>
```

```
        $(function(){
            $("div#testHTML").html(function(){
                var content = "";
                for(i = 1; i <=3; i++){
                    content += "testing " + i + "...<br />";
                }
                return content;
            });
        });
    </script>
  </head>
  <body>
    <div id="testHTML">
    </div>
  </body>
</html>
```

Code snippet is from html-with-function-argument.txt

In this last example, the body consists of a lone div. After selecting the testHTML div, the .html() method is passed an anonymous function which generates the following HTML:

```
testing 1...<br />
testing 2...<br />
testing 3...<br />
```

Manipulating Attributes

Attributes are the properties of an element, not to be confused with a JavaScript object property. Element attribute values are both retrieved and modified using the .attr() method. If .attr() is passed two values, one for the attribute name and one for the attribute value, then it sets an attribute, but if it's invoked with one argument (again, the attribute name), it gets a value. The following example illustrates both cases:

```
<!DOCTYPE html>
<html>
  <head>
    <style type="text/css">
      .blue {
        Background-color: blue;
      }
    </style>
    <script src="http://code.jquery.com/jquery-1.7.1.js">
    </script>

    <script>
      $(function(){
          $("p#i_am_blue").attr("class","blue");
          var attribute = $("p#i_am_blue").attr();
          console.log(attribute);
      });
    </script>
```

```
    </head>
    <body>
      <p id="i_am_blue">
        I am Blue.
      </p>
    </body>
  </html>
```

Code snippet is from atttribute-manipulation.txt

Sometimes you just don't need attributes. Yep, you guessed it, there's a method for removing an attribute too, surprisingly enough called .removeAttr(). The following code example shows .removeAttr() in action, removing the class attribute from the #i_am_not_blue div.

```
<!DOCTYPE html>
<html>
  <head>
    <style type="text/css">
      .blue {
        background-color: blue;
      }
    </style>
    <script src="http://code.jquery.com/jquery-1.7.1.js">
    </script>

    <script>
      $(function(){
          $("p#i_am_not_blue").removeAttr("class");
      });
    </script>
  </head>
  <body>
    <p id="i_am_not_blue" class="blue >
      I am not Blue.
    </p>
  </body>
</html>
```

Code snippet is from removeAttr.txt

There's no need for a console.log to verify this example. After loading this example you'll see that the text is black.

GENERATING HTML

It's also possible to generate code with the jQuery wrapper function. To do so, pass in a string to the jQuery function like so:

```
$("<p>My nifty paragraph</p>");
```

This is only half the story, because the new paragraph element added to the DOM is parentless. You'll need an additional jQuery method like `.appendTo()` in order to insert the new markup into the DOM. HTML generation, coupled with selectors and chaining, allow for some very elegant jQuery statements. The following code sample shows HTML generation, coupled with `.appendTo()` and `.attr()` used to insert a new H1 into the page.

```html
<!DOCTYPE html>
<html>
  <head>
    <style type="text/css">
      .titleText {
        color: green;
        font-family:arial;
      }
    </style>
    <script>
    </script>

    <script>
      $(function(){
        $("<h1>Have A Nice Day</h1>")
          .appendTo("body")
          .attr("class", "titleText");
      });
    </script>
  </head>
  <body>
  </body>
</html>
```

Code snippet is from generating-html.txt

SUMMARY

By now, you should have a very good idea of the efficiency and power of jQuery selectors. Effective use of all the different types of selector expressions, in harmony, greatly reduces complexity when retrieving elements for manipulation inside the DOM.

You've revisited a subset of the JavaScript language, learned about the jQuery wrapper, learned to write concise selector expressions, and found new ways of modifying element contents, solidifying your jQuery foundation. If you're using these concepts in real life, your JavaScript code should look far more concise and readable.

5

Event Handling

WHAT'S IN THIS CHAPTER?

➤ Understanding the Browser Event Model

➤ Understanding How jQuery Handles Events

➤ Working with jQuery Events

Any GUI-based modern application is inherently event-driven, and web applications are no exception. All event-driven applications follow the familiar pattern of setting up event-handling mechanisms, waiting for an interesting event to occur (such as a mouse click), and responding to that event. Beyond the normal clicking and key-pressing events, there's also page loading and other semantic events, as well as the more recently added events such as swipe gestures, which are now important given the popularity of touch devices such as iPhones and Android. Events are fundamental to the Web; the use of JavaScript is seriously limited without them. The jQuery docs categorize event methods into document loading, form events, event-handler attachments, mouse events, browser events, methods related to the Event object, and keyboard events.

Most likely, at some point in your career as a developer you've heard about the various cross-browser issues that plague web development. How different browsers manage events is one of the most significant cross-browser problems.

In this chapter you review basic JavaScript event handling, both DOM level 0 and level 2, event propagation, bubbling, and Internet Explorer's event model to get a better understanding of what's going on under the hood. Then you translate that knowledge over to jQuery's event-handling mechanism, and see how it normalizes all of the cross-browser difficulties. Finally, you apply all this to a sample application.

UNDERSTANDING THE BROWSER EVENT MODEL

Before getting into how jQuery handles events, and how it saves you a lot of grief, let's review JavaScript event models. JavaScript was originally introduced as LiveScript back in 1995. Getting in the DeLorean and jumping back in time to 1996, Netscape Navigator and Microsoft Internet Explorer 3 were all the rage among the young crowd. Table 5-1 illustrates the various event models in play during those primordial days of web scripting.

TABLE 5-1: DOM Level Events

DOM LEVEL	DESCRIPTIONS
0	Original event models developed by Netscape. All browsers support this model.
2	Standard event model, more advanced than level 0, but not supported by IE.
IE Model	A separate event model that only IE browsers use.

DOM level 0 refers to the document model support given by Netscape Navigator 2.0, which is also adopted by later browsers. This level is not a formal standard, but all major browsers are level 0 compatible. The DOM provides an interface for accessing and modifying the content, style, and structure of an HTML document. DOM level 0 events are handled either inline, with an "on" attribute added to the element with JavaScript code as the attribute value, or by selecting the element inside JavaScript code and then binding an anonymous function as the event handler. The following snippet demonstrates the former method:

Available for
download on
Wrox.com

```
<html>
  <head>
    <style type="text/css">
      .clickDiv {
        width:100px;
        height:100px;
        background-color:blue;
      }
    </style>
    <script type="text/javascript">
      function hitMe(){
        var txtNode = document.createTextNode(" clicked ");
        var br = document.createElement("br");
        document.getElementsByTagName("body")[0].appendChild(txtNode);
        document.getElementsByTagName("body")[0].appendChild(br);
      }
    </script>
  </head>
  <body>
<div class="clickDiv" onclick="hitMe();">
</div>
  </body>
</html>
```

Code snippet is from onclick.txt

The JavaScript in this example is obviously intrusive. I've bound to the `onclick` event the `hitMe()` method. The previous example can also be written as:

```html
<html>
  <head>
    <style type="text/css">
      .clickDiv {
        width:100px;
        height:100px;
        background-color:blue;
      }
    </style>
    <script type="text/javascript">
      document.getElementById("clickDiv").onclick = function(event){
        document.getElementsByTagName("body")[0].appendText("clicked");
      }
    </script>
  </head>
  <body>
    <div id="clickDiv" class="clickBox">Click Here</div>
  </body>
</html>
```

Code snippet is from better-onclick.txt

which now separates the control logic from the structure. This still suffers from a few serious setbacks. The function bound to the `onclick` event accepts a `vent` object. While most browsers accept the standard `event` object, Internet Explorer uses *window.event*, or in other words, binds the event object to the global window object. Using feature detection, preferred over browser detection, your event handler script should do something like the following:

```
var evt = (window.event ? window.event : event);
```

Furthermore, the standard `event` object is not the same as IE's `Event` object, and supports a slightly different set of properties. For cross-browser scripts, this is very annoying and breaks compatibility. Table 5-2 illustrates some of the similarities/differences between the IE `Event` object and the standard `Event` object.

TABLE 5-2: Firefox Event Object (In) Compatibilities

NAME	PROPERTY OR METHOD?	IE EQUIVALENT
stopPropagation()	Method	cancelBubble()
layerX, layerY	Property	offsetX, offset
Target	Property	srcElement
Type	Property	Type
preventDefault()	Method	returnValue()

continues

TABLE 5-2 *(continued)*

NAME	PROPERTY OR METHOD?	IE EQUIVALENT
altKey, ctrlKey, shiftKey	Property	altKey, ctrlKey, shiftKey
Button	Property	Button
charCode	Property	keyCode
relatedTarget	Property	fromElement, toElement
Bubbles	Property	N/A

At times, you may want to bind several different handlers to the onclick event of the same element. In DOM level 0, binding will overwrite any other method already bound to the event.

The solution is found in DOM level 2 events. You probably noticed a lack of DOM level 1 events; it's because they don't exist. Level 2, on the other hand, is a more advanced model than level 0, and is supported by most browsers except for IE version 8 and earlier; more on this deviation later. In this model, instead of assigning an event handler function as an object property each page element in the DOM has a method called .addEventListener(), which allows you to add more than one event handler to an element. For example:

Available for
download on
Wrox.com

```html
<html>
  <head>
    <script src="http://code.jquery.com/jquery-1.7.1.js"></script>
    <script>
      $(function(){
        var eventType = "click";
        var useCapturePhase = false;
        var handler1 = function(event){ /* handler code here */ };
        var handler2 = function(event){ /* handler code here */ };

        $("#element").addEventListener(eventType, handler1, useCapturePhase);
        $("#element").addEventListener(eventType, handler2, useCapturePhase);
      });
    </script>
  </head>
  <body>
  </body>
</html>
```

Code snippet is from addEventListener.txt

The addEventListener() accepts three arguments: the event type (in this case it's "click"), the function that will handle the event, and a Boolean value for using the capturing phase. "What's that?" you ask.

Event Capturing and Bubbling

Consider the situation of nested elements with the same kind of event type, for example an `onclick` event type. Which element should have its `onclick` event handler executed first, the inner element or the outer element? Originally, Netscape decided that the handling should be from outer to inner, called *capturing*, as Figure 5-1 illustrates.

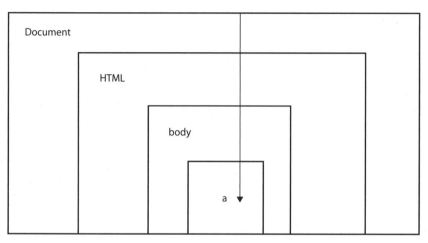

FIGURE 5-1

Microsoft went with the opposite approach where the inner element's "onclick" handler should be executed before the outer element's, or the *bubbling* phase, as shown in Figure 5-2.

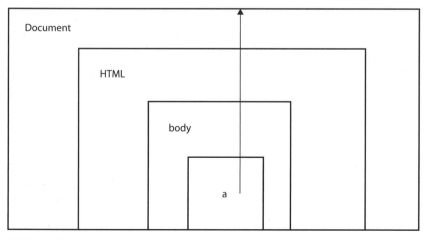

FIGURE 5-2

The third argument to the `.addEventListener()` method is a Boolean flag to determine whether or not you should use the capture phase.

But, you may not want event propagation or bubbling to occur at all; this can also be controlled in JavaScript. In browsers that follow the W3C standard, a call to the method `.stopPropagation()` is used. In older versions of IE, the property `cancelBubble` of the event object is assigned a value of true.

The following example demonstrates event capturing:

```html
<html>
  <head>
    <style type="text/css">
      .div1Class {
        width: 300;
        height: 300;
        background-color: blue;
      }

      .div2Class {
        width: 200;
        height: 200;
        background-color: green;
      }

      .div3Class {
        width: 100;
        height: 100;
        background-color: red;
      }
    </style>

    <script src="http://code.jquery.com/jquery-1.7.1.js"></script>
    <script>
      $(function(){
        function f(id){
          document.body.innerHTML += "<p>executing handler for div " + id + "</p>";
        }

        document.getElementById("div1").onclick = function(){
          f("1");
        }

        document.getElementById("div2").onclick = function(){
          f("2");
        }

        document.getElementById("div3").onclick = function(){
          f("3");
        }
      });
    </script>
  </head>
  <body>
```

```
        <div id="div1" class="div1Class">
          <div id="div2" class="div2Class">
            <div id="div3" class="div3Class">
            </div>
          </div>
        </div>
      </body>
    </html>
```

Code snippet is from stop-propagation.txt

The previous example is tested with Google Chrome; you can see the results in Figure 5-3. After clicking on div 3 each successive handler is called.

IE8 and below do not support DOM level 2 like most other browsers. For example, the IE event model uses `attachEvent` instead of `addEventListener`. As mentioned earlier, IE's `Event` object doesn't completely support all the same methods and properties of the other W3C-compliant browsers; even the event names differ. IE offers an event propagation similar to bubbling, but not exactly the same.

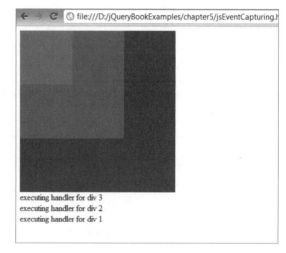

executing handler for div 3
executing handler for div 2
executing handler for div 1

FIGURE 5-3

UNDERSTANDING HOW JQUERY HANDLES EVENTS

All this talk of propagation, event model inconsistencies, and so on, is enough to drive anyone mad. The logical next step is to abstract away the differences in event-handling mechanisms, which is precisely what jQuery does. You have a few options for binding event handlers in jQuery: `.bind()`, `.live()`, one of the several event methods such as `.click()`, `.load()`, or `.mouseout()`, or the new unified `on()` and `off()` API introduced in jQuery 1.7.

Just like DOM level 2, you can bind more than one event handler to the same event using `.bind()`:

Available for download on Wrox.com

```
<html>
  <head>
    <script src="http://code.jquery.com/jquery-1.7.1.js"></script>
    <script>
      $(function(){
        $("#aDiv").bind('click', function(){
          console.log("Handler 1");
        });

        $("#aDiv").bind('click', function(){
```

```
        console.log("Handler 2");
      });
    });
  </script>
</head>
<body>
  <div id="aDiv" class="boxDiv">Press Me
  </div>
</body>
</html>
```

Code snippet is from bind.txt

The superfluous "on" is removed from the event name, so instead of onclick() you use click(). In this example, upon clicking the div, aDiv, you will see both logs. Because jQuery is handling all of the behind-the-scenes details, .bind(), .click(), and so on are the same independent of which browser is interpreting your code. Quite a relief!

jQuery's mechanism for handling events has a consistent naming for all the different event types independent of the browser, and like the DOM level 2 model, allows for multiple event handlers on the same element and event type. The Event object passed into the handlers is also normalized and is of the type *jQuery.Event*, and is guaranteed to contain the properties outlined in Table 5-3 independent of browser/platform:

TABLE 5-3: Properties Independent of Browser/Platform

altKey	Detail	pageY
attrChange	eventPhase	prevValue
attrName	fromElement	relatedNode
Bubbles	Handler	relatedTarget
Button	keyCode	Screen
Cancelable	layerX	shiftKey
charCode	layerY	srcElement
Client	metaKey	Target
Client	newValue	toElement
ctrlKey	Offset	View
currentTarget	originalTarget	wheelDelta
Data	pageX	which

APPLYING JQUERY EVENT HANDLERS

The jQuery way to bind a function to an event is through the `.bind()` method, which accepts three arguments: the event type, data, and the function handler. For example, to bind a `mouseover` event:

```
$("#objId").bind('mouseover', function(event){
    // code here…
});
```

In this example, an element, `objId` is selected by `id`, and has a `mouseover` event bound to an anonymous function.

Table 5-4 lists all the available jQuery event handlers.

TABLE 5-4: jQuery Events

`.blur()`	`.mouseenter()`
`.focus()`	`.mousemove()`
`.select()`	`.mouseout()`
`.submit()`	`.mouseover()`
`.click()`	`.mouseup()`
`.dblclick()`	`.toggle()`
`.focusin()`	`.error()`
`.focusout()`	`.resize()`
`.hover()`	`.scroll()`
`.mousedown()`	

It's also possible for you to remove any bindings with `.unbind()`, which accepts a string denominating the event type to unbind. Using the previous example as a reference, to remove the binding do the following:

```
$("selectorHere").unbind("mouseover");
```

This removes all events of type `mouseover` from the selected elements. If you want the capability to unbind a particular class of events, events can also be namespaced.

The element you want to bind an event handler to may not exist given the dynamic nature of JavaScript/jQuery. If this is the case, bind won't work, so instead use the corresponding method `.live()`, which will bind an event handler independently of whether it exists. This is very useful for cases where DOM elements are added on the fly as shown in the following example, where the click handler to a non-existent anchor element is bound using `.live()`. When the `.ready()` event is executed, the anchor is dynamically added and is bound to the click handler.

```
<html>
  <head>
    <scriptsrc="http://code.jquery.com/jquery-1.7.1.js"></script>
    <script>
      $(function(){
        // element doesn't exist yet, but we can create handler
        // anyways
        $("#anchor").live("click", function(event){
          console.log("I have a handler");
        });

        $(document).append("<a id='anchor'> I go no where </a>")
      });
    </script>
  </head>
  <body>
  </body>
</html>
```

Code snippet is from live.txt

Similar to `.unbind()`, `.live()` has a corresponding `.die()` method for removing the handlers
set by `.live()`. The `.live()` method cannot be chained, unlike other jQuery methods. In cases
where you want to use chaining, use the `.delegate()` method instead, which also binds a handler
independent of whether the DOM element exists.

```
<html>
  <head>
    <script src="http://code.jquery.com/jquery-1.7.1.js"></script>
    <script>
      $(function(){
        $("body").delegate("p","click",function(){
          console.log('ouch');
        }).css("color", "green");
      });
    </script>
  </head>
  <body>
    <p>Hit Me!</p>
  </body>
</html>
```

Code snippet is from delegate.txt

And again, just like `.unbind()` and `.die()`, `.delegate()` has a corresponding `.undelegate()`
method. For example, to remove the binding from the previous example you could do the following:

```
$("body").undelegate("p","click");
```

In some cases, you may want for a handler to execute only, or at most once. You can accomplish this
effect using the `.one()` method as the following snippet demonstrates. The click event handler is
executed only once for the first div.

```html
<html>
  <head>
    <style type="text/css">
      .div1 {
        width : 100;
        height : 100;
        background-color: blue;
      }

      .div2 {
        width : 100;
        height : 100;
        background-color: red;
      }
    </style>
    <script src="http://code.jquery.com/jquery-1.7.1.js"></script>
    <script>
    $(function(){
      $(".div1").one("click", function(){
        $("body").append("<p>clicked div 1 </p>");
      });

      $(".div2").bind("click", function(){
        $("body").append("<p>clicked div 2 </p>");
      });
    });
    </script>
  </head>
  <body>
    <div class="div1"></div>
    <div class="div2"></div>
  </body>
</html>
```

Code snippet is from one.txt

Figure 5-4 shows the results.

jQuery also has method shortcuts for creating event handlers.

```javascript
$("#el").bind('click', function(event){
  // do stuff
});
```

can be rewritten as:

```javascript
$("#el").click(function(event){
  // do stuff
});
```

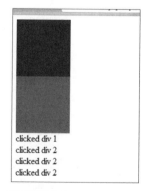

FIGURE 5-4

The same goes for hover, mouseout, mouseover, and so on. The following example shows how to make a classic "rollover" effect by chaining two event shortcuts, mouseover and mouseout:

```
<html>
  <head>
    <script src="http://code.jquery.com/jquery-1.7.1.js"></script>
    <script>
      $(function(){
        $("#text").mouseover(function(){
          $(this).css("text-decoration","underline");
        }).mouseout(function(){
          $(this).css("text-decoration","none");
        });
      });
    </script>
  </head>
  <body>
    <p id="text">I go no where</p>
  </body>
</html>
```

Code snippet is from mouseover.txt

You can also programmatically, or manually, execute handlers already bound. In other words, to initiate an event handler you don't actually need the event to occur, which is useful for testing. In the following example, three `divs` (each conveniently given a different color) are each bound to a `mouseover` event that causes a nested paragraph element to fade in and out. Following the `divs` is a button that when clicked, fires the `.trigger()` method to manually cause all of the `mouseover` handlers to execute simultaneously. The `.trigger()` method is called on a wrapped set, and accepts two arguments: a string denoting the event type to trigger, in this case `mouseover`, and an array of additional parameters to pass in. Alternatively, a `jQuery.Event` can be passed in instead. By default, event handlers executed by a call to the `.trigger()` method bubble up.

```
<html>
  <head>
    <style type="text/css">
      div {
        padding : 10 10 10 10;
        width : 100;
        height : 100;
      }

      .div1 {
        background-color : blue;
      }

      .div2 {
        background-color : yellow;
      }

      .div3 {
        background-color : green;
      }

    </style>
    <script src="http://code.jquery.com/jquery-1.7.1.js"></script>
```

```
<script>
  $(document).ready(function(){
    $("p").hide();

    $(".div1", this).mouseover(function(){
      $(this).find("p").fadeIn().fadeOut();
    });

    $(".div2", this).mouseover(function(){
      $(this).find("p").fadeIn().fadeOut();
    });

    $(".div3", this).mouseover(function(){
      $(this).find("p").fadeIn().fadeOut();
    });

    $("input").click(function(){
      $("div").trigger("mouseover");
    });
  });
</script>
</head>
<body>
  <div class="div1">
    <p>Here</p>
  </div>
  <div class="div2">
    <p>Here</p>
  </div>
  <div class="div3">
    <p>Here</p>
  </div>
  <input type="button" value="run with trigger"></input>
</body>
</html>
```

Code snippet is from trigger.txt

Figure 5-5 shows the preceding example in action.

The .trigger() method calls the browser event. For example, doing a
$("#myButton").trigger("click"); calls the default JavaScript onclick
method. Using .triggerHandler() instead, as the name implies, executes the
attached handler rather than the native method and takes the same arguments as
.trigger(). But, unlike the .trigger() method, .triggerHandler() executes
the handler of the first matched object instead of an entire matched set, and does
not bubble up.

Table 5-5 summarizes jQuery's methods for attaching event handlers.

FIGURE 5-5

TABLE 5-5: Event Handler Attachment

METHOD	DESCRIPTION
.bind()	Binds an event handler
.delegate()	Binds a handler to one or more events currently or in the future
.die()	Removes event handlers add using the .live() method
.live()	Binds a handler currently or in the future
.one()	Attaches an event handler that is executed at most once
.proxy()	Takes a function and returns another belonging to a specified context
.trigger()	Executes event handlers attached to an element for an event type
.triggerHandler()	Executes all handlers for a specific event
.unbind()	Removes event bindings created with .bind()
.undelegate()	Removes bindings created with .delegate()

WORKING WITH EVENTS

Now you get to put together not only your knowledge of events, but your cumulative work with jQuery. One of the most common features of any database-driven web application is a registration form. E-mail, social networks, or anywhere you want to post content, at the very least you'll need to provide an e-mail and a password. In this sample application, you create a skeleton that could easily serve for a more complex/complete user registration form. The form will ask for a username, e-mail, password, and password confirmation. Although the application doesn't actually save (yet), a button is provided for validating the inputs. All fields are required, and the passwords must match in order to pass validation. Optionally, the user may add location information; in this case, a simple drop-down select for U.S. state and city information.

Clicking the Add Location button generates a state drop-down and a city drop-down that are dependent — when the state value is changed, so is the list of available cities. Of course, the values available for state and city are by no means comprehensive, or even practical, considering that only the U.S. is considered. But, for the purposes of this example it suffices. Figure 5-6 demonstrates the implemented registration form.

FIGURE 5-6

First, begin with the basic markup. This should be old hat by now. After all of the regular boilerplate HTML, the body consists of a div for displaying any error messages, and a form with text inputs and two password inputs. At the bottom are two buttons. Notice that the body contains only HTML elements, and absolutely no JavaScript, as it should be.

```html
<!DOCTYPE html>
<html>
  <head>
    <title>User Registration and Validation</title>
    <script src="http://code.jquery.com/jquery-1.7.1.js"></script>
    <script>
      $(function(){
        // jQuery code will go here
      )};
    </script>
  </head>
  <body>
    <div id="msg"></div>
    <form name="userRegistrationForm">
      <label for="userName">User</label><input type="text" name="userName" /><br/>
      <label for="email">Email</label><input type="text" name="email" /><br/>
      <label for="password">Password</label><input type="text" name="password" /><br/>
      <label for="chkPassword">Re-enter Password</label>
      <input type="text" name="chkPassword" /><br/>
      <input type="button" name="validate" value="Validate Inputs" />
    </form>
    <input type="button" name="addLocation" value="Add Location" />

  </body>
</html>
```

The `$(function(){…});` as you'll recall is equivalent to using `.ready()`, which executes the enclosed code after all DOM elements are loaded, but before the full document is loaded with all assets. The first action to add is the validation of the fields. The validation will occur upon a click event of the `validate` button. Using the jQuery attribute selector to get the `validate` button as wrapped object, you then apply a `click` event with anonymous function as its handler. Whenever the `validate` button is clicked the `msg` div has its content removed using the `.html()` method to get rid of any old messages. Then all of the input values are extracted using `.val()`.

Using `&&` operators to simplify the conditional tests, when a value of any of the inputs is empty (null), some text is appended to the `msg` div, and the CSS styling of the font color is changed to red on the fly. The second check confirms that both passwords match using the identity operator (`===`), and just like the previous validation, upon failure adds a text message to the `msg` div. Only one of the two messages is ever shown, never both at the same time. Figures 5-7 and 5-8 illustrate each of the messages being shown, individually.

```javascript
...
$( 'input[name="validate"]' ).click(function(){
        // clear message div
        $("#msg").html("");

        // get values for all input boxes
        var userName = $( 'input[name="userName"]' ).val();
        var email = $( 'input[name="email"]' ).val();
```

```
var pass1 = $( 'input[name="password"]' ).val();
var pass2 = $( 'input[name="chkPassword"]' ).val();

// no empty values permitted
var hasValue = userName && email && pass1 && pass2;
if( !hasValue ){
    $("#msg")
    .append("All Fields are required.")
    .css("color","red");
    return false;
}

// check that passwords match
var passwordMatch = false;
if( pass1 === pass2 ) {
    passwordMatch = true;
}

if( !passwordMatch ){
    $("#msg").append("<p>Passwords don't match.</p>").css("color", "red");
    return false;
}
});
...
```

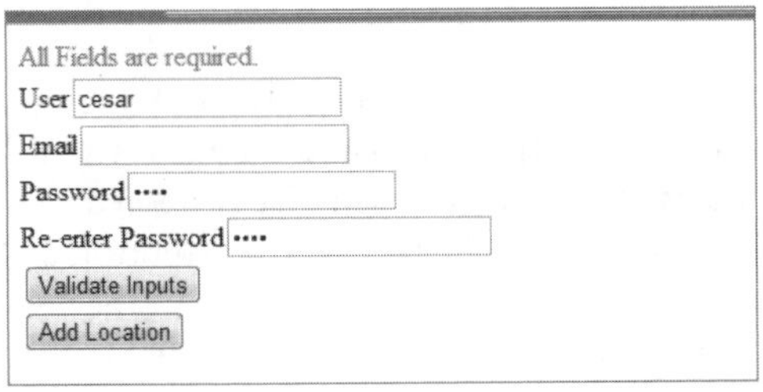

FIGURE 5-7

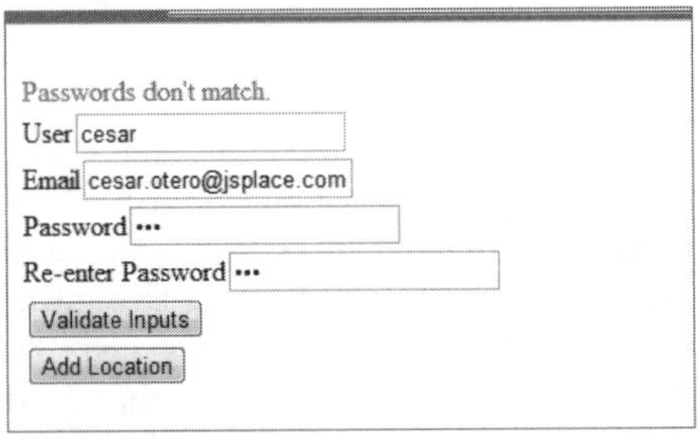

FIGURE 5-8

Now for the tricky part; neither of the drop-downs exists in the DOM until the Add Location button is clicked. Hence, the elements must be generated by jQuery, but this also means that the event handlers must be created using .live() rather than .bind().

```
$( "input[name='addLocation']" ).click(function(){
    $( "body" )
        .append( "<select name='stateCombo'>"
            + "<option>Select State</option></select>" );
```

Here, .append() is used to create the select element inside of the click event handler (listener) for the Add Location button. Clicking this button multiple times will continue to append select elements to the document body. To prevent a user from doing this, you can disable the button after a single click:

```
$(this).attr("disabled", "disabled");
```

For the limited location options, I've picked three states: California, Florida, and New York. A string for each is kept in an array, which is iterated over when generating the select list. Simultaneously, a second select list (for the city) is also appended to the document body, without any data.

```
// add some sample states
var states = ["California", "Florida", "New York"];

$.each(states, function(index, value){
    $("[name='stateCombo']")
    .append("<option value='"+index+"'>" + value + "</option>");
});

// add another empty select list
$("body")
.append("<select name='cityCombo'><option>Select City</option></select>");
});
```

Notice that some concatenation of strings is required here for the HTML strings. This is a perfect place to use a more readable jQuery string template, which you'll see in Chapter 11. In the next snippet, the "change" event is bound to the state select element, or combo box, using the .live() method. This way you don't have to worry about whether the select element actually exists at load time.

Three string arrays with city names for each of the different states are stored in transient variables. Depending on which state is selected (0 for California, 1 for Florida, and 2 for New York) determines which array is saved to the cities array, which in turn is then used to load the city select element. Each time the state changes, the city select element, cityCombo, is emptied, or in other words, all of its children are removed from the DOM altogether.

```
// use .live() since states select box doesn't exist yet
$("[name='stateCombo']").live("change", function(event){
    // get name of state and fill with some data
    var selectedState = $(this).val();

    var CA_Cities = ["San Francisco", "Los Angeles", "Mountain View"];
    var FL_Cities = ["Fort Lauderdale", "Miami", "Orlando"];
    var NY_Cities = ["New York", "Buffalo", "Ithica"];
    var cities = [];

    if(selectedState == 0){
       cities = $.extend([], CA_Cities);
    } else if(selectedState == 1){
       cities = $.extend([], FL_Cities);
    } else if(selectedState == 2){
       cities = $.extend([],NY_Cities);
    }

    // clear cityCombo of any previous values
```

```
        $("[name='cityCombo']").empty();
        $.each(cities, function(index, value){
            $("[name='cityCombo']").append("<option value='"+index+"'>"
                                            +value+"</option>");
        });
    });
```

Now, you can put all this together into the complete application, shown in the final code snippet of this chapter. Several improvements come to mind, such as a mask for the e-mail address field, perhaps by use of a third-party plugin, but for demonstrating handlers for dynamically generated elements, as well as some of the more common events, such as mouse clicks and ready, this example works just fine.

```
<!DOCTYPE html>
<html>
    <head>
        <title>User Registration and Validation</title>
        <script src="http://code.jquery.com/jquery-1.7.1.js"></script>
        <script>
            $(function(){
                $( 'input[name="validate"]' ).click(function(){
                    // clear message div
                    $("#msg").html("");

                    // get values for all input boxes
                    var userName = $( 'input[name="userName"]' ).val();
                    var email = $( 'input[name="email"]' ).val();
                    var pass1 = $( 'input[name="password"]' ).val();
                    var pass2 = $( 'input[name="chkPassword"]' ).val();

                    // no empty values permitted
                    var hasValue = userName && email && pass1 && pass2;
                    if( !hasValue ){
                        $("#msg")
                        .append("All Fields are required.")
                        .css("color","red");
                        return false;
                    }

                    // check that passwords match
                    var passwordMatch = false;
                    if( pass1 === pass2 ) {
                        passwordMatch = true;
                    }

                    if( !passwordMatch ){
                        $("#msg").append("<p>Passwords don't match. </p>").css("color", "red");
                        return false;
                    }
                });

                $( "input[name='addLocation']" ).click(function(){
                    $( "body" ).append( "<select name='stateCombo'><option>"
```

```
                                          + "Select State</option></select>" );

             // disable add location button so that we don't get
             // more than one drop-down
             $(this).attr("disabled", "disabled");

             // add some sample states
             var states = ["California", "Florida", "New York"];
             $.each(states, function(index, value){
                     $("[name='stateCombo']").append("<option value='"
                                                 + index
                                                 + "'>"
                                                 + value
                                                 + "</option>");
             });

             // add another empty select list
             $("body").append("<select name='cityCombo'>"
                             + "<option>Select City</option></select>");
      });

      // use .live() since states select box doesn't exist yet
      $("[name='stateCombo']").live("change", function(event){
             // get name of state and fill with some data
             var selectedState = $(this).val();

             var CA_Cities = ["San Francisco", "Los Angeles", "Mountain View"];
             var FL_Cities = ["Fort Lauderdale", "Miami", "Orlando"];
             var NY_Cities = ["New York", "Buffalo", "Ithica"];
             var cities = [];

             if(selectedState == 0){
                cities = $.extend([], CA_Cities);
             } else if(selectedState == 1){
                cities = $.extend([], FL_Cities);
             } else if(selectedState == 2){
                cities = $.extend([],NY_Cities);
             }

             // clear cityCombo of any previous values
             $("[name='cityCombo']").empty();
             $.each(cities, function(index, value){
                $("[name='cityCombo']").append("<option value='"
                                           +index
                                           +"'>"
                                           +value
                                           +"</option>");
             });
      });
   });
   </script>
</head>
<body>
   <div id="msg"></div>
   <form name="userRegistrationForm">
```

```
            <label for="userName">User</label>
            <input type="text" name="userName" /><br/>
            <label for="email">Email</label>
            <input type="text" name="email" /><br/>
            <label for="password">Password</label>
            <input type="password" name="password" /><br/>
            <label for="chkPassword">Re-enter Password</label>
            <input type="text" name="chkPassword" /><br/>
            <input type="button" name="validate" value="Validate Inputs" />
        </form>
        <input type="button" name="addLocation" value="Add Location" />
    </body>
</html>
```

Code snippet is from event-handling.txt

JQUERY'S NEW EVENT API

Starting with version 1.7, jQuery has made an effort to simplify the API for setting events. While you'll still be able to `.bind()` and `.unbind()`, `.live()` and `.die()` and set `.click()` and `.blur()` the old way, there's now a unified API which bundles all the various functionalities under one, consistent API. The two new methods are `.on()` and `.off()`. Moving forward, these two new methods represent the preferred API, so it's worth learning about them now so that any new projects you kick off going forward start by using the recommended API.

The beauty of `.on()` is that it replaces the functionality of all the event methods covered in this chapter with a single, flexible API. The following code sample shows a basic example of `.on()`, using it to bind a click event to an element already present in the DOM. IT accepts two arguments in this example, an `eventType` and a `handler` function to execute.

This would compare to directly using `.bind("click")` or `.click()` and as proof, this sample rewrites the `.bind()` example from earlier in the chapter.

```
<html>
  <head>
    <script src="http://code.jquery.com/jquery-1.7.1.js"></script>
    <script>
      $(function(){
        $("#aDiv").on('click', function(){
          console.log("Handler 1");
        });

        $("#aDiv").on('click', function(){
          console.log("Handler 2");
        });
      });
    </script>
  </head>
```

```
<body>
  <div id="aDiv" class="boxDiv">Press Me
  </div>
</body>
</html>
```

Code snippet is from on-click.txt

Beyond that basic example, `on()` also exposes the same functionality present in `.delegate()` and `.live()` and does so with the exact same syntax. To use `.on()` like `delegate()` or `.live()`, simply add a second, optional `selector` argument representing the target element for the event. This first example shows `on()` used to replace our example of `live()` from earlier in the chapter. In it, `on()` is used to listen for `clicks` on the `document` and fire the provided `handler` function if the click originates from an element with the ID `#anchor`. Since the listener is set on the document, it will work whenever and wherever the `#anchor` appears.

Available for
download on
Wrox.com

```
<html>
  <head>
    <script src="http://code.jquery.com/jquery-1.7.1.js"></script>
    <script>
      $(function(){
        // element doesn't exist yet, but we can create handler
        // anyways
        $(document).on("click", "#anchor", function(event){
          console.log("I have a handler");
        });

        $("body").append("<a id='anchor'> I go no where </a>")
      });
    </script>
  </head>
  <body>
  </body>
</html>
```

Code snippet is from on-live.txt

Using `on()` like `delegate()` uses the exact same syntax as the `live()` replacement in the previous example. This illustrates one of the benefits of the new, simplified events API. Instead of remembering two separate methods and their associated arguments, you simply remember the one `on()` method and adjust your arguments accordingly. If you truly need to bind events to generic elements across the whole page, you just use `.on()` on the `document` and pass in your generic p or a `selector`. If you want to follow the more performant delegate pattern, you simply apply `.on()` to a more focused `selector`.

Rewriting the earlier `.delegate()` example to use `.on()` is shown in the following code sample. In it, `.on()` is used to listen for `clicks` on the `#delegate` div and fires the provided `handler` function if the click originates on a p.

```html
<html>
  <head>
    <script src="http://code.jquery.com/jquery-1.7.1.js"></script>
    <script>
      $(function(){
        $("#delegate").on("click", "p" , function(){
          console.log('ouch');
        }).css("color", "green");
      });
    </script>
  </head>
  <body>
   <div id="delegate">
    <p>Hit Me!</p>
   </div>
  </body>
</html>
```

Code snippet is from on-delegate.txt

Removing events is as simple as reversing the process with `.off()`, the same way you would use `.unbind()` or `.die()`. The following code shows how to remove the events set in the previous examples.

```
$("#delegate").off("click", "p");
$(document).off("click", "#anchor");
$("#aDiv").off('click');
```

As you can see, this new event API radically simplifies the way jQuery handles events. All the same power and convenience you've learned about in this chapter is still available, it's just presented in a more straightforward, consistent manner.

SUMMARY

At this point your jQuery scripts are taking on a whole new dimension. You can select elements in any number of ways, traverse the DOM, manipulate the classes and attributes of any element, and apply a uniform event-handling mechanism, independent of browser types.

In this chapter you also learned about the historical differences of how event handling is different across browsers; about event propagation, the Event object, and how jQuery helps cut through the haze and deliver a simple solution to managing events easily. Finally, you put together all this event know how into a useful example.

In the next step of your journey, you'll use your knowledge of events to work with data and forms, and learn about submission of forms via Ajax, a cornerstone of modern web development.

NOTES

https://developer.mozilla.org/en/Gecko_DOM_Reference/
http://msdn.microsoft.com/en-us/ie/ff468705#_IntroEnhancedDOM
http://en.wikipedia.org/wiki/DOM_events#Event_handling_models
http://www.quirksmode.org/js/dom0.html
http://www.w3.org/TR/DOM-Level-3-Core/
http://catcode.com/domcontent/events/capture.html
http://www.quirksmode.org/js/events_order.html
http://www.javascriptkit.com/jsref/event.shtml
http://stackoverflow.com/questions/4579117/jquery-live-vs-delegate
http://jquerybyexample.blogspot.com/2010/08/bind-vs-live-vs-delegate-function.html
http://en.wikipedia.org/wiki/Internet_Explorer
http://api.jquery.com/on/

HTML Forms, Data, and Ajax

WHAT'S IN THIS CHAPTER?

➤   jQuery Data Appreciation

➤   Validating Forms With jQuery

➤   Using jQuery's Ajax Methods

The three main topics of this chapter are closely related cousins. HTML forms contain and process data, an everyday operation of the Web. More often than not, form data is processed and posted to a server somewhere asynchronously, rather than the old-fashioned post-process-reload technique. Here, you explore one of the biggest revolutions in web development of the past 10 years — Ajax. You also learn how insanely easy jQuery makes it, simplifying asynchronous communication with the server side.

JQUERY DATA APPRECIATION

An often misused feature of tag elements is using attributes such as `alt` or `class` to attach useful data to an element. For example:

```
<!DOCTYPE html>
<html>
  <head>
      <script src="http://code.jquery.com/jquery-1.6.1.js"></script>
      <script type="text/javascript">
          $(function(){
              $( "#randomEl" ).attr( "alt" , "1999" );
          });
      </script>
  </head>
    <body>
        <img src="usefulImage.jpg" id="randomEl"></div>
    </body>
</html>
```

Just for the record, we're aware of the fact that we can assign "1999" directly to the `alt` attribute, but just suppose you needed to add the string programmatically. There's a semantic problem with this because the attribute used to store the data isn't meaningfully associated. Is 1999 a year, a random integer, or what? A better approach is to use jQuery's `.data()` method, which stores arbitrary data for an element with a meaningful key. It takes the following form:

```
$.data( element, key, value );
```

Or, to retrieve the stored data use:

```
$.data( element, key );
```

For example:

```
<!DOCTYPE html>
<html>
  <head>
    <script src=""></script>
    <script type="text/javascript">
      $(function(){
        $( "#randomEl" ).data( "itemPrice", "1999" );
      });
    </script>
  </head>
  <body>
    <img src="usefulImage.jpg" id="randomEl"></div>
  </body>
</html>
```

Now it's obvious that 1999 isn't a year, but rather a price. HTML5 introduces custom data attributes, where any attribute that is prefixed with `data-` can be used in a standardized, programmatic way. For example, the following div element contains the data attribute `data-age`. That's an alternative for storing information on the client side.

```
<div id="person" data-age="31"></div>
```

Microsoft contributed to the community three additional plugins that were, for a time, officially endorsed by the jQuery project; Data Link, Template, and Globalization. In a later chapter we review the Template plugin. The Data Link plugin allows two-way binding between objects. In other words, it links the field of one object to another, so changing the value of one field changes the corresponding field on the second object. You can use this feature to simplify communication between a form and an object because it removes glue code. For example:

```
<!DOCTYPE html>
<html>
  <head>
    <script src="http://code.jquery.com/jquery-1.6.1.js"></script>
    <script src="jquery.datalink.js"></script>
    <script type="text/javascript">
      $(document).ready(function(){
```

```
        var registration = {};
        $( "form" ).link(registration);

        // set some default values
        $( registration ).setField( "name", "New User Registration" );
        $( registration ).setField( "email", "i_dont_exist@mail.com" );

        $( "form" ).change(function(){
          console.log( registration.name + " " + registration.email );
        });
      });
    </script>
  </head>
  <body>
    <form method="post">
      <label for="name">User Name </label>
      <input type="text" name="name" />

      <label for="email">email </label>
      <input type="email" name="email" />

      <input type="submit" value="send it" />
    </form>
  </body>
</html>
```

Code snippet is from datalink.txt

In this example, after changing the value of the form, there's a `console.log` showing the value of the registration object, which reflects the new changes.

So you've seen that jQuery has some shortcuts and methods for working with data, but end users can't be trusted! The following section explains the ins-and-outs of data validation.

USING FORM VALIDATIONS

Form validation is important for a list of reasons, anywhere from preventing unintentionally messing up a database to securing your system from malicious injection attacks, as well as the more mundane reasons such as making sure that the data entered makes sense. For example, a first name field probably shouldn't permit special characters like $%&#@ or numbers.

Traditionally, you would use jQuery, or some form of JavaScript, to either mask a field or validate the data entered. The simplest example is to check that data has been entered for a required field:

```
if($("#myInput").val() !== ''){
// handle here
}
```

A note of caution: your carefully crafted validation is useless if end users turn off JavaScript features on their browsers. Data should be sanitized on both the server and client side before saving.

Feature Detection with Modernizr

Before going any further with HTML5 forms and jQuery, it's a good time to mention the Modernizr library. It can greatly simplify the task of detecting browser features that aren't yet implemented in all mainstream browsers. Modernizr does this by using a process called *feature detection*. Instead of relying on the old-school method of User Agent (UA) Sniffing, detecting a browser's capabilities based on the unreliable `navigator.userAgent` string, feature detection tests for specific browser capabilities. This is a much more future-proof and user-friendly method of feature testing. It doesn't matter if some new browser appears or some version of Chrome or Firefox hits the Web with a novel `navigator.userAgent` string. If the feature is supported, Modernizr will report it as being available.

For example, you could use Modernizer to detect if a browser supports the `canvas` element: In this sample, you'll see one of the great features of Modernizr. For every feature it detects it stores a Boolean flag in the Modernizr object representing the result of the test. In this example, with supporting browsers, `Modernizr.canvas` will evaluate to `true`. In addition to this Modernizr also adds CSS classes to the `html` element indicating the availability of features.

```
<!DOCTYPE html>
<html>
    <head>
        <script src="http://code.jquery.com/jquery-1.6.1.js"></script>
<!-- Link to modernizr, useful for feature detection -->
        <script  src="http://ajax.cdnjs.com/ajax/libs/modernizr/1.7/modernizr-1.7.min.js">
    </script>

        <script type="text/javascript">
          if(Modernizr.canvas){
            // code that depends on canvas here
          } else {
            // oops, canvas doesn't exist, deal with situation
            // here
          }
        </script>
    </head>
    <body>
    </body>
</html>
```

Code snippet is from modernizr.txt

Anywhere I need to use Modernizr, we link to the code using the public JavaScript CDN `ajax.cdnjs .com`. Let's put Modernizr to some use. Another great feature of HTML5 forms is the required field flag. For example, the following form:

```
<!DOCTYPE html>
<html>
    <body>
      <form>
        <input type="text" name="userName" required/>
```

```
        <input type="password" name="password" required/>
        <input type="submit" value="send it" />
      </form>
    </body>
  </html>
```

renders the message seen in Figure 6-1 in supporting browsers, in this case, Chrome, after attempting to submit a blank form.

Not all browsers support this feature, or even any of the other HTML5 features. Again, jQuery comes to the rescue for validating forms. As the following

FIGURE 6-1

code illustrates you can use feature detection to determine if a browser has the "required field" feature, and if it doesn't use jQuery techniques instead. Modernizr tests for the presence of the "required field" feature, and if it's absent, a message div is appended to the document and a simple form handler is attached to the form. This handler tests to see if any of the required fields are empty using the jQuery form utility `.val()`. If one is empty it throws up the message div, adds a small border to the form field and prevents submission of the form. This is clearly a simplified form validation example, but it illustrates the basic concepts of form validation with jQuery and the basic concepts of using feature detection to take advantage of modern browser features.

Available for download on Wrox.com

```
<!DOCTYPE html>
<html>
  <head>
    <script src="http://code.jquery.com/jquery-1.7.1.js"></script>
    <script src="http://ajax.cdnjs.com/ajax/libs/modernizr/1.7/modernizr-1.7.min.js">
    </script>

    <script type="text/javascript">
        $(function(){
    if( !Modernizr.input.required ){
      var $msg = $( "<div id='reqMessage'>Required Fields Missing</div>" );
      $msg.css( "background-color", "yellow" )
          .hide();

      $( "body" ).append( $msg );

      $( "#fDet" ).on("submit", function(e){
        $( "input[required]" ).each(function(){
          if ( $(this).val() === "" ) {
            $( "#reqMessage" ).show();
            $( this ).css( "border" , "1px solid red" );
            e.preventDefault();
          }
        });
      });
    }
});
    </script>
  </head>
<body>
```

```
<form id="fDet" action="#">
<input type="text" name="userName" required/>
<input type="password" name="password" required/>
<input type="submit" value="send it" />
</form>
</body>
<html>
```

Code snippet is from featureDetection-form.txt

WORKING WITH HTML FORM ELEMENTS

As you've seen, missing HTML5 functionality can be reconstructed using jQuery techniques. This section explores some of the additions to form elements.

It's just as important to know when not to use jQuery as when to use it. HTML5 brings to the table new form elements and functionality. Table 6-1 shows a selection of the new input types and controls.

TABLE 6-1: New HTML5 Form Controls

CONTROL TYPE	INPUT TYPE	DESCRIPTION
URL	url	A control for editing a URL.
E-mail	e-mail	A control for entering or editing an e-mail address.
Telephone	tel	A one-line plain-text edit control for entering a telephone number.
Search	search	A one-line plain-text edit control for entering one or more search terms.
Slider	range	An imprecise control for setting the element's value to a string representing a number.
Number	number	A precise control for setting the element's value to a string representing a number.
Date	date	A control for setting the element's value to a string representing a date.
Date and Time	datetime	A control for setting the element's value to a string representing a global date and time (with timezone information).
Color	color	A color-well control for setting the element's value to a string representing a simple color.

From http://www.w3.org/TR/html-markup

In addition to new input controls, HTML5 also introduces a shortcut for adding placeholder text. Placeholder text is a temporary default text message displayed inside an input field until the user focuses on the field. Before, JavaScript was necessary to achieve this effect, but the newer HTML5 browsers support this by default with a `placeholder` attribute. For example, the following code sample shows two inputs with the `placeholder` attribute set. Figure 6-2 shows these inputs rendered on the page.

FIGURE 6-2

```
<!DOCTYPE html>
<html>
  <body>
    <form>
      <input type="text" placeholder="name" >
      <input type="text" placeholder="email" >
    </form>
  </body>
</html>
```

This `placeholder` attribute solves, at the browser level, a normally hand-coded usability enhancement. It's a nice feature to have without having to write a line of code. Unfortunately, not every browser supports `placeholder` natively, so we're not at the place where we can put away the code solutions. The following code sample will show how to implement a polyfill for placeholder using jQuery. Again, you'll use Modernizr to detect if the browser supports this feature, and then use some jQuery goodness to fill in the gap for other browsers.

In a production environment, you'd likely just use one of the excellent `placeholder` polyfill plugins, like the one written by Mathias Bynens: https://github.com/mathiasbynens/ jquery-placeholder. It is still instructive to see how you might solve this problem without the use of plugins. Feature detection and polyfills are a strong piece of modern web development, so seeing how it works under the hood can enlighten in ways simply using a plugin can't.

```
<!DOCTYPE html>
<html>
  <head>
    <script src="http://code.jquery.com/jquery-1.7.1.js"></script>
    <script src="http://ajax.cdnjs.com/ajax/libs/modernizr/1.7/modernizr-1.7.min.js">
    </script>

    <script type="text/javascript">
        $(function(){
  if( !Modernizr.input.placeholder ){
    $( 'input[type=text]' ).focus(function(){
      if( $(this).val() === $( this ).attr( 'placeholder' ) ){
        $( this ).val('');
      }
    });
    $( 'input[type=text]' ).blur( function(){
    if( $( this ).val() === '' ){
      $( this ).val($( this ).attr( 'placeholder' ));
    }
    });
  }
});
    </script>
  </head>
```

```
    <body>
      <form>
        <input type="text" name="userName" placeholder="Enter your Name" />
        <input type="text" name="address" placeholder="Enter your Address" />
      </form>
    </body>
  </html>
```

Code snippet is from placeholder.txt

The next example implements an e-mail input widget. Again, there is a native HTML5 version, but that isn't implemented in all browsers.

```
<!DOCTYPE html>
<html>
  <head>
      <script src="http://code.jquery.com/jquery-1.7.1.js"></script>
      <script src="http://ajax.cdnjs.com/ajax/libs/modernizr/1.7/modernizr-1.7.min.js">
      </script>

      <script type="text/javascript">
        $(function(){
  var emailRegEx = /^([\w-\.]+@([\w-]+\.)+[\w-]{2,4})?$/;
  $( "#errorDiv" ).hide();
  If ( !Modernizr.inputtypes.email ){
    $( "input[type=email]" ).blur( function(){
      var emailValue = $( this ).val();
      if( emailValue !== '' ){
        var passes = emailRegEx.test( emailValue );
        if( !passes ){
          // display validation error message
          $( "#errorDiv" ).show();

          // disable submit button
          $( "input[type='submit']" ).attr( "disabled" );
        } else {
          $( "#errorDiv" ).hide();
          $( "input[type='submit']" ).attr( "disabled","" );
        }
      }
    });
  }
});
      </script>
  </head>
  <body>
    <form>
      <input type="email" name="companyEmail" />
      <input type="submit" />
      <div id="errorDiv">Invalid email format.</div>
    </form>
  </body>
</html>
```

Code snippet is from email-input.txt

HTML5 controls degrade gracefully. That means that if a browser doesn't support a particular control — for example, at the time of this writing only Opera supports the color control — a regular text input box is displayed.

In some cases you may want to validate against values in a database, and using Ajax you can achieve this effect. But first, the following section provides a quick review of Ajax and later on we return to form validation.

REVISITING AJAX BASICS

The definition of Ajax has evolved from its original acronym of Asynchronous JavaScript and XML, a method for sending and retrieving data (using XML) to a server asynchronously without the need to completely reload a web document. It now refers to methods for creating interactive web and dynamic applications with JavaScript, as you've seen in previous chapters, as well as asynchronous communication between the client and server. These days it's not always XML that's used to transport information between the server and client, but often other formats such as JSON.

At the heart of Ajax is the `XmlHttpRequest` object, which dates back to 2000 when Microsoft introduced an ActiveX object for asynchronous communication between server and client. In 2005, the term "Ajax" was coined by Jesse James Garrett to describe this technique.

The same disparity between the way browsers manage events is also observed with Ajax, albeit not as complex. For example, to create a new request object in Internet Explorer, you would do the following:

```
var xhr = new ActiveXObject("Microsoft.XMLHTTP");
```

or in even older versions of IE:

```
var xhr = new ActiveXObject("MSXML2.XMLHTTP");
```

In IE7 or above and any other browser that supports `XMLHttpRequest`, you use the native JavaScript `XMLHttpRequest` object:

```
var xhr = new XMLHttpRequest();
```

Luckily, the methods used between the standard `XMLHttpRequest` object and the Microsoft ActiveX object are remarkably similar, hence simplifying matters. Typically, if you were to handle the details yourself you might use bit of code like this to instantiate a request object:

```
/*
Support for the original ActiveX object in older versions of Internet Explorer
This works all the way back to IE5.
*/
if ( typeof XMLHttpRequest == "undefined" ) {
  XMLHttpRequest = function () {
    try {
        return new ActiveXObject( "Msxml2.XMLHTTP.6.0" );
    }
    catch (e) {}
```

```
    try {
        return new ActiveXObject( "Msxml2.XMLHTTP.3.0" );
    }
    catch (e) {}
    try {
        return new ActiveXObject( "Msxml2.XMLHTTP" );
    }
    catch (e) {}
    throw new Error( "No XMLHttpRequest." );
  };
}
var xhr = new XMLHttpRequest();
```

Once the details of creating the request object have been taken care of, a connection must be established with the server, using the `xhr.open()` method, which follows the form:

```
xhr.open(method, url, isAsynchronous);
```

where `method` refers to the HTTP method, the action to be performed on the specified resource. While the full list of HTTP methods (or "verbs") is much longer, Ajax requests will typically be a POST or a GET. The second parameter is the `url` used to exchange data, and `isAsynchronous` is a Boolean flag indicating whether or not the call is asynchronous. This flag indicates whether or not the request should block the execution of the rest of the script. As the name of the technique implies, this will normally be set to true. So, you can use the request object to make synchronous posts to the server, but that would be defeating the whole purpose of Ajax. After opening the connection, use the `xhr.send()` method to initiate the request to the server. It accepts a `data` argument:

```
xhr.open("POST", "/request/url/", true);
xhr.send(data);
```

Because the communication is asynchronous you can't count on sequential execution of methods. For example:

```
xhr.send(data);
doSomething();
```

The `send` method is executed and returns immediately, whereas the request and response each operate on separate threads. You won't have the response from the server when `doSomething();` gets executed. The solution is to use the callback handler `onreadystatechange`, which is invoked when there is a request state change. So, the previous snippet can be rewritten as:

```
xhr.onreadystatechange = function(){
  if( this.readyState === 4 ){
    if( this.status >== 200 && this.status < 300 ){
      doSomething();
    } else {
      // problem with communication
    }
  }
}
xhr.send( data );
```

Now, when the request is completed and successful, `doSomthing()` is executed. Table 6-2 shows the different ready states.

TABLE 6-2: The ReadyState Object

STATE	DESCRIPTION
0: Uninitialized	The object has been constructed.
1: Loading	The `open()` method has been successfully invoked. During this state request headers can be set using `setRequestHeader()` and the request can be made using the `send()` method.
2: Loaded	All redirects (if any) have been followed and all HTTP headers of the final response have been received. Several response members of the object are now available.
3: Interactive	The response entity body is being received.
4: Completed	The data transfer has been completed or something went wrong during the transfer (e.g., infinite redirects).

From: http://www.w3.org/TR/XMLHttpRequest/#states

After the request is completed and successful, you can get the response using the `xhr` object's `responseText` method. What the `responseText` returns is dependent on the server-side code. It can be text of any format, not just XML. Now given that, you can expect any data format to come from the server — HTML, XML, JSON, plain text, and so on, each with its own pros and cons for parsing data returned.

The major trend these days is toward using JSON at the data interchange format of choice. Since it's a native JavaScript object, people find it much easier to deal with programmatically. Instead of firing up DOM traversal methods to walk through the XML DOM returned by the server, you can simply use dot notation to access properties of the JSON response. Also, JSON is generally less verbose than XML so it lowers the cost of each request over the wire.

You'll still see XML, of course, and there are uses for plain text and even full blocks of HTML, but it's much more common to see JSON these days.

As you've no doubt expected, jQuery offers alternative ways of handling Ajax request and response in a more simplified manner.

APPLYING AJAX WITH JQUERY

Just as you saw in the previous chapter with event handling, jQuery abstracts away many of the details of Ajax communication. For example, you don't have to worry about how the `xhr` object is instantiated. The general jQuery method used for sending Ajax calls is (drum roll...) the `$.ajax()` method, which takes the form:

```
$.ajax(url, [settings]);
```

Or a single `settings` object:

```
$.ajax([settings]);
```

Many of the following examples require a server to respond to the Ajax calls. The samples include both Python and PHP backends to support the frontend; both are freely available. Unfortunately, explanation of either of these technologies is beyond the scope of this book.

Table 6-3 lists some of the most important available `settings`. For a full list check out the online documentation at `http://api.jquery.com/jQuery.ajax/#jQuery-ajax-settings`.

TABLE 6-3: jQuery `$.ajax()` Settings

PROPERTY	DESCRIPTION
`url`	The URL of the resource to be requested.
`type`	The HTTP method of the Ajax request. This will generally be a GET or a POST, although more esoteric HTTP methods like PUT or DELETE are possible, depending on browser support.
`data`	Data to be sent to the server.
`dataType`	The type of data that you're expecting back from the server. The available types are: "XML", "HTML", "script", "JSON", "JSONP" and "text".
`success(data, textStatus, jqXHR)`	A function to be called if the request succeeds.
`error(jqXHR, textStatus, errorThrown)`	A function to be called if the request fails.
`complete(jqXHR, textStatus)`	A function to be called when the Ajax request is completed.
`timeout`	Set a timeout (in milliseconds) for the request.

The following example sends a post to the URL `/post/2/here.html`, which receives some plain text, and logs the result on success, or displays another log on error:

```
<!DOCTYPE html>
<html>
  <head>
    <script src="http://code.jquery.com/jquery-1.7.1.js"></script>
    <script type="text/javascript">
      $.ajax({
```

```
      url : "/post/2/here.html",
      dataType: "html",
      success: function(r){
        console.log( "made it" );
      },
      error : function(r){
        console.log( "Something didn't work" );
      }
    })
  </script>
  </head>
  <body>
  </body>
</html>
```

Valid types of data that can be returned are XML, HTML, JSON, JSONP, text and script.

As you've seen in previous chapters, jQuery is particularly adept at traversing DOM trees. In a situation where the server response is XML, jQuery has the $.find() method for getting data from an XML document. Say you have an Ajax call that returns an XML document that describes a book, and you'd like to retrieve the chapter titles. The following code illustrates a use of $.find() to parse some XML data and append it into the DOM.

```
<!DOCTYPE html>
<html>
  <head>
    <scriptsrc="http://code.jquery.com/jquery-1.7.1.js"></script>
    <script type="text/javascript">
      $.ajax({
        url : "/book.html",
        dataType: "xml",
        success: function( data ){
          $( data ).find( "chapter" ).each(function() {
            $( "document" ).append($( this ).find( "title" ).text());
          });
        },
        error : function(data){
          console.log( "unable to process request" );
        }
      });
  </script>
  </head>
    <body>
    </body>
</html>
```

Code snippet is from ajax-find.txt

This example appends the titles found to the document body. The .find() method searches an XML document for the element name specified. Just like an HTML document, if you want to access an attribute use the .attr() method.

These days it's fairly common to request data in JSON format, which is completely logical considering that JSON objects are JavaScript objects. They also have the advantage of being lighter-weight than XML data. You could use the `$.ajax()` method to obtain a JSON object from the server like this:

```
$.ajax({
  url: "/jsonBook.html",
  dataType: 'json',
  data: data,
  success: function( data ){
    // process json data
  }
});
```

But, jQuery provides a shortcut method for obtaining data from the server asynchronously in JSON format — it's called `$.getJSON()`:

```
<!DOCTYPE html>
<html>
  <head>
  <script src="http://code.jquery.com/jquery-1.7.1.js"></script>
  <script type="text/javascript">
    $.getJSON("/url/2/get/json.php", function(data, text, jqXHR){
      // handle callback here
    });
  </script>
</head>
  <body>
  </body>
</html>
```

Unfortunately, there is no equivalent `$.postJSON()` method.

By now, you'll notice that many of your applications will use a common set of options. jQuery provides a method that globally sets the Ajax options called `$.ajaxSetup()`. These values will be used in any call to `$.ajax()` unless overridden. `$.ajaxSetup()` takes the form:

```
$.ajaxSetup(options);
```

where `options` is an object instance whose properties are used to set the global Ajax properties. For example, to set the default type, `dataType`, and error callback:

```
$.ajaxSetup({
    type : "GET",
    dataType : "json",
    error : universalGoofupFunction
});
```

It should be noted that `$.ajaxSetup()` overrides the settings for all Ajax requests on the page so it should be used sparingly unless you're in complete control of all the JavaScript code running on the page.

But, before continuing this is a good time to review a feature introduced in jQuery 1.5, which is deferred objects. These objects are an example of the promise pattern. A promise is an object that "promises" to give a value at a convenient future time; this is particularly useful for asynchronous computing. jQuery deferred objects, also based on the promise pattern, allow chainable callback functions.

Deferred objects begin in the unresolved state, and can change from unresolved to either resolved or rejected. Deferred objects are covered in depth in Chapter 13.

The $.ajax() method, indeed all jQuery Ajax methods, returns a promise object called a jqXHR object, which is a superset of the XmlHTTPRequest object. This allows Ajax calls to be rewritten, now, as:

```
$.ajax({url : "/go/here"})
.success(function(){ /* handle success */ })
.complete(function(){ /* handle complete method */ });
```

There are some shortcut utility methods as well, $.get() and $.post(), which send get and post requests, respectively. In the case of $.get(), instead of having to write:

```
$.ajax({
    type: "get",
  url: "/go/here.php",
  data: data,
  success: callBackFunction,
  dataType: "json"
});
```

you can instead type:

```
var jqxhr = $.get( "/go/here.php", function(data){} );
```

The general format is:

```
$.get( url, parameters, callback, type );
```

Just like $.ajax(), the $.get() method returns a jqXHR object. The corresponding shortcut for posts, $.post(), is almost identical, except for the type, of course:

```
$.post( url, parameters, callback, type );
```

jQuery also has an incredibly useful method, $.load(), for making Ajax requests and loading HTML fragments into a matched element, all in the same call. It takes the following form:

```
$( selector ).load( url, [data], [success(response, status, XHR)] )
```

It accepts a target url, an optional data object, and an optional success object, which itself will receive a response text, a status string, and an XMLHttpRequest object. For example:

```
$( "#latestNews" ).load( "/getLatest.php", dateObj, function(resp, status, XHR){
if(status === "success"){
// handle here
}
});
```

Assuming all went well on the server, the `latestNews` element will be loaded with the text obtained from the server.

The last example of this chapter is a pizza order form, and uses the new HTML5 controls and jQuery's `$.load()` Ajax method. To accommodate customers using older browsers, you'll employ jQuery to fill in the functionality, but also to validate input and post the order.

As a note, this sample doesn't handle the case of users without JavaScript. While that's an important factor to keep in mind when designing web forms, the majority of the hard work to do that properly (setting up a fallback validation service on the server) is outside the scope of a book like this.

The customer is not required to register with the pizza shop in order to get a pizza, but must fill out several fields. The order form will have the following fields:

➤ first name

➤ last name

➤ address

➤ state

➤ zip

➤ phone

➤ e-mail

➤ time of delivery

➤ cc type

➤ cc number

➤ pizza size

➤ toppings

First design the form, and instead of using labels to indicate each field, use placeholder text. All fields are required except for pizza toppings. The state field will use an Ajax autocomplete feature. In order to sniff out the browser features, you'll employ Modernizr again. To bring things around full circle, add the Data Link plugin to shorten the process of getting data from the form fields to the server. After posting to the server, if no exception is thrown, the customer is shown a receipt of the order.

The following code listing shows the markup. Remember that the full source code for this example is available at the book's website; no need to type all of this!

```
<!DOCTYPE html>
<html>
    <head>
        <script src="http://code.jquery.com/jquery-1.7.1.js"></script>
        <script src="http://ajax.cdnjs.com/ajax/libs/modernizr/1.7/modernizr-1.7.min.js">
        </script>
        <script src="jquery.datalink.js"></script>
        <script type="text/javascript">
```

```
   //Application code will go here.
    </script>
 </head>
 <body>
   <h1>Enter Order Information</h1>
   <form id="pizzaOrderForm">
     <input type="text" name="firstName" placeholder="First Name" required >
     <input type="text" name="lastName" placeholder="Last Name" required >
     <input type="text" name="address" placeholder="Address" required >
     <input type="text" name="state" placeholder="State" required >
     <input type="text" name="zip" placeholder="Zip Code" required >
     <input type="tel" name="phone"
       pattern="999-999-9999" placeholder="Phone" required >
     <input type="email" name="email" placeholder="Email" required >
     <input type="text" name="timeOfDeliver" placeholder="Time to Deliver" required >
     <select name="ccType">
       <option value="visa">Visa
       <option value="amex">AmEx
       <option value="discover">Discover
     </select>
     <input type="text" name="ccNumber" placeholder="CC Number" required >
     <input type="text" name="pizzaSize" placeholder="" required >
     <select name="pizzaSize">
       <option value="0">Pick a size
       <option value="1">personal
       <option value="2">small
       <option value="3">medium
       <option value="4">large
       <option value="5">sportsman
     </select>
     <label> Number of Pizzas
       <input type="number" name="numOfPizzas" min="0" max="99"
        value="0" placeholder="Zip Code" required ></label>
     <label>Pepperoni<input type="checkbox" name="toppings" value="pepperoni"></label>
     <label>Garlic<input type="checkbox" name="toppings" value="garlic"></label>
     <label>Mushroom<input type="checkbox" name="toppings" value="mushrooms"></label>
     <label>Sausage<input type="checkbox" name="toppings" value="sausage"></label>
     <input type="button" value="Order!" >
   </form>
   <div id="price"></div>
 </body>
 </html>
```

Building on previous examples from this chapter, this example uses the Modernizr library to determine if the email input, required, and placeholder features are present. As you'll see in the JavaScript that follows, when any of the features aren't present, jQuery is employed to fill in the missing functionality.

In order to auto-fill in the order object, the Data Link plugin is used, thereby removing some intermediate steps. This is as simple as creating an empty object that will serve as the container for the field data, selecting the form, and calling the inherited link method on the wrapper object.

```
var order = {};
$("#pizzaOrderForm").link(order);
```

We use the traditional submit method of the form and add a simple test to see if the required fields have been filled in browsers that don't support the `required` attribute. The `$.load()` method is used to make an order to the server. The response text returned is an HTML string, which is inserted inside of the `#price` div, avoiding the need to append text. The following code block demonstrates the complete JavaScript example.

```
$( "form" ).bind( "submit", function( e ){
  var valid = true;
    if(!Modernizr.input.required){
      $( "input[required]" ).each(function(){
      if ( $( this ).val() === "" ) {
        $( "#reqMessage" ).show();
        $( this ).css( "border" , "1px solid red" );
        valid = false;
      }
    });
  }
    e.preventDefault();
    if (valid) {
    $( "#price" ).load( "/process", data, function(responseTxt, status, XHR ){
      if(status === "success"){
        $( "[type=button]" ).attr( "disabled" );
      } else if(status === "error"){
        $( "#price" ).append( "unable to process request, game over man" );
      }
    });
  }
});
```

```
...
<script type="text/javascript">
$(function(){
// for browsers that don't yet process HTML5 //
// Placeholder implementation
  if(!Modernizr.input.placeholder){
    $('input[type=text]').each(function(){
      $( this ).val($( this ).attr('placeholder'));
    });    $('input[type=text]').focus(function(){
      if($( this ).val() === $( this ).attr('placeholder')){
        $( this ).val('');
      }
    });
    $('input[type=text]').blur(function(){
      if($( this ).val() === ''){
        $( this ).val($( this ).attr('placeholder'));
      }
    });
  }

// required implementation
  if(!Modernizr.input.required){
    var $msg = $( "<div id='reqMessage'>Required Fields Missing</div>" );
    $msg.css( "background-color", "yellow" )
```

```
            .hide();
        $( "body" ).append( $msg );
    }
// email input implementation
  var emailRegEx = /^([\w-\.]+@([\w-]+\.)+[\w-]{2,4})?$/;
  if( !Modernizr.inputtypes.email ){
    $('input[type=url]').blur( function(){
    var emailValue = $( this ).val();
    if( emailValue !== '' ){
      var passes = emailRegEx.test(emailValue);
      if( !passes ){
        // display validation error message
        $( "#errorDiv" ).show();
        // disable submit button
        $( "input[type='submit']" ).attr( "disabled" );
      } else {
        $( "#errorDiv" ).hide();
        $( "input[type='submit']" ).attr( "disabled","" );
      }
     }
    });
   }


// ordering stuff
  var order = {};
  $( "#pizzaOrderForm" ).link( order );
  $( "form" ).bind( "submit", function( e ){
    var valid = true;
    if(!Modernizr.input.required){
      $( "input[required]" ).each(function(){
      if ( $( this ).val() === "" ) {
        $( "#reqMessage" ).show();
        $( this ).css( "border" , "1px solid red" );
        valid = false;
      }
     });
    }
    e.preventDefault();
    if (valid) {
    $( "#price" ).load( "/process", data, function(responseTxt, status, XHR ){
      if(status === "success"){
        $( "[type=button]" ).attr( "disabled" );
      } else if(status === "error"){
        $( "#price" ).append( "unable to process request, game over man" );
      }
     });
    }
   });
});
</script>
</head>
...
```

Code snippet is from pizza-form.txt

Figure 6-3 shows a side-by-side comparison of the same form with Opera 11, which supports HTML5, and the older Firefox 2, which does not.

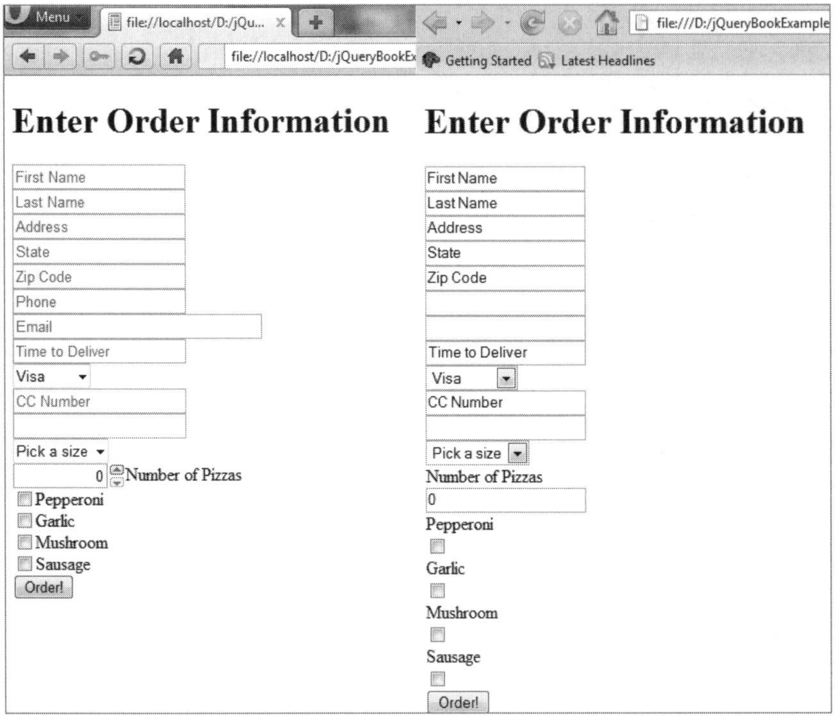

FIGURE 6-3

SUMMARY

This chapter concludes most of what you need to know about Ajax handling. You've seen how jQuery helps attach data to form elements in a meaningful way, helps form validating, and helps in the current transition from previous versions of HTML to HTML5. You've also explored the foundations of Ajax, and how jQuery makes asynchronous calls just that much easier, not to mention its many utility methods for further simplifying common operations like quick gets and posts.

NOTES

```
http://diveintohtml5.info/forms.html
http://www.bennadel.com/blog/1404-jQuery-Data-Method-Associates-Data-With-DOM-
    Elements-SWEET-ASS-SWEET-.htm
http://marcgrabanski.com/article/5-tips-for-better-jquery-code
http://www.matiasmancini.com.ar/jquery-plugin-ajax-form-validation-html5.html
```

```
http://en.wikipedia.org/wiki/Ajax_(programming)
http://www.jibbering.com/2002/4/httprequest.html
http://www.w3.org/TR/html-markup/input.email.html
http://msdn.microsoft.com/en-us/library/ms536648(v=vs.85).aspx
http://en.wikipedia.org/wiki/Hypertext_Transfer_Protocol
http://ejohn.org/blog/html-5-data-attributes/
http://www.modernizr.com/docs/#features-html5
http://wiki.commonjs.org/wiki/Promises/A
http://www.erichynds.com/jquery/using-deferreds-in-jquery/
```

7

Animations and Effects

WHAT'S IN THIS CHAPTER?

➤ Animating Elements and CSS Properties

➤ Resizing Elements

➤ Creating Custom Animations

➤ Animations with HTML5 Canvas

One of the fun parts of working with the Web is animating it. By animation we not only mean moving elements around, but also toggling their visibility, altering their properties in either a timed fashion or in reaction to an event, or even resizing an element. Web animation use to be done mostly with Flash, and JavaScript was used for minor situations such as rollovers. But, the tables have turned, and with the help of jQuery, animating the Web through JavaScript is much more predominant.

In this chapter you explore some of the shortcuts that jQuery offers for animating components in your web applications such as moving, fading, toggling, and resizing elements. You explore how to combine different animations effects in parallel with the `$.animate()` method, and then re-apply the same techniques with the new HTML5 `canvas` tag.

ANIMATING ELEMENTS

Elements, like divs, have two properties that determine their positioning on a web page: the `top` and `left` properties. The positions can be expressed in either percentage or using a unit of length like pixels or centimeters.

The following code sample illustrates the basic concept underlying an animation, programmatically adjusting the position of an element. In it, any click on the document moves the green div ten pixels to the right.

```
<!DOCTYPE html>
<html>
  <head>
    <style type="text/css">
      div {
        position: absolute;
        left:10px;
        top:10px;
        width:20px;
        height:20px;
        background-color:green;
      }
    </style>
    <script src="http://code.jquery.com/jquery-1.7.1.min.js"></script>
    <script type="text/javascript">
      $(function(){
        $(document).click(function(){
          var pos = $("div").css("left");
          pos = parseInt(pos);
          $("div").css("left", pos+10);
        });
      });
    </script>
  </head>
  <body>
    <div>
    </div>
  </body>
</html>
```

Instead of having to get the left and top position using `$.attr()` and converting the result to a number, it's better to use the `$.offset()` method, which returns an object containing numeric `left` and `top` values indicating the current position of an element relative to the document. The `$.offset()` method takes the following form:

```
$(selector).offset();
```

The following code gets the offset of a div with an `id` of `"box"`, and displays the left and top properties with an alert box:

```
<!DOCTYPE html>
<html>
  <head>
    <style type="text/css">
      div {
        position: absolute;
        left:10px;
        top:50px;
        width:20px;
        height:20px;
        background-color:green;
      }
    </style>
    <script src="http://code.jquery.com/jquery-1.7.1.min.js"></script>
```

```
<script type="text/javascript">
  $(function(){
    $("div#box").click(function(){
      var pos = $(this).offset();

      $("#watcher").text(pos.top+":"+pos.left);
    });
  });
</script>
</head>
<body>
  <p>Where is the box? <span id="watcher"></span></p><div id="box"></div>
</body>
</html>
```

Code snippet is from offset.txt

The preceding example displays the coordinates of the div when clicked. You can also use the same `offset` method to reposition an element:

```
$(selector).offset(coordinatesObject);
```

where `coordinatesObject` is any object that contains a `top` and `left` property set to integer values. For example:

```
$("div#box").offset({
  top:100,
  left:100
});
```

In the situation were you don't want to position an element relative to the document, but rather to its parent container you can use the `$.position()` method instead. The syntax for getting and setting coordinates is identical to `$.offset()`.

ANIMATING CSS PROPERTIES

Many neat effects are achieved by manipulating CSS properties in reaction to an event; for example, the showing or hiding an element. There are two different CSS properties: `display` or `visibility` control whether or not an element appears on the page. Setting `display` to none or `visibility` to hidden hides an element. The converse is to set `display` to block or `visibility` to visible.

While both "hide" an element, it should be pointed out that each method has a very different effect on the flow of the page. Elements with their `visibility` set to `hidden` remain firmly within the flow of the document. Elements that follow a `hidden` element in the document will retain their original offset. Elements with their `display` property set to `none`, on the other hand, are completely pulled out of the flow of the document.

```
$("div#message").click(function(){
  $(this).css("display", "none");
});
```

And to show the image:

```
$("div#message").ready(function(){
  $(this).css("display", "block");
});
```

A better approach is to use jQuery's `$.hide()` and `$.show()` methods. In the next example, the page displays a message box at the top. Upon clicking the div it disappears, and on clicking the container the message appears again.

```html
<!DOCTYPE html>
<html>
  <head>
    <style type="text/css">
      #message {
        position: absolute;
        left:0;
        top:0;
        width:100%;
        height:20px;
        background-color:orange;
      }
      #container {
        position:absolute;
        left:0;
        top:0;
        width:100%;
        height:500px;
      }
    </style>
    <script src="http://code.jquery.com/jquery-1.7.1.min.js"></script>
    <script type="text/javascript">
      $(function(){
        $("#message").click(function(e){
          e.stopPropagation();
          $(this).hide();
        });

        $(document).click(function(){
          $("#message").show();
        });
      });
    </script>
  </head>
  <body>
    <div id="message">
      Fill out our annoying survey! (click to dismiss)
    </div>
  </body>
```

Code snippet is from showhide.txt

Stack overflow and Twitter both have a really neat feature where messages are displayed at the top, in a similar fashion to the previous example, except for one big difference; the message box slides in. jQuery has both `$.slideDown()` and `$.slideUp()` methods for translating divs in/out of a page. Each has the following syntax:

```
$(selector).slideUp([speed,] [easing,] [callback]);
$(selector).slideDown([speed,] [easing,] [callback]);
```

All three arguments are optional. The speed, or duration of the animation, can be indicated as either a number (representing milliseconds) or as a string `'fast'` or `'slow'`. A `'fast'` animation is 200 milliseconds whereas a `'slow'` animation is 600 milliseconds. If the speed (aka duration) is omitted, the default speed is 400 milliseconds. Both `$.slideUp()` and `$.slideDown()` accept a callback function, which is executed once the `$.slideUp()` or `$.slideDown()` function has finished executing.

You can also include an optional `easing` argument, which dictates how fast the animation runs at different time points. The only defaults included at the time of this writing are linear and swing. But, there's a neat easing plugin with a variety of different easing options. Check it out at `http://james.padolsey.com/demos/jquery/easing/`. More easing functions are also included with jQuery UI.

The following example improves on the previous message box by using both `$.slideUp()` and `$.slideDown()` instead of `$.show()` and `$.hide()`:

```html
<!DOCTYPE html>
<html>
  <head>
    <style type="text/css">
      div {
        text-align: center;
        color: white;
        font-size: xx-large;
        position: absolute;
        left:0;
        top:0;
        width:100%;
        height:50px;
        background-color:orange;
      }
    </style>
    <script src="http://code.jquery.com/jquery-1.7.1.min.js"></script>
    <script type="text/javascript">
      $(function(){
        $("div#message").click(function(e){
          e.stopPropagation();
          $("div#message").slideUp('fast');
        });

        $(document).click(function(){
          $("div#message").slideDown('fast');
        });
      });
    </script>
  </head>
  <body>
```

```
            <div id="message">
               Fill out our annoying survey! (click to dismiss)
            </div>
         </body>
      </html>
```

Code snippet is from slideup-slidedown.txt

Another slick effect provided by jQuery is fading. More specifically, `$.fadeIn()` and `$.fadeOut()`. The syntax for the fade functions is almost identical to the slide functions, with the same concepts applying to speed, easing, and an optional callback function.

```
$(selector).fadeIn([speed,] [easing,] [callback]);
$(selector).fadeOut([speed,] [easing,] [callback]);
```

RESIZING ELEMENTS

You might have expected a simple utility method for resizing an element but there isn't one. The `$.resize()` method is a handler for the onresize event. Unless you're using `$.animate()`, you'll have to code your own.

To resize an element just change its height and width attributes using `$.css()`. For example, to shrink the width of an existing element you could do the following:

```
var w = $("#myElem").css("width");
w = parseInt(size.replace("px","")) - 10;
$("#myElem").css("width", w-10);
```

But this has the inherent disadvantage of returning a string with a unit, for example, pixels. By using the `$.height()` and `$.width()` methods, you can get the height and width of an element, making it easier to resize:

```
var w = $("#myElem).width() - 10;
$("#myElem").width(w);
```

DESIGNING CUSTOM ANIMATIONS

All of the previous methods for animating elements are nice, but there's a more elegant weapon for these uncivilized times, the `$.animate()` method. jQuery has a more general method for doing animations, which permits you to modify more than one attribute simultaneously. Any attribute that uses a numeric value such as top, left, height, width, and opacity is open game for manipulation by `$.animate()`. It accepts an object with the properties to be animated, the duration of the animation, a string denoting the easing algorithm to use, and a callback function executed upon completion:

```
$(selector).animate( properties, [duration,] [easing,] [complete] )
```

In the next example, a plain blue div is animated from left to right by 100px when the document is clicked; this is about as simple as it gets. Note that the position must be relative, absolute, or fixed in order for the animation to work.

```html
<!DOCTYPE html>
<html>
  <head>
    <style type="text/css">
      div {
         position: relative;
         left:0;
         top:0;
         width:10px;
         height:10px;
         background-color:blue;
      }
    </style>
    <script src="http://code.jquery.com/jquery-1.7.1.min.js"></script>
    <script type="text/javascript">
      $(function(){
        $(document).click(function(event){
          $("div#box").animate({
              left: '+=100px'
          }, 200);
        });
      });
    </script>
  </head>
  <body>
    <div id="box">
    </div>
  </body>
</html>
```

Code snippet is from custom-animation.txt

But, like we said, you can change more than one attribute at a time. The following example animates a UFO that moves right, and fades out at the same time. The fade out is accomplished by setting the final opacity to 0.

```html
<!DOCTYPE html>
<html>
  <head>
    <style type="text/css">
      img#alien {
         position: relative;
         left:0;
         background-color:blue;
      }
    </style>
    <script src="http://code.jquery.com/jquery-1.7.1.min.js"></script>
    <script type="text/javascript">
      $(function(){
        var winWidth = $(document).width();
```

```
            var duration = 1000;

            $(document).click(function(event){
              $("#alien").animate({
                  opacity: 0,
                  width: 10,
                  height: 10,
                  left: '+=1000px'
              }, duration );
            });
          });
        </script>
      </head>
      <body>
        <img id="alien" src="ufo.png">
      </body>
    </html>
```

Code snippet is from two-attributes.txt

As you can see, the UFO image moves, shrinks, and fades out simultaneously. Try changing the left and duration properties to experiment velocities and effects. Figure 7-1 illustrates the states of the animations.

FIGURE 7-1

The next example is longer, but demonstrates how you can accomplish a lot with very little code. It's a foundation for what could turn into a "Space Invaders"-style game. At the bottom of the screen is a very primitive-looking spaceship, which moves back and forth, using the left and right arrow keys. Pressing the up arrow key fires a "laser," which is really just a hidden div. At the top of the screen is an evil-looking space alien that hides when hit by the laser. Figure 7-2 shows this layout in action.

The following code sample shows this in full. There's some initial CSS necessary to get this to work and then just a few lines of JavaScript are needed to wire up the animations and interactivity.

Available for
download on
Wrox.com

```
    <!DOCTYPE html>
    <html>
      <head>
        <style type="text/css">
          body {
            background-color:black;
          }

          h1 {
            color: yellow;
          }

          img#spaceShip {
```

```
    position: absolute;
    left:0;
    top:80%;
    background-color:blue;
  }

  img#invader {
    position: absolute;
    left:25%;
    top:10%;
  }

  div#laser {
    position: absolute;
    display: none;
    left:0;
    top:0;
    width:10px;
    height:70px;
    background-color: red;
  }
</style>
<script src="http://code.jquery.com/jquery-1.7.1.min.js"></script>
<script type="text/javascript">
  $(function(){
    var winWidth = $(document).width();
    var duration = 1000;

    $(document).keydown(function(event){
      var keyCode = event.keyCode || event.which;
      var keyMap = { left: 37, up: 38, right: 39, down: 40 };

      switch (keyCode) {
        case keyMap.left:
          $("#spaceShip").animate({
            left: '-=50'
          },200);
        break;

        case keyMap.up:
          var ufoLeft = $("#spaceShip").offset().left;
          var ufoTop = $("#spaceShip").offset().top;
          $("#laser").offset({left:ufoLeft+87, top:(ufoTop-30)});
          $("#laser").css("display","block")
                  .animate({top:10}, 200, function(){
                      var invaderLeft = $("#invader").offset().left;
                      var laserLeft = $("#laser").offset().left;

                      if( laserLeft >= invaderLeft &&
                          laserLeft <= invaderLeft + 288){
                        $("#invader").hide();
                        $("body").html("<h1>Direct Hit!</h1>");
                      }

                      $("#laser").offset({left:0, top:0});
                      $("#laser").css("display","none");
                  });
```

```
          break;

        case keyMap.right:
          $("#spaceShip").animate({
            left: '+=50'
          },200);
          break;
      }
    });
  });
</script>
</head>
<body>
  <img id="spaceShip" src="spaceShip.png">
  <img id="invader" src="invader.png">
  <div id="laser"></div>
</body>
</html>
```

Code snippet is from spaceInvader.txt

FIGURE 7-2

ANIMATIONS WITH HTML5 CANVAS

If we said it once, we'll say it again. Recent developments on the Web have made giving a site that extra "wow" effect just that much easier. One of the big additions to HTML5 is the canvas tag. This element creates a space for drawing bitmap images in HTML. The markup for canvas is about as minimalistic as it gets:

```
<canvas id="drawingSpace" width="300" height="200"></canvas>
```

To get any real use out of `canvas`, you'll need JavaScript. The following example demonstrates how to create a rectangle:

```
$(function(){
  var rect_ctx = $("canvas#rect")[0].getContext("2d");
  rect_ctx.fillRect(10, 10, 50, 50);
});
```

The `canvas` object is selected, and used to get a handle on its context. Then the context is used to draw a rectangle at the point (10, 10) with a width of 50 and a height of 50. The context is an object that contains all of the drawing methods and properties for the `canvas`. In the previous example, you used the `fillRect()` method to create a rectangle using the system default color black.

The coordinate system used by `canvas` has its origin at the top-left corner of the browser window with an increasing x value toward the right and an increasing y value downward. Figure 7-3 illustrates this system.

The `strokeStyle` is the outline style, and the `fillStyle` obviously is for everything inside the drawn area. Here are a couple of different rectangles with different fill and stroke styles:

```
$(function(){
  var ctx = $("canvas#c1")[0].getContext("2d");

  ctx.fillStyle = "rgb(0,150,0)";
  ctx.strokeStyle = "rgb(200,0,0)";
  ctx.fillRect(0,0,150,150);

  ctx.fillStyle = "rgb(100,100,0)";
  ctx.fillRect(150,150,150,150);
});
```

FIGURE 7-3

You can also draw connected lines. First you map out the path, and then do the actual drawing.

```
ctx.beginPath();
ctx.moveTo(1,1);
ctx.lineTo(10,10);
ctx.stroke();
ctx.closePath();
```

To get a good primer on the `canvas` tag we recommend the canvas chapter of Mark Pilgrim's, "Dive Into HTML5." You can find it at `http://diveintohtml5.info/canvas.html`.

In the next example, you redo the same box animation, but this time you use `canvas` instead of a div. Even though this example is just a simple black box, consider that it could be a much more complex drawn object.

```
<!DOCTYPE html>
<html>
  <head>
    <style type="text/css">
```

```
      canvas {
        width:100px;
        height:100px;
        top:0;
        left:0;
        position:absolute;
      }
    </style>
    <script src="http://code.jquery.com/jquery-1.7.1.min.js"></script>
    <script type="text/javascript">
      $(function(){
        var rect_ctx = $("canvas#rect")[0].getContext("2d");
        rect_ctx.fillRect(0, 0, 50, 50);

        $(document).click(function(){
          $("#rect").animate({
            left : '+=800px'}, 200);
        });
      });
    </script>
  </head>
  <body>
    <canvas id="rect"></canvas>
  </body>
</html>
```

Code snippet is from canvas.txt

SUMMARY

In a single chapter you've learned how to draw with the canvas tag, created an animated slide-down message bar, and even a starting point for creating a "Space Invaders"-style game. Although the first half of the chapter explored how to animate DOM elements, you learned that the same techniques are applicable to canvas-drawn elements as well. In the next chapter, you continue your exploration of user interfaces with an extension of the jQuery core called jQuery UI.

NOTES

http://api.jquery.com/animate/
https://developer.mozilla.org/en/canvas_tutorial
http://www.whatwg.org/specs/web-apps/current-work/multipage/the-canvas-element
    .html#2dcontext
http://dev.opera.com/articles/view/html-5-canvas-the-basics/

PART II
Applied jQuery

8

jQuery UI
Part I—Making Things Look Slick

WHAT'S IN THIS CHAPTER?

➤ Theming and Styling with jQuery

➤ Using ThemeRoller

➤ Using jQuery UI Widgets

jQuery UI is an associated user interface library for jQuery that contains widgets, effects, animations, and interactions. Widgets in this rich set are themeable, a process simplified by the ThemeRoller web app, and have an advanced look and feel to them. The framework also includes a very complete set of CSS classes useful for theming your application. While many of these features are replicated in other plugins, the unified codebase and API, overall quality, and flexibility of jQuery UI make it an indispensible asset when building complete web applications. This chapter covers jQuery UI theming, creating custom themes, widgets, and other ways to get effects that the jQuery core doesn't provide.

THEMING AND STYLING

Getting started with jQuery UI is easy. You simply navigate over to `jqueryui .com/download` to obtain a copy. You can either download a preexisting theme or make your own. As Figure 8-1 shows, the download page also gives you the option of choosing which components to include in your download. It's the rare

FIGURE 8-1

project that makes full use of all the widgets and tools of jQuery UI, and in those cases, it's better to download only the necessary components in order to reduce the download size footprint on your final product. But for exploring and experimenting, download the complete set of options.

If you want to edit your theme, inside of the file css/*selected-theme-name*/jquery-ui-xxx.css, there is a series of commented outlines (in my file, it's around line 50) with an HTTP address. Use this address to re-create your altered theme in ThemeRoller, and continue modifying to your heart's content.

The following folders are included in the jQuery UI download:

➤ **index.html:** A "gallery" of the widgets included with jQuery UI as well as the CSS classes

➤ **js:** A folder containing a copy of the latest, full version of jQuery UI, alongside a local copy of the core jQuery library

➤ **css:** A folder containing a default jQuery UI theme

➤ **development-bundle:** A folder containing full, unminified versions of all the jQuery UI files

jQuery UI contains a comprehensive CSS framework, which gives all of the widgets a consistent look and feel.

The CSS framework files are located in two places: the css folder at the top level and the development-bundle/themes folder. The .css file found at the top level contains all of the definitions in a single place, which reduces the amount of HTTP requests required to obtain CSS definitions. The files found under the development-bundle directory contain both the base theme and the selected custom theme.

USING THEMEROLLER

jQuery UI is themeable (that's the word the jQuery maintainers use) and customizable. You have a few different approaches for modifying themes:

➤ Make a theme from scratch

➤ Use a premade theme without making any changes

➤ Alter a theme manually

➤ Use ThemeRoller to modify a premade theme

Making a theme from scratch is anything but practical given the sheer number of CSS classes you'd have to create. Using the default themes is a great option, but the out-of-the-box defaults probably don't match the colors of your application, so your best bet is to modify an existing theme. If you feel inclined, you can modify the CSS classes manually, but using ThemeRoller is much less of a hassle.

You can find ThemeRoller at http://jqueryui.com/themeroller. This page shows a preview of each of the widgets and the icon set before you download it. On the left side of the page is a panel displaying options for "Roll your own" themes, a gallery of premade themes, and a Help tab. Choose a theme that closely resembles what you'd like as a final product, and modify the options to suit your needs. When you're finished, click the Download Theme button. It's that simple.

In any event, your jQuery UI will always require the following boilerplate code, provided here for your convenience:

```html
<!DOCTYPE html>
<html>
  <head>
    <link rel="stylesheet"
          href="development-bundle/themes/base/ui.theme.css">
    <meta http-equiv="Content-Type" content="text/html; charset=utf-8">
  </head>
  <body>
  </body>
</html>
```

Code snippet is from ui.css.txt

USING JQUERY UI WIDGETS

Generally, the JavaScript for creating any of the widgets is very simple and straightforward:

```
$(selector).widgetType();
```

Each widget type may require a specific markup structure; for example, the tab widget requires a list with anchors in order to render: Table 8-1 illustrates the code needed initialize each of the jQuery UI widgets.

TABLE 8-1: Code to Intialize jQuery UI Widgets

WIDGET	METHOD CALL
button	`$('#myButton').button();`
button set	`$('input[type=radio]').buttonset();`
tabs	`$('#tabs').tabs();`
accordion	`$('#myAccordian').accordion();`
autocomplete	`$('#myText').autocomplete();`
datepicker	`$('#date').datepicker();`
dialog	`$('#myDialog').dialog();`
progressbar slider	`$('#itemLoader').progressbar();` `$('#numberSlider').slider();`

The widget sets also accept an object for configuring the many available options for fine controlling of the widgets.

Button

Browsers use the default OS native button for inputs. While this is certainly a functional choice, you'll often want to create custom styles to match your site's overall design. Figure 8-2 illustrates how the jQuery UI button class enhances the native version.

FIGURE 8-2

The `$.button()` style is applied to individual buttons whereas `$.buttonset()` is applied to button groups like radio inputs and checkboxes. Table 8-2 lists the available methods for both types of button widgets.

TABLE 8-2: Available `$.button()` and `$.buttonset()` Methods

METHOD	DESCRIPTION
`$(selector).button();` `$(selector).buttonset();`	Creates a default button widget
`$(selector).button('disable');` `$(selector).buttonset('disable');`	Disables a previously created button widget.
`$(selector).button('enable');` `$(selector).buttonset('enable');`	Enables a previously enabled button widget.
`$(selector).button('destroy');` `$(selector).buttonset('destroy');`	Removes the button widget completely. This option rolls the selected element back to its initial state.

`$(selector).button('option',`
`optionName, value);`
`$(selector).buttonset('option',`
`optionName, value);`
	Gets or sets any button option. If the third argument is omitted, acts as a getter. Otherwise, it sets the `optionName` with the provided `value`.

`$(selector).button('widget');` `$(selector).buttonset('widget');`	Returns the .ui-button element.
`$(selector).button('refresh');` `$(selector).buttonset('refresh');`	Refreshes the visual state of the button widget.

Table 8-3 shows the options available for the button and buttonset.

TABLE 8-3: `$.button()` and `$.buttonset()` Options

OPTION	ACCEPTS	DESCRIPTION
Disabled	Boolean	Disables the button widget.
Text	Boolean	Option dictating if text should be displayed or not.

OPTION	ACCEPTS	DESCRIPTION
Icons	Options	Icons displayed with button widget. Contains a primary and secondary icon.
Label	String	Button text.

As you can tell from the options list, you can also include icons with the buttons. A button may contain both a primary icon (displayed on the left side) and a secondary icon (displayed on the right side). A valid icon name must be given. For example:

Available for download on Wrox.com

```
$(selector).button({
  text : true,
  icons : {
  primary : 'ui-icon-alert',
    secondary : 'ui-icon-lightbulb'
  }
});
```

Code snippet is from ui-button-icon.txt

Tabs

Tabs are a great way to pack a dense amount of information on a single page, and help to organize the content. To create a tab widget, you need a list, either ordered or unordered, with an anchor element in each list item. In addition, each list item must contain a reference to the associated tab content. A simple tab setup would look something like the following code sample. The `href` attribute of the anchors within our tab list reference their associated tab content element ids.

Available for download on Wrox.com

```
<div id="tabs">
  <ul>
    <li><a href="#tab1">Tab #1</a></li>
    <li><a href="#tab2">Tab #2</a></li>
  </ul>
  <div id="tab1">Tab Number 1</div>
  <div id="tab2">Tab Number 2</div>
</div>
```

Code snippet is from sample-tab-markup.txt

Table 8-4 lists the available `$.tab()` methods.

TABLE 8-4: Available `$.tabs()` Methods

METHOD	DESCRIPTION
`$(selector).tabs();`	Initializes the tab widget on the selected element.
`$(selector).tabs("destroy");`	Removes the tabs completely. This option rolls the selected element back to its initial state.
`$(selector).tabs("disable");`	Disables the tab widget.
`$(selector).tabs("enable");`	Enables the tab widget.
`$(selector).tabs( "option" , optionName , [value] );`	Gets or sets any tabs option. If the third argument is omitted, acts as a getter. Otherwise, it sets the `optionName` with the provided `value`.
`$(selector).tabs("widget");`	Returns the .ui-tabs element.
`$(selector).tabs( "add" , url , label , [index]);`	Adds a new tab widget. The second `url` argument is either a fragment identifier for an in-page tab or a full URL for a remote (Ajax) tab. The `label` argument represents the text label for the new tab. The optional `index` argument is the zero-based position where to insert the new tab.
`$(selector).tabs("remove" , index);`	Removes a tab widget. The second `index` argument indicates the tab to be removed.
`$(selector).tabs("enable" , index);`	Enables a disabled tab widget. The second `index` argument indicates the tab to be enabled.
`$(selector).tabs( "disable" , index );`	Disables a tab widget. As a note, the currently selected tab cannot be disabled. The second `index` argument indicates the tab to be disabled.
`$(selector).tabs("select", index);`	Selects a tab widget, as if it were clicked. The second `index` argument indicates the tab to be selected or the `id` selector of the associated panel.
`$(selector).tabs("load", index);`	Reloads the content of an Ajax tab. The second `index` argument indicates the tab to be reloaded.
`$(selector).tabs("url", index, url);`	Changes the `url` from which an Ajax tab will be loaded. The second `index` argument indicates the tab to be removed. The third argument is the `url` to load the new content from.
`$(selector).tabs("length");`	Retrieves the number of tabs of the first matched tab widget.
`$(selector).tabs("abort");`	Terminates all running ajax requests and animations.
`$(selector).tabs( "rotate" , ms , [continuing] );`	Sets up an automatic rotation of tabs. The second `ms` argument indicates the time between rotations. The third argument, `continuing`, controls whether or not the rotation continues after a tab has been selected by a user.

The following example demonstrates a tab set with the tabs displayed at the bottom that are also reorderable. The example initializes the tabs, uses $.find() to search for elements with the class ui-tabs-nav, and then applies the $.sortable() method to them.

$.sortable() is a jQuery UI Interaction method that allows elements to be sortable by dragging them with the mouse. You'll learn about $.sortable() in Chapter 9.

The second line adjusts the CSS classes to allow the tabs to be positioned at the bottom of the content panel.

```html
<!DOCTYPE html>
<html>
<head>
  <link href="css/ui-lightness/jquery-ui-1.8.13.custom.css"
        rel="stylesheet" />
  <script src="http://code.jquery.com/jquery-1.7.1.js"></script>
  <script src="js/jquery-ui-1.8.13.custom.min.js"></script>
  <script>
    $(function() {
      $("#tabs")
        .tabs()
        .find( ".ui-tabs-nav" )
        .sortable({ axis: "x" });
      $( ".tabs-bottom .ui-tabs-nav, .tabs-bottom .ui-tabs-nav > *" )
        .removeClass( "ui-corner-all ui-corner-top" )
        .addClass( "ui-corner-bottom" );
    });

  </script>
  <style type="text/css">
    #tabs {
      height: 200px;
    }
    .tabs-bottom {
      position: relative;
    }
    .tabs-bottom .ui-tabs-panel {
      height: 140px;
      overflow: auto;
    }
    .tabs-bottom .ui-tabs-nav {
      position: absolute !important;
      left: 0;
      bottom: 0;
      right:0;
      padding: 0 0.2em 0.2em 0;
    }
    .tabs-bottom .ui-tabs-nav li {
      margin-top: -2px !important;
      margin-bottom: 1px !important;
      border-top: none;
      border-bottom-width: 1px;
    }
```

```
      .ui-tabs-selected {
          margin-top: -3px !important;
      }
  </style>

  </head>
  <body>
    <div id="tabs" class="tabs-bottom">
      <ul>
        <li><a href="#t1">Tech Notes</a></li>
        <li><a href="#t2">Startup Ideas</a></li>
        <li><a href="#t3">JS Notes</a></li>
      </ul>
      <div id="t1">
        <p>Lorum Bacon</p>
      </div>
      <div id="t2">
        <p>Lorum Bacon</p>
      </div>
      <div id="t3">
        <p>Blah blah</p>
      </div>
    </div>

    </body>
  </html>
```

Code snippet is from sortabletabs.txt

Table 8-5 lists some of the options available when working with `$.tabs()`. For the full list of options, see the documentation at `http://jqueryui.com/demos/tabs/`

TABLE 8-5: Tab Options

OPTION	ACCEPTS	DESCRIPTION
disabled	Boolean	An array containing the position of the tabs that should be disabled when the widget is initialized.
event	String	The event used for selecting a tab. This commonly allows tabs to change on mouseover instead of a standard click.
fx	Options, Array	`fx` allows you to set animations for showing and hiding tab content.
panelTemplate	String	If you're using Ajax tabs, then you can use `panelTemplate` to create default HTML from which the new tab panels will be generated.
selected	Number	This zero-based integer sets the position of the initially selected tab.

OPTION	ACCEPTS	DESCRIPTION
`spinner`	String	An HTML string used to display a "spinner" or some other indication that the tab panel is loading. Requires a `span` in the `a` tag of the title.
`tabTemplate`	String	The HTML template from which new tabs are generated.

Accordion

Accordion widgets, similarly to tabs, are a great way to display and categorize a large amount of information. This widget is an expandable/collapsible box. It's not meant to have all of its content expanded at the same time, but rather to display one "slice" of content at a time.

Table 8-6 illustrates the various accordion methods.

TABLE 8-6: Available `$.accordion` Methods

METHOD	DESCRIPTION
`$(selector).accordion();`	Initializes an accordion widget.
`$(selector).accordion( "destroy" );`	Removes the accordion widget completely. This option rolls the selected element back to its initial state.
`$(selector).accordion( "disable" );`	Disables the accordion widget.
`$(selector).accordion( "enable" );`	Enables the accordion widget.
`$(selector).accordion( "option" , optionName , [value] );`	Get or set any accordion option. If the third argument is omitted, acts as a getter. Otherwise, it sets the `optionName` with the provided `value`.
`$(selector).accordion( "widget" );`	Returns the `.ui-accordion` element.
`$(selector).accordion( "activate" , index );`	Activates a content part of the accordion widget. The `index` indicates the zero-indexed number matching the position of the header to close or a selector matching an element.
`$(selector).accordion( "resize" );`	Recomputes the heights of the accordion widget contents.

The required markup for an accordion is a div with nested headers, where each header contains a link. The content is placed in a nested div following the header, as the following example illustrates:

```html
<!DOCTYPE html>
<html>
<head>
<link href="css/ui-lightness/jquery-ui-1.8.13.custom.css" rel="stylesheet" />
<script src="http://code.jquery.com/jquery-1.7.1.js"></script>
<script src="js/jquery-ui-1.8.13.custom.min.js"></script>
<script>
$(function() {
  $( "#accordion" ).accordion();
});

</script>

</head>
<body>
  <div id="accordion">
    <h3><a href="#">First header</a></h3>
    <div>First content</div>
    <h3><a href="#">Second header</a></h3>
    <div>Second content</div>
  </div>
</body>
</html>
```

Code snippet is from accordion.txt

Table 8-7 lists some of the available options when initializing an accordion widget. For the full list of options, consult the documentation available at http://jqueryui.com/demos/accordion/.

TABLE 8-7: Accordion Options

OPTION	ACCEPTS	DESCRIPTION
disabled	Boolean	Enables (`false`) or disables (`true`) the accordion widget.
animated	Boolean, String	Sets the preferred animation. A Boolean argument enables or disables animations altogether.
event	String	The type of event used to fire the accordion. This commonly allows tabs to change on mouseover instead of a standard click.

Autocomplete

Given the large amount of data on the web, the quicker you can get to your results, the better. The autocomplete feature shows a pre-populated list of selectable options as the user types in characters. If you've ever used a search engine, you've experience autocomplete. Figure 8-3 shows a familiar implementation of autocomplete functionality in action on Google.com.

FIGURE 8-3

The following code sample shows a simple implementation of the autocomplete widget. It leverages the `source` option to reference a local datasource, in this case an array. Other than that, it's nothing more than a simple call to `$.autocomplete` and this powerful feature is immediately available. There's probably no better illustration of the power of jQuery UI. One line of code and you've significantly enhanced the usability of your site or application.

Available for download on Wrox.com

```
<!DOCTYPE html>
<html>
<head>
  <script src='http://code.jquery.com/jquery-1.7.1.js'></script>
  <link href="css/ui-lightness/jquery-ui-1.8.13.custom.css" rel="stylesheet" />
  <script src="js/jquery-ui-1.8.13.custom.min.js"></script>
  <script >
  $(window).load(function(){
    $(function() {
      var stageWinners = [
        "Eddy Merckx","Bernard Hinault",
        "André Leducq","Lance Armstrong",
        "André Darrigade","Mark Cavendish",
        "Nicolas Frantz","François Faber",
        "Jean Alavoine","Jacques Anquetil",
        "René Le Greves","Charles Pelissier",
        "Freddy Maertens","Philippe Thys",
        "Louis Trousselier","Gino Bartali",
        "Mario Cipollini","Miguel Indurain",
```

```
                "Robbie McEwen","Erik Zabel",
                "Jean Aerts","Louison Bobet",
                "Raffaele Di Paco","Maurice Archambaud",
                "Charly Gaul","Walter Godefroot",
                "Gerrie Knetemann","Antonin Magne",
                "Henri Pelissier","Jan Raas",
                "Joop Zoetemelk","Thor Hushovd"
            ];
            $( "#tdf" ).autocomplete({
                source: stageWinners
            });
        });
    </script>
</head>
<body>
    <div>
        <label for="tags">Tags: </label>
        <input id="tdf">
    </div>
</body>
</html>
```

Code snippet is from autocomplete.txt

Table 8-8 lists the full selection of `$.autocomplete()` methods.

TABLE 8-8: Available `$.autocomplete` Methods

METHOD	DESCRIPTION
`$(selector).autocomplete()`	Initializes an autocomplete widget.
`$(selector).autocomplete( "destroy" )`	Removes the autocomplete widget completely. This option rolls the selected element back to its initial state.
`$(selector).autocomplete( "disable" )`	Disables the autocomplete widget.
`$(selector).autocomplete( "enable" )`	Enables the autocomplete widget.
`$(selector).autocomplete( "option" , optionName , [value] )`	Gets or sets any autocomplete option. If the third argument is omitted, acts as a getter. Otherwise, it sets the `optionName` with the provided `value`.
`$(selector).autocomplete( "widget" )`	Returns the `.ui-autocomplete` element.
`$(selector).autocomplete( "search" , [value] )`	Triggers a search event. If data is available, this will display the autocomplete suggestions.
`$(selector).autocomplete( "close" )`	Closes the autocomplete widget menu.

Table 8-9 lists the available autocomplete options.

TABLE 8-9: Autocomplete Options

OPTION	ACCEPTS	DESCRIPTION
disabled	Boolean	Enables (false) or disables (true) the accordion widget.
appendTo	Selector	The element to append the menu to.
autofocus	Boolean	Indicates whether or not the first item should be automatically focused.
delay	Integer	The delay, in milliseconds, after a keystroke before the autcomplete opens.
minLength	Integer	The minimum number of characters a user has to type before the autocomplete fires.
position	Object	Indicates the position of the widget in relation to the associated input element.
source	String, Array, callback function	Indicates the preferred data source. This can be an array containing local data, a string specifying a URL, or a callback function

Datepicker

The datepicker is one of the more versatile jQuery UI widgets. Chances are, if you've made a reservation online for a flight or hotel, you've used a JavaScript datepicker.

The "out of the box" version of the datepicker is incredibly useful, but there's a mind-numbing amount of additional features and options that extends its capabilities. Besides the various ways of presenting the datepicker, it also includes a set of utility functions and keyboard shortcuts for navigation. You could call the default datepicker like so:

```
$(selector).datepicker();
```

and get a really nice widget like the one shown in Figure 8-4.

It looks cool, but you have so much more control over the datepicker outside of the default functionality. Table 8-10 gives the full list of $.datepicker methods.

FIGURE 8-4

TABLE 8-10: Available `$.datepicker()` Methods

METHOD	DESCRIPTION
`$(selector).datepicker();`	Initializes the datepicker widget.
`$(selector).datepicker( "destroy" );`	Removes the datepicker widget completely. This option rolls the selected element back to its initial state.
`$(selector).datepicker( "disable" );`	Disables the datepicker widget.
`$(selector).datepicker( "enable" );`	Enables the datepicker widget.
`$(selector).datepicker( "option" , optionName , [value] );`	Gets or sets any datepicker widget option. If the third argument is omitted, acts as a getter. Otherwise, it sets the `optionName` with the provided `value`.
`$(selector).datepicker( "widget" );`	Returns the `.ui-datepicker` element.
`$(selector).datepicker( "dialog" , date , [onSelect] , [settings] , [pos] );`	Opens a datepicker in a "dialog" box. This method accepts several arguments of its own. `dateText`: the initial date for the datepicker. `onSelect`: A callback function when a date is selected. `settings`: Settings for the datepicker. `pos`: The position of the top/left of the dialog as [x, y].
`$(selector).datepicker( "isDisabled" );`	Determines whether or not a datepicker widget has been disabled.
`$(selector).datepicker( "hide" );`	Hides a datepicker widget.
`$(selector).datepicker( "show" );`	Shows a hidden datepicker widget.
`$(selector).datepicker( "refresh" );`	Refreshes the datepicker widget.
`$(selector).datepicker( "getDate" );`	Returns the current selected date for the datepicker. Returns `null` if no date is selected.
`$(selector).datepicker( "setDate" , date );`	Sets the current date for the datepicker.

Table 8-11 lists all the available options for the datepicker widget.

TABLE 8-11: Datepicker Options

OPTION	ACCEPTS	DESCRIPTION
disabled	Boolean	Enables/disables datepicker functionality.
altField	Selector, jQuery, element	An alternative field that will be updated in addition to the main field. Use a selector or jQuery wrapper object to specify the alternative field. Use in conjunction with the `altFormat` option.
altFormat	String	The date format used for the alternative field (`altField`) specified. Does not need to match the format of the principal text input field. For the full list of options for formatting dates, see the documentation for the `$.datepicker.formatDate()` method `http://docs.jquery.com/UI/Datepicker/formatDate`.
appendText	String	Text appended to the end of the date field, used to let the user know the date format.
autoSize	Boolean	Option specifying whether or not the date field should be resizable to fit the length of the date text of the current format.
buttonImage	String	A URL string for the pop-up button image.
buttonImageOnly	Boolean	When `true`, an image to trigger the calendar is placed after the input field. When `false`, the image is combined with a button element.
buttonText	String	The text shown on the trigger button.
calculateWeek	Function	A custom function for calculating the week for a particular date.
changeMonth	Boolean	Add a drop-down for selecting the month.
changeYear	String	Add a drop-down for selecting the year.
closeText	String	Text to be displayed on the close button on the display panel. The display panel must be set to true.
constrainInput	Boolean	Allow constraining of input to character set specified in `dateFormat`.
currentText	String	Text to display for "current day" button on the button panel.
dateFormat	String	The format of both the parsed and displayed date formats.
dayNames	Array	An array of the long name days.
dayNamesMin	Array	An array list of the minimized day names.

continues

TABLE 8-11 *(continued)*

OPTION	ACCEPTS	DESCRIPTION
dayNamesShort	Array	An array of shortened day names.
defaultDate	Date, Number, String	Sets the default date to highlight when the datepicker is opened. Valid input options include a date object, an input string matching the `dateFormat`, number of days from the current day, a string of values, or null.
Duration	String, Number	Value indicating the speed at which the datepicker appears or disappears.
firstDay	Number	Option specifying the first day of the week, starting with Sunday at 0.
gotoCurrent	Boolean	When `true`, the current day button links to the currently selected day rather than today.
hideIfNoPrevNext	Boolean	Hides the next/previous buttons instead of disabling in circumstances where the next/previous buttons are not applicable.
isRTL	Boolean	True when the current language is read from right to left. This is a renationalization option.
maxDate	Date, Number, String	The maximum selectable date.
minDate	Date, Number, String	The minimum selectable date.
monthNames	Array	An array of the full month names, used by `dateFormat`.
monthNamesShort	Array	An array of shortened month names used on the header of the datepicker. When `true`, the `$.datepicker.formatDate()` function is applied to the `prevText`, `nextText`, and `currentText` values before being displayed.
navigationAsDateFormat	Boolean	
nextText	String	The text for the next month link.
numberOfMonths	Number, Array	Option denoting the number of months to display; default is one. Accepts either an integer or an array for specifying number of rows by columns.
prevText	String	The text for the previous month link.

OPTION	ACCEPTS	DESCRIPTION
selectOtherMonths	Boolean	When true, allows the selection of dates in months other than the current month.
shortYearCutoff	String, Number	Sets the cutoff year for determining the century for a date.
showAnim	String	An option for setting the show/hide animation.
showButtonPanel	Boolean	Shows/hides the button panel.
showCurrentAtPos	Number	When more than one month is displayed, specifies in which month to select. Zero-based, starting at top left.
showMonthAfterYear	Boolean	Whether or not to show the year after the month in the datepicker header.
showOn	String	Valid options are focus, button, or both. Determines what action will trigger the appearance of the datepicker by focusing on the text input, clicking the mouse button, or both.
showOptions	Options	Additional options for showAnim if using jQuery UI effects for displaying the datepicker.
showOtherMonths	Boolean	Shows dates from the previous or next month, but not selectable. To make these days selectable, set selectOtherMonths to true.
showWeek	Boolean	Displays the week number.
stepMonths	Number	Number of months to skip over (step through) after clicking the previous/next links.
weekHeader	String	Used in conjunction with showWeek, the string shown for the week header. The default is Wk.
yearRange	String	The permissible range of years to display.
yearSuffix	String	Text displayed after the year. For example, BC or AD.

The following example shows how to create a 2 × 2 datepicker, with a button panel:

```
<!DOCTYPE html>
<html>
  <head>
    <meta http-equiv="Content-Type" content="text/html; charset=iso-8859-1" />
    <link href="css/ui-lightness/jquery-ui-1.8.13.custom.css"
        rel="stylesheet" />
```

```
<script src="http://code.jquery.com/jquery-1.7.1.js"></script>
<script src="js/jquery-ui-1.8.13.custom.min.js">
</script>
<script>
  $(function(){
      $('input#mainField').datepicker({
          appendText : '(mm/dd/yyyy)',dateFormat : 'dd/mm/yy',
          closeText : 'X',
          showOn : 'button'
          currentText : 'Now',
          numberOfMonths : [2,2],
          selectOtherMonths : true,
          showOtherMonths : true,
          showWeek : true,
          weekHeader : 'Week'

      });
  });
</script>
</head>
<body>
  <input type="text" id="mainField">
</body>
</html>
```

Code snippet is from datepicker.txt

You should see something similar to Figure 8-5.

FIGURE 8-5

Dialog

The jQuery UI dialog looks infinitely better than the default JavaScript alert box.

A nice replacement for the native JavaScript alert box might go something like this:

```html
<!DOCTYPE html>
<html>
<head>
  <link href="css/ui-lightness/jquery-ui-1.8.13.custom.css"
      rel="stylesheet" />
  <script src="http://code.jquery.com/jquery-1.7.1.js"></script>
  <script src="js/jquery-ui-1.8.13.custom.min.js">
  </script>
  <script>
    $(function() {
        $( "#dialog" ).dialog({
            modal: true,
            buttons: {
                Ok: function() {
                    $( this ).dialog( "close" );
                }
            }
        });
    });

</script>
</head>
  <body>
    <div id="dialog" title="A sample dialog">
        Message Goes here
    </div>
  </body>
</html>
```

Code snippet is from dialog.txt

This displays a dialog box with a message and an OK button. The callback function simply closes the dialog. Of note is the `modal` property. In this case, it's set to `true`, which indicates that the rest of the page will be inaccessible while the dialog is open.

The full list of `$.dialog()` options can be seen in Table 8-12.

TABLE 8-12: Available `$.dialog()` Methods

METHOD	DESCRIPTION
`$(selector).dialog()`	Initializes the dialog widget.
`$(selector).dialog( "destroy" )`	Removes the dialog widget completely. This option rolls the selected element back to its initial state.
`$(selector).dialog( "disable" )`	Disables the dialog widget.

continues

TABLE 8-12 *(continued)*

METHOD	DESCRIPTION
`$(selector).dialog( "enable" )`	Enables the dialog widget.
`$(selector).dialog( "option" , optionName , [value] )`	Gets or sets any dialog widget option. If the third argument is omitted, acts as a getter. Otherwise, it sets the `optionName` with the provided `value`.
`$(selector).dialog( "widget" )`	Returns the `.ui-dialog` element.
`$(selector).dialog( "close" )`	Closes the dialog widget.
`$(selector).dialog( "isOpen" )`	Returns `true` if the dialog widget is currently open.
`$(selector).dialog( "moveToTop" )`	In the case of multiple dialog widgets on a page, this method moves the selected dialog widget to the top of the dialog stack.
`$(selector).dialog( "open" )`	Opens the selected dialog widget.

Table 8-13 lists all the available dialog widget options.

TABLE 8-13: Dialog Options

OPTION	BOOLEAN	DESCRIPTION
`disabled`	Boolean	Disables (`true`) or enables (`false`) the dialog widget.
`autOpen`	Boolean	Set to `true`, the dialog widget will open automatically.
`buttons`	Object, Array	Specifies which buttons should be displayed on the dialog widget. With a single object, the property of the object is a string indicating the type of button and the value is the callback methods to fire when the button is clicked. Alternatively, an array of button/callback pairs can be passed in to indicate a series of buttons to be presented in the dialog widget.
`closeOnEscape`	Boolean	Specifies whether or not the dialog widget should close when the user presses the escape key.
`closeText`	String	Specifies the text for the close button.
`dialogClass`	String	Specifies the CSS class to be added to the dialog. This allows for more detailed theming of dialog widgets.
`draggable`	Boolean	Indicates whether or not the dialog widget is draggable.
`height`	Number	The height, in pixels, of the dialog widget.
`hide`	String, Object	The effect to be used when the dialog widget is hidden.

OPTION	BOOLEAN	DESCRIPTION
maxHeight	Number	The maximum height, in pixels, of the dialog widget.
minHeight	Number	The minimum height, in pixels, of the dialog widget.
maxWidth	Number	The maximum width, in pixels, of the dialog widget.
minWidth	Number	The minimum width, in pixels, of the dialog widget.
modal	Boolean	Set to `true`, the dialog widget will display modal behavior: interaction with other elements on the page will be disabled.
position	String, Array	Specifies the position of the dialog.
resizable	Boolean	Indicates whether or not the dialog widget is going to be resizable.
show	String, Object	Shows the dialog widget.
stack	Boolean	Indicates whether or not the dialog widget will stack on top of other dialogs.
title	String	The title of the dialog widget.
width	Number	The width, in pixels, of the dialog widget.
zIndex	Number	The starting z-index of the dialog widget.

PROGRESSBAR

Users want to be informed. They want to know whether a page is loading, an operation is being performed, or if it's stuck. A progress bar is a classic tool for communicating this information to the end user. It's important to keep in mind that the value of the progress bar displayed should be somewhat accurate, or you'll still anger your users, at which point they may leave your page.

The progressbar widget is fairly simple in comparison with the other widgets studied so far, and only accepts two options, as summarized in Table 8-14.

TABLE 8-14: Progressbar Options

OPTION	ACCEPTS	DESCRIPTION
Disabled	Boolean	Disables (`true`) or enables (`false`) the progressbar.
Value	Number	Indicates the initial value of the progressbar widget

Expectedly, to change the "percent finished" of the progress bar, change the value option. The following example shows a progress bar that slowly increments to 100 percent after page load:

```html
<!DOCTYPE html>
<html>
<head>
  <link href="css/ui-lightness/jquery-ui-1.8.13.custom.css" rel="stylesheet" />
<script src="http://code.jquery.com/jquery-1.7.1.js"></script>
  <script src="js/jquery-ui-1.8.13.custom.min.js"></script>
  <script>
    $(function() {
      $( "#bar" ).progressbar({ value: 0 });
        setTimeout( updateProgress, 500 );
      });

    function updateProgress() {
      var progress;
      progress = $( "#bar" ).progressbar( "option","value" );
      if (progress < 100) {
        $( "#bar" ).progressbar( "option", "value", progress + 1 );
        setTimeout( updateProgress, 500 );
      }
    }
  </script>
</head>
<body>
  <div id="bar">
  </div>
</body>
</html>
```

Code snippet is from progressbar.txt

SLIDER

Sliders are a more restricted way of inputting numeric values, as shown in Table 8-15. The old-fashioned method of using text fields with masks or validations has drawbacks. Using a slider is visually cleaner and intuitive. The sliders are either vertical or horizontal.

TABLE 8-15: Slider Options

OPTION	ACCEPTS	DESCRIPTION
disabled	Boolean	Disables (`true`) or enables (`false`) the slider widget.
animate	Boolean, String, Number	Whether to slide the handle smoothly when the user clicks on the slider widget outside of the hit area represented by the handle.

OPTION	ACCEPTS	DESCRIPTION
min	Number	The minimum value of the slider widget.
max	Number	The maximum value of the slider widget.
orientation	String	The orientation of the slider widget. Widgets can be either horizontal or vertical.
range	Boolean, String	If true, the slider will detect if you have two handles and create a range element between these two handles.
step	Number	Determines the size of intervals between the min and max of the slider widget.
value	Number	Indicates the value of the slider.
values	Array	Used to define multiple handles.

In the following example, three vertical sliders are created, and positioned side by side to give a visual "mixer" look:

Available for
download on
Wrox.com

```
<!DOCTYPE html>
<html>
<head>
  <link href="css/ui-lightness/jquery-ui-1.8.13.custom.css" rel="stylesheet" />
<script src="http://code.jquery.com/jquery-1.7.1.js"></script>
  <script src="js/jquery-ui-1.8.13.custom.min.js"></script>
  <style type="text/css">
    div {
      float : left;
      margin-left : 30px;
      margin-right : 30px;
    }
  </style>
  <script type="text/javascript">
    $(function(){
      $( '#slider1' ).slider({
        orientation : "vertical"
      });

      $( '#slider2' ).slider({
        orientation : "vertical"
      });

      $( '#slider3' ).slider({
        orientation : "vertical"
      });
    });
  </script>
</head>
<body>
```

```
    <div id="slider1"></div>
    <div id="slider2"></div>
    <div id="slider3"></div>
  </body>
  </html>
```

Code snippet is from slider.txt

Your output should look something like Figure 8-6.

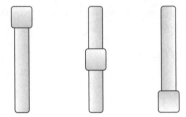

FIGURE 8-6

SUMMARY

This intro to jQuery UI has given you a quick glance at the structure of a jQuery UI project, the themes, as well as the very complete CSS framework. Also, you've explored the sophisticated set of jQuery UI widgets that help normalize the look and feel of widgets across browsers while each widget presents a broad range of useful options. In the following chapter, you explore jQuery UI further with mouse interactions.

NOTES

```
http://jqueryui.com/docs/Theming
http://jqueryui.com/docs/Theming/API
http://jquery-ui.googlecode.com/svn/trunk/tests/static/icons.html
http://www.petefreitag.com/cheatsheets/jqueryui-icons/
http://docs.jquery.com/UI/Datepicker/formatDate
http://www.ajaxlines.com/ajax/stuff/article/jquery_progressbar.php
```

jQuery UI
Part II—Mouse Interactions

WHAT'S IN THIS CHAPTER?

➤   Dragging and Dropping Elements

➤   Sorting

➤   Resizing Elements

➤   Making Elements Selectable

In this chapter, you continue exploring jQuery UI features centered on moving, sorting, resizing, and selecting elements with the mouse. Different from the plugins mentioned in the previous chapter, these aren't widgets, but rather, interesting behaviors you can add to DOM elements.

By default, divs, spans, and the like can't be dragged across a web page or resized. You need the help of JavaScript to make these elements dynamic, and with the help of jQuery UI, it becomes a trivial issue to do these kinds of operations that were once reserved for the desktop environment.

In this chapter, you review dragging, dropping, sorting, resizing, and making elements selectable. As you'll see, most of the details of implementing these operations are taken care of for you; yet you're given a healthy set of options to accommodate these interactions to your needs.

DRAGGING AND DROPPING

Dragging and dropping an element usually go together. There might be moments where just dragging around an element is enough, but usually you'll want both features. A draggable DOM element can be moved around by clicking and then moving the mouse. Droppable elements can accept draggable elements.

Dragging and dropping aren't features that are available to web pages by default, although they are very common idioms of everyday computer use. Thankfully, jQuery UI makes it simple and approachable. Although the actions are coupled, they require separate calls.

A component is made draggable by calling the jQuery UI draggable method, `$(selector)`
`.draggable()`, as simple as that. Like many of the method calls you've seen in this book, the `.draggable()` method is overloaded, reducing namespace clutter. (See Table 9-1.)

TABLE 9-1: `$.draggable()` Methods

METHOD	DESCRIPTION
`$(selector).draggable();`	Makes selected element draggable.
`$(selector).draggable("destroy");`	Removes the draggable functionality completely. This option rolls the selected element back to its initial state.
`$(selector).draggable("disable");`	Disables the draggable element.
`$(selector).draggable("enable");`	Enables the draggable element.
`$(selector).draggable("option", optionName, "value");`	Gets or sets any draggable element option. If the third argument is omitted, acts as a getter. Otherwise, it sets the `optionName` with the provided `value`.
`$(selector).draggable("widget"); //`	Returns the `.ui-draggable` element.

Table 9-2 shows the different options for draggable elements.

TABLE 9-2: Draggable Elements

OPTIONS	ACCEPTS	DESCRIPTION
`disabled`	Boolean	Enables/disables the draggable functionality.
`addClasses`	Boolean	Prevents adding the `ui-draggable` class when set to `false`.
`appendTo`	Element, Selector	Defines where the helper element is appended to during the drag.
`axis`	String	Constrains movement to either the x or y axis.
`cancel`	Selector	Prevents dragging from starting on specified elements.
`connectToSortable`	Selector	Allows the selected draggable element to be dropped on a sortable element.

OPTIONS	ACCEPTS	DESCRIPTION
containment	Selector, Element, String, Array	Limits dragging to a contained area. Valid options are window, document, parent, or an array in the form of [x1,y1,x2,y2].
cursor	String	The CSS cursor type used during the drag. For example, crosshair.
cursorAt	Object	Adjust the dragging helper offset position, relative to the mouse position.
delay	Integer	Delay time, in milliseconds, before drag goes into effect.
distance	Integer	The distance the mouse must move after mousedown before dragging begins to work.
grid	Array	When specified, the dragging helper snaps to a grid, which is spaced every x and y pixels. Expects an array of the form [x,y].
handle	Element, Selector	Gives the element a drag "handle"; in other words, restricts where an element can be dragged from to an element/area.
helper	String, Function	Allows for a helper element to be used for dragging display.
iframeFix	Boolean, Selector	Prevents iframes from capturing the mousemove events during a drag.
opacity	Float	The opacity level of the helper while being dragged.
refreshPositions	Boolean	When true, on every mousemove, the droppable position is calculated. Degrades the application's performance.
revert	Boolean, String	If set to true, the draggable element will return to its original position when dragging stops.
revertDuration	Integer	The duration, in milliseconds, of the revert animation.
scope	String	Used to group sets of draggable and droppable items.
scroll	Boolean	If set to true, container auto-scrolls while dragging.
scrollSensitivity	Integer	Distance, in pixels, from the edge of the viewport after which the viewport should scroll.
scrollSpeed	Integer	The speed at which the window should scroll once the mouse pointer gets within the scrollSensitivity distance.

continues

TABLE 9-2 *(continued)*

OPTIONS	ACCEPTS	DESCRIPTION
snap	Boolean, Selector	Indicates whether or not a draggable element should snap to the edges of the selected element.
snapMode	String	Defines the edges which snap elements will adhere to. Possible values are `inner`, `outer`, or `both`.
snapTolerance	Integer	Defines the distance, in pixels, from the edges of the snap element where the snap should occur.
stack	Selector	Controls the z-index of the matched elements.
zIndex	Integer	z-index for the element being dragged.

In a very similar fashion, the `$.droppable()` method is also overloaded. Table 9-3 lists all available `$.draggable()` methods.

TABLE 9-3: `$.draggable()` Methods

METHOD	DESCRIPTION
`$(selector).droppable();`	Makes selected element droppable.
`$(selector).droppable("destroy");`	Removes the droppable functionality completely. This option rolls the selected element back to its initial state.
`$(selector).droppable("disable");`	Disables the droppable element.
`$(selector).droppable("enable")`	Enables the droppable element.
`$(selector).droppable("option", optionName, "value");`	Get or set any droppable element option. If the third argument is omitted, acts as a getter. Otherwise, it sets the `optionName` with the provided `value`.
`$(selector).droppable("widget");`	Returns the `.ui-droppable` element.

All draggable components have a class of `ui-draggable`. While in a dragging state, the class changes to `ui-draggable-dragging`.

The following example uses both drag and drop to demonstrate a visual way of dividing tasks. At the top are square elements that each represent a task. At the bottom are the different states of a task: in progress or finished. By making the tasks draggable, the end user can intuitively organize tasks. Upon dropping a task box, the task box changes color. Figure 9-1 shows the output of this code.

```html
<!DOCTYPE html>
<html>
  <head>
    <link type="text/css"
      href="css/ui-lightness/jquery-ui-1.8.13.custom.css" rel="stylesheet" />

    <script src="http://code.jquery.com/jquery-1.7.1.js"></script>
    <script src="js/jquery-ui-1.8.13.custom.min.js"></script>
    <style type="text/css">
      div {
        width : 150px;
        margin-bottom : 20px;
        margin-right : 20px;
        float: left;
      }

      #flow {
        float: left;
        height : 400px;
      }

      #task3 {
        clear: both;
      }

    </style>
    <script type="text/javascript">
      $(function(){
        $('div[id^="task"]').draggable({
          snap : 'div',
          snapMode : 'both'
          // snap tolerance
        });

        $('#flow').droppable({
          drop : function( event, ui ) {
            $( this ).addClass( "ui-state-highlight" );
          }
        });
      });
    </script>
  </head>
  <body>
    <div id="task1" class="ui-widget-content">
      <p>Task 1</p>
    </div>
    <div id="task2" class="ui-widget-content">
      <p>Task 2</p>
    </div>
    <div id="task3" class="ui-widget-content">
      <p>Task 3</p>
    </div>
    <div id="flow" class="ui-widget-content">
      <p class="ui-widget-header">In Progress</p>
    </div>
```

```
    <div id="flow" class="ui-widget-content">
      <p class="ui-widget-header">Finished</p>
    </div>
  </body>
</html>
```

Code snippet is from drag-drop.txt

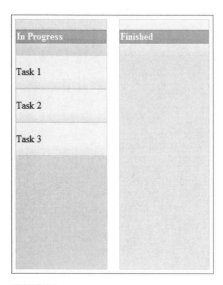

FIGURE 9-1

SORTING

A group of sortable elements are reorderable drag/drop components; for example, a list, a grid of elements, or even sorting an interconnected set of elements. Table 9-4 shows the different methods available for sortable elements.

TABLE 9.4: `$.sortable()` Methods

METHOD	DESCRIPTION
`$(selector).sortable();`	Makes selected element sortable.
`$(selector). sortable ("destroy");`	Removes the sortable functionality completely. This option rolls the selected element back to its initial state.
`$(selector). sortable ("disable");`	Disables the sortable element.
`$(selector). sortable ("enable")`	Enables the sortable element.

METHOD	DESCRIPTION
`$(selector). sortable ("option", optionName, "value");`	Gets or sets any sortable element option. If the third argument is omitted, acts as a getter. Otherwise, it sets the `optionName` with the provided `value`.
`$(selector). sortable ("widget");`	Returns the `.ui-sortable` element.
`$(selector) .sortable("serialize",[options]);`	Converts the sortable elements to a string suitable for form submission.
`$(selector).sortable("toArray");`	Converts the sortable elements to an array.
`$(selector).sortable("refresh");`	Refreshes the sortable elements.
`$(selector) .sortable("refreshPositions");`	Refreshes the cached positions of the sortable items.
`$(selector).sortable("cancel");`	Cancels a change in the current sortable elements.

Along with the different call methods, you also have a nice long list of options available for configuration, as shown in Table 9-5. These options give you control over the sensitivity and tolerance of the sortable elements. Sortable elements can also be interconnected between two different sets.

Sortable elements are built on top of the drag-and-drop functionality, but with a bit more specific behavior.

TABLE 9-5: Sortable Options

OPTION	ACCEPTS	DESCRIPTION
`disabled`	Boolean	Enables or disables the sortable element.
`appendTo`	String	Defines where the helper element is appended to during the drag.
`axis`	String	Constrains movement to either the x or y axis.
`cancel`	Selector	Prevents sorting on specified elements.
`connectWith`	Selector	Connects the sortable element with another sortable element matching the supplied `selector`.
`containment`	Element, String, Selector	Constrains dragging to within the bounds of the specified element.

continues

TABLE 9-5 *(continued)*

OPTION	ACCEPTS	DESCRIPTION
cursor	String	Defines the cursor shown when sorting.
cursorAt	Object	Adjust the dragging helper offset position, relative to the mouse position.
delay	Integer	Delay time, in milliseconds, before drag goes into effect.
distance	Integer	The distance the mouse must move after mousedown before dragging begins to work.
dropOnEmpty	Boolean	If false, items from this sortable can't be dropped to an empty linked sortable.
forceHelperSize	Boolean	If true, forces the helper to have a size.
forcePlaceholderSize	Boolean	If true, forces the placeholder to have a size.
grid	Array	When specified, the dragging helper snaps to a grid, which is spaced every x and y pixels. Expects an array of the form [x,y].
handle	Selector, Element	Gives the element a drag "handle"; in other words, restricts where an element can be dragged from to an element/area.
helper	String, Function	Allows for a helper element to be used for dragging display.
items	Selector	Specifies which items inside the element should be sortable.
opacity	Float	The opacity level of the helper while being dragged.
placeholder	String	Class that gets applied to the otherwise white space.
revert	Boolean/Integer	If set to true, the draggable element will return to its original position when dragging stops.
scroll	Boolean	If set to true, container auto-scrolls while dragging.
scrollSensitivity	Integer	Distance, in pixels, from the edge of the viewport after which the viewport should scroll.
scrollSpeed	Integer	The speed at which the window should scroll once the mouse pointer gets within the scrollSensitivity distance.

OPTION	ACCEPTS	DESCRIPTION
tolerance	String	This is the way the reordering behaves during drag. Possible values: `'intersect'`, `'pointer'`. In some setups, `'pointer'` is more natural.
zIndex	Integer	z-index for the element being dragged.

The following example revisits the task list. Each of the individual task boxes now has a "portlet" style interface. When reordering one of the component boxes, the new position of the orderable component is highlighted with a different style. An example of the reordering in process can be seen in Figure 9-2.

```html
<!DOCTYPE html>
<html>
  <head>
    <link href="css/ui-lightness/jquery-ui-1.8.13.custom.css"
      rel="stylesheet" />
    <script src="http://code.jquery.com/jquery-1.7.1.js"></script>
    <script src="js/jquery-ui-1.8.13.custom.min.js"></script>
    <style type="text/css">
      .column {
        width: 170px;
        float: left;
        padding-bottom: 100px;
      }
      .portlet {
        margin: 0 1em 1em 0;
      }
      .portlet-header {
        margin: 0.3em;
        padding-bottom: 4px;
        padding-left: 0.2em;
      }
      .portlet-header .ui-icon {
        float: right;
      }
      .portlet-content {
        padding: 0.4em;
      }
      .ui-state-highlight {
        height: 1.5em;
        line-height: 1.2em;
      }
    </style>
    <script>
      $(function(){
        $( ".portlet" )
          .addClass( "ui-widget ui-widget-content"
            + "ui-helper-clearfix ui-corner-all" )
```

```
            .find( ".portlet-header" )
            .addClass( "ui-widget-header ui-corner-all" )
            .prepend( "<span class='ui-icon ui-icon-minusthick'></span>")
             .end()
             .find( ".portlet-content" );
        $('.column').sortable({ placeholder: "ui-state-highlight" });
      });
    </script>
  </head>
  <body>
<div class="column">
    <div class="portlet">
       <div class="portlet-header">Task 1</div>
       <div class="portlet-content">...</div>
    </div>
    <div class="portlet">
       <div class="portlet-header">Task 2</div>
       <div class="portlet-content">...</div>
    </div>
    <div class="portlet">
       <div class="portlet-header">Task 3</div>
       <div class="portlet-content">...</div>
    </div>
    <div class="portlet">
       <div class="portlet-header">Task 4</div>
       <div class="portlet-content">...</div>
    </div>
</div>
    </body>
  </html>
```

FIGURE 9-2

Code snippet is from sortable.txt

RESIZING ELEMENTS

When "resizing" is applied to an element, the element is given a handle and can be visually resized using a mouse. You've already seen this ability indirectly with the dialog widget, which is a resizable widget. Table 9-6 lists all available $.resizable() methods.

TABLE 9-6: $.resizable() Methods

METHOD	DESCRIPTION
$(selector).resizable();	Makes selected element resizable.
$(selector).resizable.("destroy");	Removes the resizable functionality completely. This option rolls the selected element back to its initial state.
$(selector).resizable("disable");	Disables the resizable element.

METHOD	DESCRIPTION
`$(selector).resizable("enable")`	Enables the resizable element.
`$(selector).resizable("option", optionName, "value");`	Gets or sets any resizable element option. If the third argument is omitted, acts as a getter. Otherwise, it sets the `optionName` with the provided `value`.
`$(selector).resizable("widget");`	Returns the `.ui-resizable` element.

Given that resizing is such a basic operation, you might be surprised at how many options are available, as shown in Table 9-7. Like the other mouse interactions in this chapter, the default utility fits many needs, but it still allows for many flexible options.

TABLE 9-7: Resizable Options

OPTION	ACCEPTS	DESCRIPTION
`disabled`	Boolean	Enables/disables the resizable functionality.
`alsoResize`	Selector, jQuery, Element	Additionally, resizes the selected elements when resizing.
`animate`	Boolean	If `true`, animates to the final size after resizing.
`animateDuration`	Intefer, String	Duration time for the animation, in milliseconds. Other possible values are `slow`, `normal`, and `fast`.
`animateEasing`	String	The easing effect to use for the animation.
`aspectRatio`	Boolean, Float	If set to `true`, resizing is constrained by the element's original aspect ratio.
`autoHide`	Boolean	If set to `true`, automatically hides the selection handles except when the mouse hovers over the element.
`cancel`	Selector	Prevents resizing from starting on specified elements.
`containment`	String, Element, Selector	Constrains resizing to within the bounds of the specified element.
`delay`	Integer	Delay time, in milliseconds, before resize event goes into effect.

continues

TABLE 9-7 *(continued)*

OPTION	ACCEPTS	DESCRIPTION
distance	Integer	The distance the mouse must move after mousedown before resize event begins to work.
ghost	Boolean	If set to `true`, a semi-transparent helper element is shown for resizing.
grid	Array	When specified, the resizing helper snaps to a grid, which is spaced every x and y pixels. Expects an array of the form [x,y].
handles	String, Object	If specified as a string, should be a comma-spearated list of any of the following: `n`, `e`, `s`, `w`, `ne`, `se`, `sw`, `nw`, or `all`. If specified as an object, the same arguments are available as keys. The value of any specified keys should be a jQuery selector matching the child element of the resizable to use as that handle.
helper	String, Function	Allows for a helper element to be used for resizing display.
maxHeight	Integer	This is the maximum height the resizable should be allowed to resize to.
maxWidth	Integer	This is the maximum width the resizable should be allowed to resize to.
minHeight	Integer	This is the minimum height the resizable should be allowed to resize to.
minWidth	Integer	This is the minimum width the resizable should be allowed to resize to.

In the following example, you create a resizable widget with an animation, a minimum width and height of 300 pixels, ghosting, and a red box helper outline. The filled-in text uses the "bacon ipsum" text generator. Lorem ipsum is nice but bacon ipsum is tastier.

```
<!DOCTYPE html>
<html>
  <head>
    <link
    type="text/css"
    href="css/ui-lightness/jquery-ui-1.8.13.custom.css"
    rel="stylesheet" />
```

```
<script src="http://code.jquery.com/jquery-1.7.1.js"></script>
<script src="js/jquery-ui-1.8.13.custom.min.js"></script>
<style type="text/css">
  .ui-resizable-helper {
    border: 1px solid red;
  }

  #resize_me {
    border: 1px solid black;
    overflow : hidden;
  }
</style>
<script type="text/javascript">
  $(function(){
    $('div#resize_me').resizable({
      animate: true,
      ghost : true,
      helper: "ui-resizable-helper",
      minWidth: 300,
      minHeight : 300
    });
  });
</script>
</head>
<body>
  <div id="resize_me" class="ui-widget-content">
    <h2 class="ui-widget-header">Pork and Stuff</h2>
Bacon ipsum dolor sit amet pastrami flank short ribs tongue, salami ham short loin shank
Pancetta venison bacon shankle, swine jerky beef cow pork pork loin ham fatback beef rib
salami ham hock. Salami beef bacon pork brisket, t-bone flank ball tip. Ham hock beef
venison, t-bone andouille ribeye sirloin salami pork shankle. Ground round beef ribs
tip, sirloin venison rump pork loin shoulder boudin salami flank chuck ham corned beef
tenderloin. Tongue pork loin boudin, turkey ribeye salami pig biltong ham ham hock strip
steak. Beef ribs short ribs turkey, pancetta swine pork meatloaf strip steak ham bacon
corned beef short loin salami.
  </div>
  </body>
</html>
```

Code snippet is from resizable.txt

Is that slick or what? Figure 9-3 shows the resizable widget.

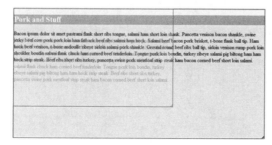

FIGURE 9-3

MAKING ELEMENTS SELECTABLE

Yet another desktop paradigm brought to the web environment is selectable. A selectable component is selected by clicking and holding a blank area and dragging the mouse up to another area and releasing the mouse button. Or you can just click inside of the component.

Clicking on an outside area deselects a group, and holding Ctrl + click (or Command + click on Apple computers) enables you to select multiple items, as shown in Table 9-8. Selected elements are given the class `ui-selected`.

TABLE 9-8: Selectable Options

OPTION	ACCEPTS	DESCRIPTION
disabled	Boolean	Enables/disables the selectable functionality.
autoRefresh	Boolean	This determines whether to refresh the position and size of each selected element at the beginning of each selection operation.
cancel	Selector	Prevents selection from starting on specified elements.
delay	Integer	Delay time, in milliseconds, before selection goes into effect.
distance	Integer	The distance, in pixels, for when selecting should start.
filter	Selector	The matching child elements will be able to be selected.

The following example shows a combination of a div, anchor (link), and list items all made selectable.

Available for
download on
Wrox.com

```
<!DOCTYPE html>
<html>
  <head>
    <meta http-equiv="Content-Type" content="text/html; charset=iso-8859-1" />
    <link
    type="text/css"
    href="css/ui-lightness/jquery-ui-1.8.13.custom.css"
    rel="stylesheet" />
    <script src="http://code.jquery.com/jquery-1.7.1.js"></script>
    <script src="js/jquery-ui-1.8.13.custom.min.js"></script>
    <style type="text/css">
        #selectable div {
          width   : 150px;
          height  : 30px;
          padding : 10px;
          margin  : 10px;
          border  : 1px solid;
        }

        #selectable div.ui-selecting {
          background: blue;
        }
```

```
        #selectable div.ui-selected {
          background: lightblue;
        }

    </style>
    <script type="text/javascript">
      $(function(){
        $( "#selectable" ).selectable();
      });
    </script>
  </head>
  <body>
    <div id="selectable">
      <div class="ui-widget-content unselectable">Item 1</div>
      <div class="ui-widget-content">Item 2</div>
      <div class="ui-widget-content">Item 3</div>
      <div class="ui-widget-content">Item 4</div>
      <div class="ui-widget-content">Item 5</div>
      <div class="ui-widget-content">Item 6</div>
      <div class="ui-widget-content">Item 7</div>
    </div>
  </body>
</html>
```

Code snippet is from selectable.txt

Figure 9-4 illustrates the selectable items in the state of being selected, and after selection. The first item is not selectable, which is accomplished by giving that item the CSS class unselectable.

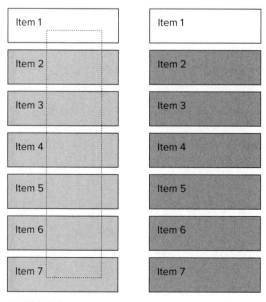

FIGURE 9-4

SUMMARY

This chapter concludes your brief tour of jQuery UI. You've seen how the interactive components, such as drag and drop, build on top of one another to create more complex interactions such as reorderable. It's also easy to see how you can create your own window-style widgets with similar operations on the web. Tasks that were once an enormous undertaking are now as simple as calling a method. A good portion of this chapter was dedicated to also documenting the myriad options for configuring each of the interaction helpers, which demonstrates the flexibility that jQuery UI offers.

10

Writing Effective jQuery Code

WHAT'S IN THIS CHAPTER?

➤ JavaScript Optimization Techniques

➤ Using JavaScript Patterns

➤ The $.data() Method

Now that you've walked through the breadth of what jQuery has to offer, it's time to look at some specific ways in which you can improve your jQuery code.

In this chapter, you learn a variety of techniques, best practices, and patterns that you can apply to your code immediately to make it more efficient, maintainable, and clear.

You'll discover optimization techniques pulled from an understanding of JavaScript fundamentals, an understanding of the relationship between the DOM and the JavaScript engine in web browsers, and from the way CSS selectors are parsed by Sizzle and other selector engines.

You also learn about common jQuery patterns and how best to use them to create maintainable, clear code for use in projects of all shapes and sizes.

Finally, you are introduced to the jQuery `$.data()` method, which enables you to store and retrieve application data in a clear, standardized way.

After reading this chapter, your code will be faster and your coworkers will applaud you for your code organization.

OPTIMIZATION TECHNIQUES

This section focuses on a variety of simple optimization techniques to keep in mind when writing jQuery, or, in many cases, pure JavaScript code.

Be warned — once you start to pay strict attention to performance, it can infect all of your coding.

Your users will love you.

Minimize DOM Updates

One of the most fundamental concepts of optimized front-end code is to keep the number of DOM updates in any given interaction down to the absolute minimum. Crossing over from the JavaScript engine into the DOM is a costly proposition. This is especially true if the operation is going to cause a repaint or reflow.

If you're unfamiliar with the concept of reflows and repaints, pay particular attention to the next section. Understanding these concepts, how they differ, and how they affect both perceived and clock performance of a web page or application, is vital knowledge for the serious front-end engineer.

Reflows and Repaints

Two common, but potentially expensive operations in the life of a web page are reflows and repaints. Reflows and repaints happen when the browser needs to update its rendering model (the combination of the DOM and the CSS rules that make up the style component of the page). This happens at least once a page load (because the browser *must* draw something at least once), but can happen many more times in the case of dynamic applications.

The two events are related, but slightly different. Understanding the difference can make or break performance of a page:

➤ A *repaint* is caused by a stylistic change to the page that doesn't change the overall page geometry. Hiding an element or changing an element's background color would cause a repaint.

➤ A *reflow* is caused by a structural update to the page. Adding or removing an element from a document, changing its dimensions, or changing its display property can all cause a reflow. This is the more expensive of the two events because it involves calculating page geometry using the current DOM/CSS landscape.

Minimizing DOM Updates in Practice

You can see a dramatic and simple illustration of the performance penalty for DOM updates in Listing 10-1. The first example appends 10,000 rows to a table by calling `$.append()` during every iteration of the `for` loop. The second example creates a string, entirely in the JavaScript domain, and then writes the results to the DOM *once*, after the loop is completed.

LISTING 10-1: Minimizing DOM updates

```
for ( var i=0; i < 10000; i++ ){
    $( "#main table" ).append( "<tr><td>My job is to log table rows, this is row #"
    +i
    +"</tr></td>" );
```

```
}

var tableRows= "";
for ( var i=0; i < 10000; i++ ){
  tableRows += "<tr><td>My job is to log table rows, this is row #"+i+"</tr></td>";
}
$( "#main table" ).append( tableRows );
```

Code snippet is from minimize-dom-updates.txt

Looking at Table 10-1, you can see that the difference is dramatic, especially in Internet Explorer 8, where the example using multiple DOM updates takes nearly a full minute to complete.

TABLE 10-1: The Importance of Minimizing DOM Manipulations

BROWSER	10,000 APPENDS	1 APPEND
Firefox 7.0	5,673 ms	421.5 ms
Chrome 15	9,372 ms	119.8 ms
Internet Explorer 8	50,783 ms	773 ms

Average of 10 runs

Leverage DOM Hyperspace

Another, related way to improve DOM manipulations is to do them in what's been referred to as "DOM Hyperspace." Basically, this boils down to creating and/or manipulating DOM elements entirely on the JavaScript side of the bridge and crossing over to the DOM itself only once manipulations are complete. You can do this by creating loaded jQuery nodes as variables to be manipulated or by using $().detach() to pull elements out of the DOM to manipulate. In each case, the fragments are inserted after the operations are completed. The basic idea behind each technique is shown in Listing 10-2.

Available for
download on
Wrox.com

LISTING 10-2: Creating and manipulating elements in JavaScript

```
//Using detach to pull elements out of the document.
var $sideBar = $( "#sidebar" ).detach();
/*
Populate the sidebar with menus, ads, and other miscellaneous elements
*/
$( "#main" ).append( $sideBar )


//Creating DOM elements with jQuery to later append to the document
var $sideBar = $( "<aside id='sidebar'></aside>" ).detach();
/*
Populate the sidebar with menus, ads, and other miscellaneous elements
```

continues

LISTING 10-2 *(continued)*

```
*/
//insert it into the DOM
$( "#main" ).append( $sideBar )
```

Code snippet is from dom-hyperspace.txt

More Effective Looping

Before you get into this particular optimization, it should be pointed out that, most of the time, using the jQuery convenience method $.each() on a collection is a perfectly acceptable solution to iterating over the members of an array.

Sometimes, however, using $.each() isn't acceptable. With larger collections where speed is an issue, using traditional control structures is a more effective solution.

$.each() and Array.forEach(): Trading Convenience for Speed

All implementations of this functionality, whether it's the aforementioned jQuery convenience method or the EcmaScript 5th Edition Array method forEach(), are slower than an associated for loop. To understand why this is, it's useful to understand the scope in which the looped code runs.

The Price of Function Creation and Adding Levels to Symbol Lookup

Take a look at the simple example in Listing 10-3 that looks through a collection of integers and tests to see if they're multiples of the number 5. One test is done with a traditional for loop, one with [].forEach(), and the other is done with $.each().

LISTING 10-3: $.each() vs. [].forEach() vs. a traditional for loop

```
/*
* Here's the setup function which populates an array with integers
*/

var numbers = [],
    fives = [];
for ( var i=0; i<1000000; i++ ){
  numbers.push( Math.round( Math.random()*i ) );
}

/*
* First we use a traditional for loop,
* caching the length
*/

var test = numbers.length;
for ( var j = 0; j<test; j++ ){
  if ( ( numbers[j] % 5 ) === 0  && numbers[j] !== 0 ) {
    fives.push( numbers[j] );
```

```
      }
    }

    /*
     * Now we use the ES5 forEach method.
     * This is actually what jQuery falls back on if it's available
     */

    numbers.forEach(
      function( e,I ){
        if ( ( e % 5 ) === 0  && e !== 0 ) {
          fives.push( e );
        }
      }
    )

    /*
     * Finally we use the $.each, convenience method.
     */

    $.each( numbers,
      function( i,e ){
        if ( ( e % 5 ) === 0  && e !== 0 ) {
          fives.push( e );
        }
      }
    )
```

Code snippet is from looptest.txt

The difference in speed between the three versions is shown in Table 10-2. As you can clearly see, the for loop is significantly faster than the convenience methods.

TABLE 10-2: for loop, forEach, and $.each (Higher is Better)

SELECTOR	FF8	SAFARI 5	CHROME 15	IE9
for loop	9,885	13,608	22,444	25,118
[].forEach	3,504	6,794	8,957	10,550
$.each	1,981	6,794	3,609	4,268

http://jsperf.com/book-loops

The difference comes down to two things that, when understood, can help you write more effective JavaScript code. The first is being wary of extraneous function creation. Because they accept functions as arguments, the convenience methods require the JavaScript engine to create a new execution context for each step in the loop. Compare that to the traditional loop, which executes in the containing scope without the overhead of a new execution context.

Scope is the second piece. Because the operations are happening inside a function, any variables that reference the outer scope are now placed one level away in the scope chain. The looped code has to constantly walk the scope chain up a level to validate references. Because the traditional loop executes in one scope, any variables defined outside the loop still remain in the current scope.

Caching Objects

Building on the idea of using local variables to speed up your script, you'll also want to think of caching objects in local scope to avoid additional script overhead. In general, if you're going to use an object more than once in a function, it's useful to cache that object in a local variable. It shortens lookup time, and if the variable is the result of a jQuery call, it cuts down on the number of times jQuery needs to do its selector magic.

It's very common to need to do this with $(this) because the object bound to a function is often the subject of multiple operations in a function.

As a matter of style, when the object being saved to a local variable is a jQuery object, it's also helpful to append a $ to the variable name. This indicates to anyone else on the project that it's more than just a plain variable and has jQuery methods baked right in. Listing 10-4 shows a simple example that illustrates this technique on two separate variables.

LISTING 10-4: Caching objects for repeated use

Available for
download on
Wrox.com

```
var $this = $( this ),
    $active = $( ".active" );
if ( $this.hasClass( "detail" ) ){
  if ( $this.hasClass( "next" ) ){
    $active
      .toggleClass( "hidden" )
      .removeClass( "active" )
      .next( ".details" )
      .toggleClass( "hidden" )
      .addClass( "active" );
  } else if ( $this.hasClass("prev") ){
    $active
      .toggleClass( "hidden" )
      .removeClass( "active" )
      .prev( ".details" )
      .toggleClass( "hidden" )
      .addClass( "active" );
  }
}
```

Code snippet is from caching-objects.txt

Use Efficient Selectors

It's not often that a 10-year-old article causes a ripple that spreads across the web development community, but that's exactly what happened when people sat up and took notice of an article written in April 2000 by Mozilla engineer David Hyatt. Entitled "Writing efficient CSS for use in the Mozilla UI" (`https://developer.mozilla.org/en/Writing_Efficient_CSS`), the article lays out the way in which the browser parses the elements in a CSS selector and outlines several selector patterns that are particularly expensive.

The basic takeaways from this article are:

➤ The engine evaluates each rule from right to left, starting with the "key" selector and moving through each selector until it finds a match or gives up.

➤ Using fewer rules is generally more efficient.

➤ Be as specific as possible — IDs are better than tags.

➤ Avoid unnecessary redundancy.

What's interesting is that JavaScript selector engines, including Sizzle and even the built-in `document.querySelectorAll`, also use some of the same techniques and also benefit from the same attention to efficiency.

In general, keeping your selectors short and sweet (leveraging IDs, for example) and keeping your key selectors as specific as possible will speed up your site whether you're working with JavaScript or CSS.

Table 10-3 illustrates applying these general selector rules to jQuery. As you can clearly see, no matter what browser you're using, leveraging IDs and single classes are by far the fastest ways to select an element. Anything more complicated than that is going to be much slower in every browser. It's not always possible to use an ID or single class, but it's fastest when you can.

TABLE 10-3: jQuery Selector Performance (Higher is Better)

SELECTOR	FF8	IE6	IE7	IE8	IE9
`$( "#id" )`	177,115	7,497	47,530	52,402	294,060
`$( ".class" )`	26,574	146	839	13,441	80,945
`$( "section div div div #id" )`	8,933	976	7,343	13,441	20,291
`$( "section div div div .class" )`	5,819	146	773	12,148	17,915
`$( "section div div div p" )`	6,369	803	2,642	12,598	21,104
`$( "section div div div p.class" )`	5,819	1,028	5,492	12,598	19,301
`$( "section div div div p#id" )`	6,369	1,164	7,101	13,092	20,938
`$( "section div div div p:not (.class)" )`	8,933	608	2,436	1,798	17,915

continues

TABLE 10-3 *(continued)*

SELECTOR	ANDROID 2.3	SAFARI 5	FF 3.6	CHROME 15
`$( "#id" )`	26,022	229,363	47,530	323,018
`$( ".class" )`	6,051	66,117	3,683	63,522
`$( "section div div div #id" )`	3,734	46,699	7,343	31,207
`$( "section div div div .class" )`	1,565	21,535	2,734	12,148
`$( "section div div div p" )`	1,633	21,104	2,734	13,652
`$( "section div div div p.class" )`	1,633	23,087	2,734	14,666
`$( "section div div div p#id" )`	3,734	46,262	2,866	23,646
`$( "section div div div p:not (.class)" )`	1,565	19,981	2,866	12,042

http://jsperf.com/book-selector-tests

jQuery-Specific Selector Performance

To be as efficient as possible, it's also important to understand jQuery's strategy for selectors. In general, jQuery wants to pass the selector immediately on to a native DOM method. As you saw in the previous section, if you're using `#id` as a selector, jQuery passes that directly to `document.getElementById("id")`. As you saw in Table 10-3, that's extremely fast. Selectors that can be passed along to `document.getElementsByTagName` and `document.getElementsByClassName` are also fast for the same reason.

As an aside, if you know your browser feature lists, you'll know that the latter isn't supported in older versions of IE, so that explains why class selectors are so slow in Internet Explorer 6 and 7.

document.querySelectorAll and jQuery Extensions

Selectors that can be passed to `document.querySelectorAll` (QSA) when it's available are also very fast. The thing to keep in mind is that every available jQuery selector isn't necessarily available in the native implementations of QSA. Because they're hand-rolled implementations and not browser-optimized, these jQuery extensions to the CSS3 selectors are comparatively slow.

The jQuery extensions to the CSS3 selection engine are listed in Table 10-4. Use them with care. When using these selectors, it's suggested that you pass a pure CSS selector to jQuery and then use `.filter()` to gather your specific results.

TABLE 10-4: jQuery Extensions to CSS3 Selectors

SELECTOR	SELECTS
`:animated`	All elements that are in the progress of an animation at the time the selector is run
`[name!="value"]`	Elements that either don't have the specified attribute, or do have the specified attribute but not with a certain value
`:button`	All button elements
`:checkbox`	All checkbox elements
`:eq()`	The element at index *n* within the matched set
`:even`	Even elements
`:file`	All file elements
`:first`	The first matched element
`:gt()`	All elements at an index greater than the argument index within the matched set
`:has()`	Elements that contain at least one element that matches the specified selector
`:header`	All header elements
`:hidden`	All hidden elements
`:image`	All image elements
`:input`	All input, textarea, select, and button elements
`:last`	The last matched element
`:lt()`	All elements at an index less than index within the matched set
`:odd`	Odd elements
`:parent`	All elements that are the parent of another element
`:password`	All password elements
`:radio`	All radio elements
`:reset`	All reset elements
`:selected`	All selected elements
`:submit`	All submit elements
`:text`	All text elements
`:visible`	All visible elements

`http://api.jquery.com/category/selectors/jquery-selector-extensions/`

Give Your Selectors a Context

By default, when you pass a selector into jQuery, it traverses the entire DOM. There's an underused, second possible `context` argument into jQuery that limits that search to a specific section of the DOM. As a note, it helps to pass in fast selectors as the additional context. It doesn't much help to speed things up with a context if the context itself is slow to be reached.

This traverses the whole DOM:

```
$(".className");
```

This searches only `element#id`:

```
$(".className","#id")
```

As Table 10-5 shows, adding in a context is always faster than a whole DOM selector or a selector with two (or more) elements.

TABLE 10-5: jQuery Selector Performance (Higher is Better)

SELECTOR	FF8	IE6	IE7	IE8
`$( ".class" )`	6,487	21	99	1,997
`$( "#id .class" )`	2,595	1,376	8,457	2,697
`$( ".class", "#id" )`	33,289	1,688	12,174	11,762
SELECTOR	**IE9**	**ANDROID 2.3**	**SAFARI 5**	**CHROME 15**
`$( ".class" )`	10,198	418	4,255	3,312
`$( "#id .class" )`	3,313	420	5,100	5,199
`$( ".class", "#id" )`	38,295	4,100	49,468	46,880

```
http://jsperf.com/context
```

Consider Skipping jQuery Methods Entirely

If performance is of primary concern to your site or application, it's useful to keep in mind the places where it's safe to skip jQuery methods entirely, falling back to quicker core JavaScript methods and properties. One common example is using `attr()` to get the `href` attribute and then using `attr()` to apply it to another element:

```
$( "#baz" ).attr( "href", $( this ).attr( "href" ) );
```

If you know core JavaScript methods, the preceding line can be rewritten as follows:

```
document.getElementById("baz").href = this.href;
```

As you can see, two calls to jQuery are removed because you use `document.getElementById` to reference the element in question and then use direct lookups to the `href` attribute of each element instead of `attr()`. As Table 10-6 shows, even with this simple example, using native methods is faster in all major browsers.

TABLE 10-6: Going Native (Higher is Better)

	FF8	IE6	IE7	IE8
Native	8,153	798	4,565	4,431
jQuery Methods	5,954	575	3,537	3,778

	IE9	SAFARI 5	CHROME 15
Native	7,512	14,905	11,796
jQuery Methods	6,532	12,166	10,801

`http://jsperf.com/sometimes-native-is-nice`

Clearly, this isn't going to be an option for every statement as there are cross-browser issues and you lose the ability to chain methods. If it was possible for everything, you wouldn't be using jQuery in the first place. It's just a good idea to know where you can fall back to the native methods to get a performance tweak. Simple property lookups to grab a string for later manipulation or to test against (`this.id`, `this.className`) are a common area, but look for examples in your own code. If performance becomes an issue, there might be easy gains waiting for you.

DRY

"Don't repeat yourself" (or DRY) is an oft-repeated mantra in software development. It's an important principle for maintenance and performance. With the simple elegance of the jQuery API, it's important stylistically as well. One place where jQuery can encourage repetition is with the liberal use of anonymous functions. Because it's so common to pass an anonymous function in as an event handler, it's not uncommon to see several short functions doing the same thing in a block of code. Although this may feel faster and convenient in the short term, it's in your best long-term interest to simplify the repeated code. You don't want to wade through a thousand lines later to make edits to similar code that lives in five places in your application.

A typical example is shown in Listing 10-5. The function changes the class of the bound element, fires off an Ajax request, and then shows a jQuery UI dialog indicating the results of the request. Writing it once as an anonymous function makes sense. It's short and full of common code. If it appears several times throughout your site, it's time to simplify.

LISTING 10-5: Repeating yourself

```
$( "#foo" ).click(
  $( this ).addClass( "active" );
  $.get( "/my/app/service/", function( data ){
    $( "#dialog" ).text( data.status ).dialog( "open" );
  }
```

continues

LISTING 10-5 *(continued)*

```
);
$( "#bar" ).click(
  $( this ).addClass( "active" );
  $.get( "/my/app/service/", function( data ){
    $( "#dialog" ).text( data.status ).dialog( "open" );
  }
);
$( "#baz" ).click(
    $( this ).addClass("active");
    $.get( "/my/app/service/", function( data ){
    $( "#dialog" ).text( data.status ).dialog( "open" );
  }
);
```

Code snippet is from repeating-yourself.txt

You can simplify this code by collecting the selectors in use:

```
$( "#baz, #bar, #foo" ).click(
    $( this ).addClass( "active" );
    $.get( "/my/app/service/", function( data ){
        $( "#dialog" ).text( data.status ).dialog( "open" );
    }
);
```

Code snippet is from dry.txt

Alternatively, if the events are spread out across your site or application, you can create a callable function accessible from anywhere:

```
function ourHandler(){
  $( this ).addClass( "active" );
  $.get( "/my/app/service/", function( data ){
    $( "#dialog" ).text( data.status ).dialog( "open" )
  }
}

$( "#baz" ).click( ourHandler );
```

Code snippet is from dry-callable-function.txt

Keeping code DRY takes a bit of vigilance, but once you start to recognize areas where it typically starts to creep in, you can stay ahead of it by immediately making the more maintainable solution.

USE JAVASCRIPT PATTERNS

Although the subject of software design patterns is far too broad a topic to cover here in depth, understanding and implementing basic patterns can go a long way toward making your code more maintainable.

For more on software design patterns in general, the classic "Gang of Four" book, *Design Patterns: Elements of Reusable Object-Oriented Software* by Erich Gamma, Richard Helm, Ralph Johnson, and John Vlissides, is the indispensable reference. Check it out if anything in the following section strikes a chord with you.

In this section, you learn about techniques that limit global namespace pollution, provide logical module initialization, and allow for easier collaboration among multiple developers.

Creating an Application Namespace with a Singleton

One of the simplest techniques you can use to structure your code is to use well-chosen namespaces. This pattern is commonly called a *singleton*.

Before you look at the singleton, look at the unstructured approach it approves upon. This style of code is still common and was especially prevalent in the earliest days of JavaScript programming. For a long time, it was typical to simply present a series of function declarations defined at the global space. This throwback approach is shown in Listing 10-6.

Available for download on Wrox.com

LISTING 10-6: The old-school approach

```
function myAppInit(){
   //code to initialize your application
}

function myAppDashboard(){
  //your dashboard feature goes here
}

function myControlPanel() {
  //control panel code goes here
}

function myAppSettings(){
  //code that updates settings goes here
}

//kicked off with the ready() function
$( document ).ready(myAppInit)
```

Code snippet is from multiple-functions.txt

Though there's nothing wrong about this pattern in a technical sense, it does present some compatibility hurdles.

To see the compatibility issues, you can just pop open Firebug and navigate to the DOM tab. There you'll see all the functions created available in the global namespace. This is illustrated in Figure 10-1.

FIGURE 10-1

It doesn't take long for a JavaScript developer to discover that populating the global namespace with multiple variables can cause serious issues. For an obvious example, imagine naming a variable i, _, or $ in the global namespace. That's going to cause a problem somewhere down the line.

More obscure names might be safer, but they're still not safe, so don't think that naming your variables after characters from Jabberwocky is going to save you from variable collisions.

Just wait until you have two Lewis Carroll freaks on a project.

So, instead of merely dropping a series of functions into a global namespace, you can alternatively leverage a single variable to hold all of your application code. In the simplest example, this variable is an object literal, which in turn will contain your application modules and properties. A simple example is shown in Listing 10-7.

LISTING 10-7: A singleton

```
var myApp = {
    init :  function(){
        //code to initialize your application
    },
    dashboard:  function(){
        //your dashboard feature goes here
    },
    controlPanel:  function() {
        //control panel code goes here
    },
    appSettings:  function(){
        //code that updates settings goes here
    }

}
//kick it off with ready()
$( document ).ready( myApp.init )
```

Code snippet is from singleton.txt

Firing up Firebug with this new structure shows that there's only the single myApp variable in the global namespace. You can see this in Figure 10-2.

Even in this simplified example, that cuts down the possibilities of a variable name collision significantly. If your application has dozens or even hundreds of similar methods and properties, the benefit of an application namespace is even greater.

FIGURE 10-2

There's more to namespaces than preventing bugs. This simple singleton can be expanded to create separate objects for individual application features and/or site sections.

This allows for multiple developers to work in a single application namespace across multiple files, allowing for greater maintainability and less chance of conflicts in version control or otherwise stepping on each other's toes. Though individuals might be able to get away with it, teams working with a monolithic JavaScript file can cause disasters.

You can see the simple object literal you've been working with broken out into multiple application objects in Listing 10-8. Structurally, each site section would be broken out into a separate file. These would be `common.js`, `dashboard.js`, `controlPanel.js`, and `settings.js` in this example. With the exception of `common.js`, individual developers could own each site section and file without really worrying about what anyone else was doing. `common.js` would be owned by the project lead, both for the sake of maintenance and because the question of what's truly "common" has some nuance to it.

LISTING 10-8: A simple application framework

```javascript
var myApp = {
//a common object holds code common to all application sections
  common : {
    init :  function(){
      //common code to initialize your application
    }
  }
};
myApp.dashboard = {
//your dashboard feature has an init function as well.
  init : function(){
    //init code
  },
  update : function(){
    //code to update the dashboard
  },
  render :  function(){
    //code to render the dashboard
  }
};

myApp.controlPanel = {
//your control panel feature has an init function as well.
  init : function(){
```

continues

LISTING 10-8 *(continued)*

```
    //init code
    },
    settings : function(){
      //code for control panel settings
    }
};
myApp.settings = {
//your settings page has an init as well
    init : function(){
        //init code
    },
    update : function(){
      //code to update site settings
    }
}
```

Code snippet is from a-simple-application-framework.txt

One thing to note is that, although working in multiple files is a best practice, actually serving multiple files to your users is definitely *not* suggested. If you're working in multiple files in your project, it's worth looking at ways to automatically concatenate (and minify) your files together into a single file. A good starting point for this kind of task is the HTML5 Boilerplate project and its associated build script. You can find it at `http://html5boilerplate.com/`. As an alternative to a static build script, a script loader like LABjs `http://labjs.com/` offers a JavaScript-based method for loading files on an as-needed basis.

The Module Pattern

A variation on the singleton, the module pattern was created by Douglas Crockford, Chief JavaScript Architect at Yahoo! and author of the JSON data interchange format. It was popularized in a post by Eric Miraglia on the Yahoo! User Interface Blog in June 2007 (`http://www.yuiblog.com/blog/2007/06/12/module-pattern/`) and is cover in depth in Crockford's book, *JavaScript: The Good Parts* (O'Reilly Media, 2008). It enhances the encapsulation provided by the singleton and adds the ability to create private methods and properties.

The module pattern consists of three main components: a namespace similar to the one leveraged in the previous example, a function that immediately executes, and the function's return object, which contains publicly available methods and properties. You can see a simplified example in Listing 10-9.

LISTING 10-9: The JavaScript module pattern

```
//Our app namespace. We pass in the jQuery object to shorten lookups
var myApp = function ( $ ) {
    // private variables and methods, only available within this myApp
    var message = "not directly accessible from outside the module";
    function multiplier ( x,y ) {
      return x * y
    };
```

```
    //the return object contains the public
    //properties and public methods
      return  {
        init : function(){
           //initialize the app
        },
        prop : "42",
        specialNumber : function () {
          //access to our private method
          var num = multiplier( 7 , 6 );
          return "Our special number is definitely " + num;
        },
        //we provide controlled access to private variables
        shareMessage : function( arg ){
          if ( arg === "open sesame" ) {
            return message + ",unless you know the magic word";
          } else {
            throw new Error( "You need to know the magic word" );

          }
        }
      };
    }( jQuery );
```

Code snippet is from module-pattern.txt

Examining this sample app on the console illustrates the way the module works. The private variables can be referenced within the module body, but can't be called directly from the outside. You are able to grant access in special cases through methods exposed in the return object. As you can see in Listing 10-10, examining the module using `console.log` illustrates both cases.

LISTING 10-10: Examining the module pattern in the JavaScript console

```
>>> console.log( myApp.message )
undefined

>>> console.log( myApp.multiplier() )
TypeError: myApp.privateMethod is not a function

>>> console.log( myApp.shareMessage( "please?" ) )
"You need to know the magic word"

>>> console.log( myApp.shareMessage( "open sesame" ) )
not directly accessible from outside the module,unless you know the magic word

>>> console.log( myApp.prop );
42

>>> console.log( myApp.specialNumber() );
Our special number is definitely 42
```

Extending the pattern to additional modules is straightforward. Listing 10-11 illustrates a dashboard module, complete with a private configuration object and a public method to allow gated access to dashboard configuration based on a set of predefined criteria. If you've got experience with languages like C#, Java, and C++, then you're familiar with the usage of the `private` and `public` keywords. This pattern allows JavaScript to provide similar functionality. It's not every day that you'll need to use this kind of protected access, but it's important to know that it's there when the need does arise.

LISTING 10-11: A dashboard module

```
myApp.dashboard = function ( $ ) {
  // private variables and methods
  var config = {
    "color" : "blue",
    "title" : "my dashboard",
    "width" : "960px"
  };
  return  {
    init : function(){
      //initialize the dashboard
    },
//updateConfig allows for monitored configuration
//of the private config object
    updateConfig : function( obj ) {

if ($.inArray(obj.color, ["red", "blue", "green", "purple"] !== -1))
{
      config.color = obj.color;
    }
    config.title = obj.title || config.title;
    config.width = obj.width || config.width;

    },
    render : function() {
      //renders the dashboard
      var $dashboard = $( "<div/>" ).html( "<h1/>" )
      $dashboard.text( config.title )
        .css(
          { "width" : config.width,
            "color" : config.color }
        );
        $( "#main" ).append( $dashboard );
    }
  };
}( jQuery );
```

Code snippet is from advanced-module.txt

The Garber-Irish Implementation

The following pattern expands on the singleton and module pattern with cleverly chosen markup and style hooks to create a seamless initialization pattern for sites and applications.

This pattern was introduced by in 2009 by Paul Irish in a blog post entitled "Markup-based unobtrusive comprehensive DOM-ready execution" (http://paulirish.com/2009/markup-based-unobtrusive-comprehensive-dom-ready-execution/) and later modified by Jason Garber in a blog post entitled "Extending Paul Irish's comprehensive DOM-ready execution" (http://www.viget.com/inspire/extending-paul-irishs-comprehensive-dom-ready-execution/).

In short, it leverages a small utility script and either CSS classes or HTML5 data attributes on the body element to selectively fire `init()` events depending on the site section or page type. This pattern alleviates the problem of trying to hunt down multiple `$(document).ready()` calls strewn throughout an application, instead providing a consistent, structured approach that works across multiple domains (server code, JavaScript, and style).

You can use either version, depending on your taste, so I'll share both flavors. First up is Paul's original version.

The Original Recipe

The pattern starts with a typical object literal. This variation has a couple of specific enhancements that are shown in Listing 10-12. Take note of the sections with `init` methods and the common section, which contains a method called `finalize`. The `init` methods are designed to fire on `$( document ).ready()` when the relevant section or feature is needed. This need is determined by the HTML structure you'll see shortly. The `finalize` methods are for code that needs to execute as soon as possible but doesn't affect the initial load of the page.

LISTING 10-12: Object literal enhanced for "markup-based unobtrusive comprehensive DOM-ready execution."

```javascript
myApp = {
  common : {
    init : function(){
      //init()
    },
    finalize : function(){
      //we're saving these for a little later
    }
  },
  dashboard : {
    init : function(){
      //dashboard init
    },
    settings: function(){
      //dashboard settings
    },
    render : function(){
      //render
    },
```

continues

LISTING 10-12 *(continued)*

```
    }
}
```

Code snippet is from garber-irish-object-literal.txt

The next component is a small utility script, which parses the `body id` and `className` and attempts to fire functions based on the patterns exposed. This code, taken directly from Paul's original post, is shown in Listing 10-13.

LISTING 10-13: "Markup-based unobtrusive comprehensive DOM-ready execution."

```
/* from
 * http://paulirish.com/2009/markup-based-unobtrusive-comprehensive-dom-ready-execution/
 * License: CC0 1.0 Universal (CC0 1.0) Public Domain Dedication
 */

UTIL = {

  fire : function(func,funcname, args){

    var namespace = myApp;  // indicate your obj literal namespace here

    funcname = (funcname === undefined) ? 'init' : funcname;
    if (func !== '' && namespace[func]
        && typeof namespace[func][funcname] == 'function'){
      namespace[func][funcname](args);
    }

  },

  loadEvents : function(){

    var bodyId = document.body.id;

    // hit up common first.
    UTIL.fire('common');

    // do all the classes too.
    $.each(document.body.className.split(/\s+/),function(i,classnm){
      UTIL.fire(classnm);
      UTIL.fire(classnm,bodyId);
    });

    UTIL.fire('common','finalize');

  }

};

// kick it all off here
$(document).ready(UTIL.loadEvents);
```

Code snippet is from irish.txt

The final piece is an HTML document with a `body` tag with a `class` and an `id` that correspond to site sections or features mapped out in the object literal:

```
<body id="settings" class="dashboard">
```

Putting them all together would fire events in the following order:

➤   `myApp.common.init()`

➤   `myApp.dashboard.init()`

➤   `myapp.dashboard.settings()`

➤   `myapp.common.settings()`

This pattern can expand beyond the single class shown in the previous example. Multiple classes can be strung together, which allows multiple features to fire automatically. This is especially cool because once it's in place, it allows JavaScript features to be initialized without having to touch a line of JavaScript code. An engineer working in PHP or Java can simply append a class to a page and know that the proper initialization code for a module will fire.

Using HTML5 Data Attributes Instead of CSS Classes and IDs

Jason Garber's variation is very similar, with the key difference that it uses HTML5 data attributes to trigger the execution.

If you're unfamiliar with them, HTML5 data attributes are defined methods for storing custom data in HTML attributes. Application developers had long stored string data in custom attributes, so this is a case of the Web Hypertext Application Technology Working Group (WHATWG) "paving the cowpaths" and standardizing common developer behavior. The benefit of standardization is that the `data-*` prefix allows for predictable programmatic access to the custom attributes. You learn more about that in an upcoming section, but for now, you see the slight difference in the body tag:

```
<body data-controller="dashboard" data-action="render">
```

Instead of using CSS classes and IDs, this method maps controllers to actions. This is a very elegant method, especially if you're building a Ruby on Rails (or similar) application where consistent naming conventions are a high priority. It also allows body IDs and classes to be used for other methods, if the need arises.

The one downside is that leveraging data attributes for section-specific styling is awkward. In a sense, it's a case of choosing where the one-to-one correspondence will be — on the server with your Ruby on Rails controllers and actions or in your CSS file with section-specific classes and IDs.

Regardless of what specific example you choose, this pattern provides an elegant addition to your toolset, adding in a consistent, scalable, and maintainable method of running code on `$(document).ready()`.

USING $.DATA()

As you saw in the previous section, the new HTML5 data attribute is designed for structured, programmatic access to custom attributes. jQuery provides a straightforward method to do just that with `$.data()`. Any data attributes set on an HTML element are immediately available to be retrieved with `$.data()`. Though that's extremely convenient, `$.data()` also provides the ability to bind *any* data to a DOM element. This allows arrays and complicated objects to be stored as well as the string values previously possible with hand-rolled custom attributes. It should be noted that while `$.data()` can read HTML5 data attributes, it doesn't actually write values to elements in the form of `data-` attributes. This makes sense because arbitrary arrays and objects don't lend themselves to being stored as string values of HTML attributes.

This is extremely powerful, and if you've been doing this for a while, it should feel like something you've been searching for your whole career.

If you've ever passed an object as an argument between several methods, you'll be happy to know you'll never have to do that again if you learn to embrace the `$.data()` method. Gone are the days of managing application state with function argument chains spreading across a half dozen method calls. Now, you can simply bind application or component data directly on the DOM element itself for convenient, direct access throughout the application life cycle.

Additionally, it's important to note that the data API stores data in a way that's safe from circular references, which prevents memory leaks.

A note on support: HTML5 data attribute support was added in jQuery 1.4.3 and a revision was released to match the W3C spec more closely in jQuery 1.6.

The Basics of the .data() API

Like many jQuery methods, `$.data()` can be used as both a setter and a getter. If two arguments, as a name/value pair, or an object of name/value pairs is passed in, `$.data()` will set the data values accordingly. A single string passed in will return the value of named data property. Some basic examples, including strings, Boolean, arrays, and objects being used as values for the `$.data()` method, are shown in Listing 10-14.

LISTING 10-14: Simple .data() examples

```
$('#dashboard').data('updated', 1321358806453);


$('body').data('fantastic', true);

$('#settings').data('faves', [1,4,6,8,9,14,27,42]);


$('#boston').data('bostonTeams', {
  'nba' : 'Celtics', 'nhl' : 'Bruins', 'mlb' : 'Red Sox', 'nfl' : 'Patriots' });
```

Code snippet is from data-examples.txt

Although the basics of the API are straightforward, the power and convenience can't be understated. Having a coherent, standard method of storing and retrieving application data clears up years of awkward coding and disparate patterns. The following section lays out this benefit with a more realistic example.

Before we look at that example, it should be noted that though $.data() allows for storing page-level data, it does not help you at all with storing persistent data. To store persistent data, you'll still have to deal with cookies or the new TML5 storage API, which are the standards for persistent data in the browser.

Fully Leveraging the Data API

Listing 10-15 illustrates an application fragment. This piece initializes a small Google Maps application. In it, you create a Google Map and use the W3C's new Geolocation API to place a marker on the map based on the user's latitude and longitude.

Throughout this example, the .data() method is used to capture variables, objects, and even instantiated Google Maps objects.

Initially, you store a reference to the map itself. Every Google Maps API call works off of an instantiated object; for example, a map, geocoder, or marker. Storing the reference to your map simplifies later map manipulations. You also store the initial mapOptions object. This is a simple scheme to store the initial state of the map if you need to reset it for any reason.

Later on, in both the success and failure functions, you store a geocoder object and an initialLocation. The geocoder can be used for any later address lookups without the cost of instantiation, and the initialLocation can be used to reset or recenter the map based on the updated latitude and longitude provided by the geolocation lookup.

LISTING 10-15: Using .data() in an application context

```
var loadMap = {
  init : function() {
    var GM = google.maps,
        defaultPosition = new GM.LatLng(42, -71),
        mapOptions = {
        zoom: 12,
        center: defaultPosition,
        mapTypeId: GM.MapTypeId.ROADMAP
        },
        map = new GM.Map( document.getElementById( 'map' ), mapOptions);

    $( "#map" ).data({ "map" : map, "mapOptions" : mapOptions } );
    var success = function( data ){
      var position = new GM.LatLng(
            data.coords.latitude,
            data.coords.longitude ),
          niceAddress = "Your location",
          geocoder = new GM.Geocoder();
      $( "#map" ).data( "geocoder" , geocoder );
```

continues

LISTING 10-15 *(continued)*

```
      geocoder.geocode(
        { 'latLng': position },
        function( results, status ) {
          if ( status == GM.GeocoderStatus.OK ) {
            if (results[0]) {
              niceAddress = results[0].formatted_address;
            }
          }
          var infowindow = new GM.InfoWindow({
            map: map,
            position: position,
            content: niceAddress
          });
          $( "#map" ).data( "infowindow" , infowindow  )
        });
      map.setCenter( position );
      $( "#map" ).data( "initialLocation" , position  )


    },
    failure = function( error ){
      var formResponse = function(e){

        var geocoder = new GM.Geocoder(),
            position = defaultPosition,
            niceAddress = "Sorry We Couldn't Find Your Location";
        $( "#map" ).data( "geocoder" , geccocoder );
        geocoder.geocode(
          { 'address': $("#location").val() },
          function( results, status ) {
            if ( status == GM.GeocoderStatus.OK ) {
              //set position
            }
            var options = {
              map: map,
              position: position,
              content: niceAddress
            },
            infowindow = new google.maps.InfoWindow(options);
            $( "#map" ).data( "infowindow" , infowindow  )
            map.setCenter( options.position );
            $( "#map" ).data( "initialLocation" , position  )
            $( "#geocode" ).hide();
          }
        )
      return false;
    }
    var $fallback = $( "<from id='geocode'></form>" );
    if ( error ) {
      switch( error.code ) {
        /* error handling */
      }
    }
```

```
        fallback.append("<label for='location'>Enter Your Location"
          +  "<input type='text' id='location' /></label>"
          +  "<input type='submit' />");
        fallback.bind("submit",formResponse);
        $("#main").append( $fallback );
    };
   if (navigator.geolocation){
     navigator.geolocation.getCurrentPosition(
       success,
       failure,
      {timeout:5000});
   } else {
     failure();
     }
   },
   reset : function(){
     var map = $( "#map" ).data( "map" ),
         position = $( "#map" )
           .data( "initialLocation" ),
         infowindow = $( "#map" )
           .data( "infowindow" , infowindow  );
     infowindow.close()
     map.setCenter( position );
   }
 }
 $( document ).ready( loadMap.init );
```

Code snippet is from data-api.txt

In just this small example, you've stored a wealth of data about your application in an accessible, standard way. Accessing it in the simple `reset` method, you have immediate access to the current `map`, `infowindow`, and the original latitude and longitude coordinates supplied when the map was created, allowing you to quickly reset the map to its original state. Once you start to leverage the `$data()` method across an application, you'll wonder how you ever survived without it.

SUMMARY

This chapter exposed you to a variety of techniques to improve your jQuery and JavaScript code. You now have an understanding of common techniques and approaches that will produce faster, more efficient code. From understanding the way the browser updates the DOM, to the price of convenience and a variety of selector optimizations, you should have a strong cache of techniques to speed up your site or application.

Additionally, you have an understanding of some common JavaScript design patterns that will allow you to create more maintainable, consistent code.

Finally, you had a glimpse at the power of the jQuery Data API, which allows you to conveniently and safely store application data associated with DOM elements in a standardized way.

11

jQuery Templates

WHAT'S IN THIS CHAPTER?

➤ Why Use Templates?

➤ The Past, Present, and Future of jQuery Templates

➤ Creating and Using Templates

In this chapter, you learn about the jQuery Template plugin. jQuery Templates are a standard way of marrying data and markup snippets. If you're familiar with template engines like Freemarker or Mustache, you'll recognize a lot of what jQuery Templates try to accomplish. If you've done any Ajax-based development, you've had to build blocks of HTML for insertion into the document based on the result of an Ajax request or other user interaction. Typically, this has meant concatenating strings or building elements using native DOM methods and then inserting them into the DOMr. jQuery Templates simplify and standardize this common task.

In this chapter, you learn about the two ways to create templates: using specially crafted script tags to define them and using pure JavaScript to define them using JavaScript strings. You'll also explore the template tags available for greater control over content and you learn strategies for implementing templates in the most efficient way possible. You also get a look at the planned roadmap for the new version of the Template plugin.

TAMING A TANGLE OF STRINGS

If you've done JavaScript development for any length of time, you've run into code similar to the following sample. In it, a collection of data about a comic book series is looped through to build out new content to be appended to the document.

```
<!doctype html>
<html>
<head>
<meta charset="utf-8">
</head>
<body>
<div id="main"> </div>
<script src="http://code.jquery.com/jquery-1.7.1.min.js"></script>
<script src="//ajax.aspnetcdn.com/ajax/jquery.templates/beta1/jquery.tmpl.min.js">
</script>
<script>
  $(function(){
    var comics = [
      {
        imgSrc : "cover1.jpg",
        title : "Captain Templates",
        year : "2010",
        number : "1"
      },
      {
        imgSrc : "cover2.jpg",
        title : "Captain Templates",
        year : "2011",
        number : "2"
      },
      {
        imgSrc : "cover3.jpg",
        title : "Captain Templates",
        year : "2012",
        number : "3"
      }
    ]
    for( var i=0; I < comics.length; i++ ){
      $( "#main" ).append( '<div class="comic"><img src='
        + comics[i].imgSrc
        + '/><div class="details"><div class="title"><h3>'
        + comics[i].title
        + '</h3></div><div class="year">'
        + comics[i].year
        + '</div><div class="number">'
        + comics[i].number
        + '</div></div></div>'
      );
    }
  }
);
</script>
</body>
</html>
```

Code snippet is from no-templates.txt

The preceding code takes the comics array, iterates through its members, and builds blocks of HTML to add to the document. This is done by simply concatenating strings of HTML with data references. Although this is a common solution, jQuery Templates improve on the pattern in some important ways.

Separation of Content and Behavior

jQuery Templates allow for a further separation of content and behavior.

One of the central tenets of modern web development is the separation of code that describes the structure and content of the page (the HTML) from the code that defines the style (CSS) and code that manages the behavior (JavaScript). Historically, this separation has most often been in the context of moving from style-based HTML elements like `font` and patterns like table-based layouts to pure CSS layouts. Secondarily, it's also been seen as a movement away from using inline CSS and JavaScript in HTML files. Though these are positive steps, the trend toward more dynamic sites and applications has introduced a new battlefront. As more and more developers rely on JavaScript to drive sites, more and more style, content, and structure are starting to work their way into JavaScript files.

This is acceptable when you're working on a small codebase, but once your application gets into the thousands or tens of thousands of lines, and more and more developers are expected to be able to manage them, this can quickly cause issues as the question "Where is this markup coming from?" becomes more frequent.

As you'll see, the jQuery Template plugin allows for a complete break between structure and program logic. This is a key to writing maintainable code.

Code Reuse

With the capability to define templates once and to apply them multiple times, including mixing and matching with other templates, you have many more opportunities to create reusable markup patterns with a template engine.

Aesthetics and Clarity

A good template system is simply easier to read. Instead of focusing on balancing quotation marks, plus signs, and data references, the focus with jQuery Templates is once again on creating clean, consistent markup.

The Past, Present, and Future of jQuery Templates

Before you get into the nuts and bolts, a little background is in order.

jQuery Templates started out in March 2010, when John Resig posted a prototype. Starting in May 2010, Boris Moore started working on a fork of the plugin. His fork was eventually merged into the main branch and branded a jQuery Official Plugin. Work continued on it, eventually reaching beta stage.

As of April 2011, activity on the jQuery Template plugin stopped, leaving it permanently in that beta state. In the blog post announcing the change (`http://blog.jquery.com/2011/04/16/`

official-plugins-a-change-in-the-roadmap/), it was noted that development of a new Template plugin was being initiated under the aegis of the jQuery UI project.

The Future

The driving force behind the original jQuery Template plugin, Boris Moore, has continued working on the problem of templates along with the jQuery UI team. In October 2011, Moore wrote a blog post (http://www.borismoore.com/2011/10/jquery-templates-and-jsviews-roadmap.html), updating the community on the new plugin's progress. In it, he stated the solution will eventually be in two parts:

➤   JsRender templates are described as "Next-generation jQuery Templates, optimized for high-performance pure string-based rendering, without DOM or jQuery dependency."

➤   JsViews are described as "Interactive data-driven views, built on top of JsRender templates."

This new solution promises speed improvements, greater flexibility, and a better separation of presentation and behavior.

The Present

Although we have confidence in this newer effort, having a sane templating system is vital *right now* to modern web development. It's therefore sensible to leverage the existing plugin until the newer effort is mature enough to supplant it.

Creating Templates

You can use two basic methods for creating jQuery Templates. Which one you use depends on the nature of your project, the makeup of your team, and the performance demands on your site or application.

Creating Inline Templates

The cleanest way to create templates is through the use of a specially crafted script tag:

Available for download on Wrox.com

```
<script id="comics" type="text/x-jquery-tmpl">
  <div class="comic"><img src="${imgSrc}" />
    <div class="details">
      <div class="title">
        <h3>${title}</h3>
      </div>
      <div class="year">
        ${year}
      </div>
      <div class="number">
        ${number}
      </div>
    </div>
  </div>
</script>
```

Code snippet is from script-tag-template.txt

This example creates a jQuery Template with the name `comics`. The `id` is tied to the name of the template in the templating engine. The special `type` indicates to jQuery that it's a template script block. The browser itself ignores that script block because it doesn't know what to do with a script of type `text/x-jquery-tmpl`. This example also introduced the first template tag, `${}`, which exposes variables to the template structure.

This is the cleaner of the two patterns, representing a pretty full break between structure and behavior. This the recommended pattern if you don't have many templates or if you need to expose templates to team members who may not spend a lot of time poking around JavaScript files.

As a note, it's also possible to create templates in any element (a DIV with `display:none` as a CSS rule, for example), but such markup might cause unexpected errors.

Creating Templates with the $.template() Method

Alternatively, you can create templates directly in your JavaScript files using the `$.template()` method:

Available for download on Wrox.com

```
$.template('comics' , '<div class="comic">
<img src="${imgSrc}" /><div class="details"><div class="title">
<h3>${title}</h3></div><div class="year">${year}</div>
<div class="number">${number}</div></div></div>');
```

Code snippet is from template-method.txt

Both examples use the same template format, with variables encapsulated in `${}` blocks. The difference here is that the template string passed as the second of a pair of arguments to the `$.template()` method. The first argument is the `id` of the template, analogous to the `id` attribute of the script tag in the first example.

Because it's not as clean a separation, this method is suggested only if you have many templates in your site or application and want to leverage browser caching for the template definitions. Because the previously illustrated specially formatted script blocks are included inline in the markup, they're downloaded and parsed each time a page is loaded.

Placing your templates in a script file enables them to be downloaded once and then retrieved from memory on each subsequent page view, saving network connection and download time. This may not matter if your templates are focused on individual pages or site sections in a single-page application, but if you have many templates spread across a large site, it might be preferable to have them served in a cacheable manner.

Making the $.template() Method Maintainable

If you find yourself needing to use the `$.template()` method, we suggest looking at something similar to the following pattern. It uses a single function to initialize all templates for the site or application. This way, while the markup being kept in JavaScript files is not the best possible solution, it's at least kept in a single, more maintainable location. You always know where your templates are. The following code illustrates this pattern. The basic pattern should be familiar from Chapter 10's discussion of the Garber-Irish implementation. In it you have a `common` object which holds code common to all pages. One piece of that code is a method called `init`. `init`, among any other functions it needs to call to start up your app, also initializes all the templates for your site by firing the `myApp.common.templates()` method.

```
var MyApp = {
  common :
    init : function(){

        myApp.common.templates();

    },
      templates: function(){
        $.template('comics' ,
'<div class="comic"><img src="${imgSrc}" /></div><div class="details">
<div class="title"><h3>${title}</h3></div><div class="year">${year}</div>
<div class="number">${number}</div></div></div>');
        $.template('author' , '<div class="author">
<div class="name"><h3>${author}</h3></div><div class="bio">
<p>${authorBio}</p></div></div>');
      },
    }
}
```

Code snippet is from template-maintenance.txt

Applying Templates with $.tmpl()

Once you've created your site's templates, it's time to start using them in your pages. You have two different contexts from which to apply templates.

If you've created your templates inline, you can pass a selector representing the script tag holding your template. This is illustrated in the following code sample. In it, you have a template tag with the id `#comics`. To apply it, you get a reference to it using the id selector and then you call the `$.tmpl()` method, passing the `comics` array as an argument. Then it's simply a matter of calling `$.appendTo()` to insert it into the document.

```
<!DOCTYPE html>
<html>
<head>
<meta charset="utf-8">
</head>
<body>
<div id="main"> </div>
<script src="http://code.jquery.com/jquery-1.7.1.min.js"></script>
<script src="//ajax.aspnetcdn.com/ajax/jquery.templates/beta1/jquery.tmpl.min.js">
</script>
<script>
  $(function(){
    var comics = [{
      imgSrc : "cover1.jpg",
      title : "Captain Templates",
      year : "2010",
      number : "1"
```

```
      },
      {
        imgSrc : "cover2.jpg",
        title : "Captain Templates",
        year : "2011",
        number : "2"
      },
      {
        imgSrc : "cover3.jpg",
        title : "Captain Templates",
        year : "2012",
        number : "3"
      }];
      $("#comics").tmpl(comics).appendTo("#main");
    }
  );
</script>
<script id="comics" type="text/x-jquery-tmpl">
  <div class="comic"><img src="${imgSrc}" />
    <div class="details">
      <div class="title">
        <h3>${title}</h3>
      </div>
      <div class="year">
        ${year}
      </div>
      <div class="number">
        ${number}
      </div>
    </div>
  </div>
</script>
</body>
</html>
```

Code snippet is from inline.html

This page produces the output shown in Figure 11-1.

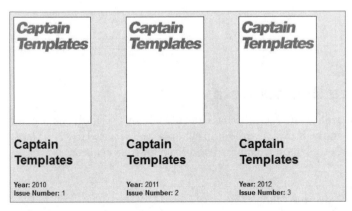

FIGURE 11-1

The second method is to use compiled templates. Pass the name of a template created with `$.template()` into `jQuery.tmpl()` along with a data object, and it will be applied in exactly the same way.

```html
<!DOCTYPE html>
<html>
<head>
<meta charset="utf-8">
</head>
<body>
<div id="main"> </div>
<script src="http://code.jquery.com/jquery-1.7.1.min.js"></script>
<script src=" //ajax.aspnetcdn.com/ajax/jquery.templates/beta1/jquery.tmpl.min.js">
</script>
<script>
  $(function(){
    var comics = [{
      imgSrc : "cover1.jpg",
      title : "Captain Templates",
      year : "2010",
      number : "1"
    },
    {
      imgSrc : "cover2.jpg",
      title : "Captain Templates",
      year : "2011",
      number : "2"
    },
    {
      imgSrc : "cover3.jpg",
      title : "Captain Templates",
      year : "2012",
      number : "3"
    }];
    $.template( 'comics' , '<div class="comic">
<img src="${imgSrc}" /><div class="details"><div class="title">
<h3>${title}</h3></div><div class="year">${year}</div>
<div class="number">${number}</div></div></div>' );
    $.tmpl( "comics",comics ).appendTo( "#main" );
);
</script>
</body>
</html>
```

Code snippet is from template-method.txt

Applying Templates Using Remote Data

Most of the examples in this chapter illustrate a JavaScript array defined in a script block for clarity, and the ability to run the examples in the browser without firing up a web server. However, most of the time, you'll be applying templates to dynamic data retrieved from an Ajax request.

Although the template patterns are the same, it's useful to walk through a simple example using an Ajax request to illustrate the way it might be handled.

In this example, you'll be working with a `data.json` file with the following structure:

```json
{
    "comics" : [
      {
        "imgSrc":"cover1.jpg",
        "title":"Captain Templates",
        "year":"2010",
        "number":"1"
      },
      {
        "imgSrc":"cover2.jpg",
        "title":"Captain Templates",
        "year":"2011",
        "number":"2"
      },
      {
        "imgSrc":"cover3.jpg",
        "title":"Captain Templates",
        "year":"2012",
        "number":"3"
      }
    ]
}
```

Code snippet is from data.json

In your script file, you simply grab the data using `$.ajax` and then pass the data to the success function, `populate`, which is set up to handle the data with `.tmpl()`:

```html
<!DOCTYPE html>
<html>
<head>
<meta charset="utf-8">
</head>
<body>
<div id="main"> </div>
<script src="http://code.jquery.com/jquery-1.7.1.min.js"></script>
<script src=" //ajax.aspnetcdn.com/ajax/jquery.templates/beta1/jquery.tmpl.min.js">
</script>
<script>
  $(function(){
    var populate = function( data ){
      $( "#comics" ).tmpl(data.comics).appendTo( "#main" );
    }
    $.ajax({
      type : 'get',
```

```
      url : 'data.json',
      success : populate,
      dataType : "json"
    });
    }
  );
</script>
<script id="comics" type="text/x-jquery-tmpl">
  <div class="comic"><img src="${imgSrc}" />
    <div class="details">
      <div class="title">
        <h3>${title}</h3>
      </div>
      <div class="year">
        <strong>Year:</strong> ${year}
      </div>
      <div class="number">
        <strong>Issue Number:</strong> ${number}
      </div>
    </div>
  </div>
</script>
</body>
</html>
```

Code snippet is from ajax.txt

Template Tags

With the basics of templates out of the way, it's time to look at some of the further features available with the Template plugin. Simply mapping data to markup in a consistent way is useful, but several other features are available that allow for greater control.

Adding Simple Logic to Your Templates with {{if}} {{else}}

{{if}} and {{else}} provide conditional inclusion of content in templates. It renders content between the {{if}} and closing {{/if}} tag only if a provided value is not null. {{else}} indicates alternative content to be rendered if the provided expression is false. The following example illustrates using {{if}} and {{else}} to conditionally include a thumbnail image. If the thumbnail isn't set in the data source, a default image will be included.

```
<!DOCTYPE html>
<html>
<head>
<meta charset="utf-8">
</head>
<body>
<div id="main"> </div>
<script src="http://code.jquery.com/jquery-1.7.1.min.js"></script>
<script src=" //ajax.aspnetcdn.com/ajax/jquery.templates/beta1/jquery.tmpl.min.js">
</script>
```

```
<script>
  $(function(){
    var comics = [{
      imgSrc : "cover1.jpg",
      title : "Captain Templates",
      year : "2010",
      number : "1"
    },
    {
      imgSrc : "cover2.jpg",
      title : "Captain Templates",
      year : "2011",
      number : "2"
    },
    {
      title : "Captain Templates",
      year : "2012",
      number : "3"
    }];
    $( "#comics" ).tmpl(comics).appendTo("#main");
  }
);
</script>
<script id="comics" type="text/x-jquery-tmpl">
  <div class="comic">
    {{if imgSrc}}
      <img src="${imgSrc}" />
    {{else}}
      <img src="default.jpg" />
    {{/if}}
    <div class="details">
      <div class="title">
        <h3>${title}</h3>
      </div>
      <div class="year">
        ${year}
      </div>
      <div class="number">
        ${number}
      </div>
    </div>
  </div>
</script>
</body>
</html>
```

Code snippet is from if.txt

Applying the template to the data produces the output shown in Figure 11-2.

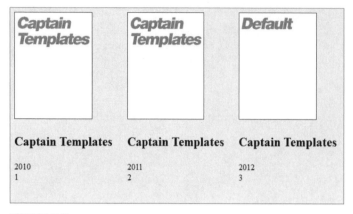

FIGURE 11-2

Iterate Over Data Objects with {{each}}

Like $.each(), {{each}} is used to iterate over a data array. It renders content between the opening and closing template tags once for each data item. As the following code sample shows, the data structure exposes an array of "themes" for each comic. The associated inline template uses {{each}} to list out a series of one or more themes for every template element. Each theme is wrapped in a list item.

```
<!DOCTYPE html>
<html>
<head>
<meta charset="utf-8">
</head>
<body>
<div id="main"> </div>
<script src="http://code.jquery.com/jquery-1.7.1.min.js"></script>
<script src=" //ajax.aspnetcdn.com/ajax/jquery.templates/beta1/jquery.tmpl.min.js">
</script>
<script>
  $(function(){
    var comics = [{
      imgSrc : "cover1.jpg",
      title : "Captain Templates",
      themes : [
        "code reuse" ,
        "separation of content and behavior" ,
        "template tags"
      ],
      year : "2010",
      number : "1"
    },
    {
      imgSrc : "cover2.jpg",
```

```
            title : "Captain Templates",
            themes : [
              "code reuse" ,
              "moustaches" ,
              "templating for fun and profit"
            ],
            year : "2011",
            number : "2"
          },
          {
            imgSrc : "cover3.jpg",
            title : "Captain Templates",
            themes : [ "threes" ],
            year : "2012",
            number : "3"
          }];
          $( "#comics" ).tmpl( comics ).appendTo( "#main" );

        }
      );
      </script>
      <script id="comics" type="text/x-jquery-tmpl">
        <div class="comic"><img src="${imgSrc}" />
          <div class="details">
            <div class="title">
              <h3>${title}</h3>
            </div>
            <div class="year">
              <strong>Year:</strong> ${year}
            </div>
            <div class="number">
              <strong>Issue Number:</strong> ${number}
            </div>
            <div class="themes">
              <strong>Themes</strong>
              <ul>
                {{each themes}}
                  <li>${$value}</li>
                {{/each}}
              </ul>
            </div>
          </div>
        </div>
      </script>
      </body>
      </html>
```

Code snippet is from each.txt

Applying the template to the data with $.tmpl() generates the output shown in Figure 11-3.

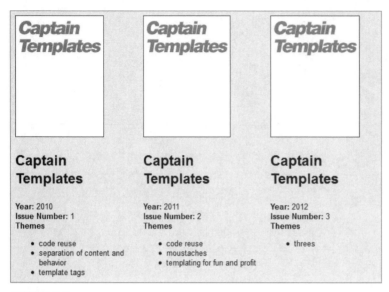

FIGURE 11-3

Additionally, {{each}} exposes an `index`, which allows for the integration of a counter in the template itself. The following variation of the previous template illustrates this:

```html
<!DOCTYPE html>
<html>
<head>
<meta charset="utf-8">
</head>
<body>
<div id="main"> </div>
<script src="http://code.jquery.com/jquery-1.7.1.min.js"></script>
<script src=" //ajax.aspnetcdn.com/ajax/jquery.templates/beta1/jquery.tmpl.min.js">
</script>
<script>
  $(function(){
    var comics = [{
      imgSrc : "cover1.jpg",
      title : "Captain Templates",
      themes : [
        "code reuse" ,
        "separation of content and behavior" ,
        "template tags"
      ],
      year : "2010",
      number : "1"
    },
    {
```

```
            imgSrc : "cover2.jpg",
            title : "Captain Templates",
            themes : [
              "code reuse" ,
              "moustaches" ,
              "templating for fun and profit"
            ],
            year : "2011",
            number : "2"
          },
          {
            imgSrc : "cover3.jpg",
            title : "Captain Templates",
            themes : [ "threes" ],
            year : "2012",
            number : "3"
          }];
          $( "#comicsIndex" ).tmpl( comics ).appendTo( "#main" );

        }
      );
    </script>
    <script id="comicsIndex" type="text/x-jquery-tmpl">
      <div class="comic"><img src="${imgSrc}" />
        <div class="details">
          <div class="title">
            <h3>${title}</h3>
          </div>
          <div class="year">
            <strong>Year:</strong> ${year}
          </div>
          <div class="number">
            <strong>Issue Number:</strong> ${number}
          </div>
          <div class="themes">
            <strong>Themes</strong>
            {{each themes}}
              <strong>${$index + 1}</strong>. ${$value}
            {{/each}}
          </div>
        </div>
      </div>
    </script>
  </body>
</html>
```

Code snippet is from each-index.txt

Applying the template with $.tmpl() produces the output shown in Figure 11-4.

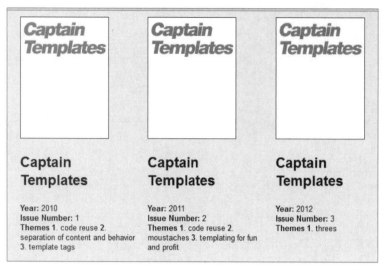

FIGURE 11-4

Nesting Templates with {{tmpl}}

The `{{tmpl}}` template tag enables you to nest templates. This allows for much greater code reuse. If, for example, you had a common structure for displaying thumbnails and titles across several separate templates, you could define the thumbnail and title as one template and reference it wherever needed.

Following are the three inline templates. The first, `headerTemplate`, defines a common header used in the other two templates, `comicsConcise` and `comicsExtended`.

Available for
download on
Wrox.com

```
<!DOCTYPE html>
<html>
<head>
<meta charset="utf-8">
</head>
<body>
<div id="main"> </div>
<script src="http://code.jquery.com/jquery-1.7.1.min.js"></script>
<script src=" //ajax.aspnetcdn.com/ajax/jquery.templates/beta1/jquery.tmpl.min.js">
</script>
<script>
  $(function(){
    var comics = [{
      imgSrc : "cover1.jpg",
      title : "Captain Templates",
      themes : [
        "code reuse" ,
        "separation of content and behavior" ,
        "template tags"
      ],
      year : "2010",
      number : "1"
```

```
      },
      {
        imgSrc : "cover2.jpg",
        title : "Captain Templates",
        themes : [
          "code reuse" ,
          "moustaches" ,
          "templating for fun and profit"
        ],
        year : "2011",
        number : "2"
      },
      {
        imgSrc : "cover3.jpg",
        title : "Captain Templates",
        themes : [ "threes" ],
        year : "2012",
        number : "3"
      }];
      $( "#comicsConcise" ).tmpl( comics ).appendTo( "#main" );
      $( "#comicsExtended" ).tmpl( comics ).appendTo( "#main" );
    }
);
</script>
<script id="headerTemplate" type="text/x-jquery-tmpl">
  <header>
    <h1>${title}</h1>
    <img src="${imgSrc}" />
  </header>
</script>
<script id="comicsConcise" type="text/x-jquery-tmpl">
  <section class="comic">
    {{tmpl "#headerTemplate"}}
    <div class="details">
      <div class="year">
        <strong>Year:</strong> ${year}
      </div>
      <div class="number">
        <strong>Issue Number:</strong> ${number}
      </div>
    </div>
  </section>
</script>
<script id="comicsExtended" type="text/x-jquery-tmpl">
  <section class="comic extended">
    {{tmpl "#headerTemplate"}}
    <div class="details">
      <div class="year">
        <strong>Year:</strong> ${year}
      </div>
      <div class="number">
        <strong>Issue Number:</strong> ${number}
      </div>
      <div class="themes">
        <strong>Themes</strong>
```

```
        <ul>
          {{each themes}}
            <li>${$value}</li>
          {{/each}}
        </ul>
      </div>
    </div>
  </section>
</script>
</body>
</html>
```

Code snippet is from tmpl.txt

Taking advantage of this ability to piece templates together with smaller chunks of code makes your code much more maintainable. Identify the common elements, break them out into their own templates, and then you're able to update a single template instead of poking around multiple templates looking for markup to change.

Embed HTML Into Your Templates with {{html}}

Occasionally, entire sections of HTML are included in data returned from a web service. Using the {{html}} template tag enables you to insert this prerendered HTML directly into your templates. Without {{html}}, then text like <a href='http://jquery.com'>jquery.com</a> would appear literally, e.g. &gta href=…, and thus would not have the intended effect.

In the following code, the data includes a description field that contains HTML text. Areas where HTML is to be output directly are bracketed by {{html}} template tags.

```
<!DOCTYPE html>
<html>
<head>
<meta charset="utf-8">
</head>
<body>
<div id="main"> </div>
<script src="http://code.jquery.com/jquery-1.7.1.min.js"></script>
<script src=" //ajax.aspnetcdn.com/ajax/jquery.templates/beta1/jquery.tmpl.min.js">
</script>
<script>
  $(function(){
    var comics = [{
      imgSrc : "cover1.jpg",
      title : "Captain Templates",
      themes : [
        "code reuse" ,
        "separation of content and behavior" ,
        "template tags"
      ],
      year : "2010",
      number : "1",
      description : "<p>In this thrilling origin issue Captain
```

```
Templates saves the day by using templates instead of a bunch of
<strong>awkward</strong> string concatenation</p>"
      },
      {
        imgSrc : "cover2.jpg",
        title : "Captain Templates",
        themes : [
          "code reuse" ,
          "moustaches" ,
          "templating for fun and profit"
        ],
        year : "2011",
        number : "2",
        description : "<p>In battling his <em>arch nemesis</em>
 <strong>Doctor Plus Sign</strong> Captain Templates falls into
 a coma. </p><p>A thrilling issue with a cliffhanger ending</p>"
      },
      {
        imgSrc : "cover3.jpg",
        title : "Captain Templates",
        themes : [ "threes" ],
        year : "2012",
        number : "3",
        description : "<p>Captain Templates awakens from his coma
 and defeats the evil <strong>Doctor Plus Sign</strong></p>"
      }];
      $( "#comics" ).tmpl( comics ).appendTo( "#main" );
  }
);
  </script>
<script id="comics" type="text/x-jquery-tmpl">
  <section class="comic">
    <header>
      <img src="${imgSrc}" />
      <h3>${title}</h3>
    </header>
    <div class="details">
      <div class="year">
        <strong>Year:</strong> ${year}
      </div>
      <div class="number">
        <strong>Issue Number:</strong> ${number}
      </div>
      <div class="description">
        {{html description}}
      </div>
    </div>
  </section>
</script>
</body>
</html>
```

Code snippet is from html.txt

This produces the output shown in Figure 11-5.

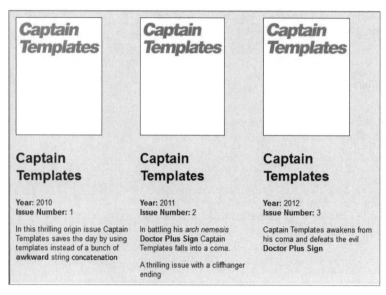

FIGURE 11-5

SUMMARY

Now you should have an understanding of the benefits of using a templating system to separate content and behavior. You should also have a good understanding of how to implement templates in jQuery with the existing jQuery Template plugin and be able to leverage template tags to render data more accurately.

This chapter also explained the current state of the Template plugin and gave you an idea of the direction of the feature moving forward, so you'll be ready for the transition whenever the new plugins are ready for prime time.

12

Writing jQuery Plugins

WHAT'S IN THIS CHAPTER?

➤ Plugin Basics

➤ Plugin Best Patterns and Practices

➤ The jQuery UI Widget Factory

In this chapter, you learn how to write jQuery plugins. Being able to extend the power of jQuery with custom methods is a fundamental skill for a top jQuery developer.

A large part of the popularity of jQuery comes from the community-driven plugin ecosystem and the wide array of functionality available to expand on jQuery's core functionality.

From subtle user-interface enhancements like those provided by hoverIntent to full-featured components like those available as part of the jQuery UI project, the plugin environment in jQuery is a vibrant, vital resource. It's easy enough to take part and create plugins of your own. This chapter outlines how.

You learn about the different methods of extending jQuery, common plugin conventions, and advanced options and patterns to further expand your plugin possibilities.

After reading through this chapter, you'll be ready to extend and enhance jQuery on your own, and will have a variety of resources available to help you in pretty much any plugin situation you're likely to experience.

THE PLUGIN BASICS

At the most basic level, creating a jQuery plugin is remarkably easy. After just the first page or two of this chapter, you should have enough knowledge to create a simple plugin.

Don't be fooled by the ease of the basic level. "Easy" to do a basic version doesn't mean it's easy to do it right. Following a number of best practices will ensure optimized performance, cut down on bugs, and provide the highest degree of interoperability between your code and the rest of the jQuery environment in which your code is running. This first section goes through some important plugin fundamentals.

Applying jQuery Plugin Naming Conventions

Imagine that after reading this chapter, you're full of knowledge about plugin development and you're happy to be sitting down to write your first jQuery plugin. You fire up your favorite editor or IDE, and create a new script file. Depending on your editor of choice, you may have the option of creating a filename there and then or you may not have the option until you save. Regardless of the reality in your particular editor, you'll want to know in *advance* how to name your files. The answer is straightforward, but it's nice to be prepared.

Generally, jQuery plugins are named with the following pattern:

```
jquery.pluginName.js
```

Minified versions are similarly named, adding a `min` flag:

```
jquery.pluginName.min.js
```

The reasoning for including `jquery` in the name is simple. It's a jQuery plugin, so it's convenient to indicate compatibility right in the filename. Some plugins come with support for multiple libraries, so this is an important touch.

Adding the `.min.` to minified versions allows for two versions to exist side by side, which is very handy because it enables developers to switch between full and minified versions while debugging.

How to Extend jQuery

Now that you know how to name your files, it's time to actually get down to the business of extending jQuery.

jQuery offers two separate, simple patterns for extending jQuery and one more complicated, but very powerful, option to extend jQuery.

The first, and most common, is a simple alias for the prototype property of the jQuery function, `jquery.fn`. The second is the method `jQuery.extend()`. The third, more complicated option is the powerful jQuery UI Widget Factory.

Using jQuery.fn

If you've ever looked at the jQuery source, you'll have seen the following very early in the source code. As of version 1.7.1, it's visible on line 97:

```
jQuery.fn = jQuery.prototype = { //jquery goes here //}
```

Code snippet is from jquery.fn.txt

If you're unfamiliar with the concept of prototypal inheritance, it's the key element of JavaScript inheritance.

Simply defined, the `prototype` of a JavaScript object is another object that contains properties and functions native to that type of object. The core JavaScript natives all have their own `prototype` property. The following code example illustrates a common use of a native prototype. In this case, the example illustrates an enhancement of `Array.prototype`, a polyfill for missing EcmaScript functionality in nonconforming browsers. Running this code adds an `[].every()` method to all arrays created in *the future* or *past* on the containing page.

```javascript
//from https://developer.mozilla.org/en/JavaScript/Reference/Global_Objects/Array/every

if (!Array.prototype.every){
  Array.prototype.every = function(fun /*, thisp */){
    "use strict";
    if (this === void 0 || this === null) {
      throw new TypeError();
    }
    var t = Object(this),
        len = t.length >>> 0;
    if (typeof fun !== "function"){
      throw new TypeError();
    }
    var thisp = arguments[1];
    for (var i = 0; i < len; i++){
      if (i in t && !fun.call(thisp, t[i], i, t)){
        return false;
      }
    }
    return true;
  };
}
```

Code snippet is from every.txt

One interesting thing to note is that `fn/prototype` is *live*. Any and all elements created of that type are going to receive access to any prototype properties or methods added or updated at any time. JavaScript's dot operator is specified to search the expression on the left of the operator for the key on the right, walking up the "prototype chain" until it finds a hit. Instances of objects have their internal "classes" as their prototypes, which is what makes the changes "live" for instances. This explains why you're able to instantiate a copy of jQuery at one point and then add features and functionality to jQuery via scripts loaded later on in the page life cycle — even seconds or minutes later.

The most basic usage of `jQuery.fn` is as follows:

```javascript
jQuery.fn.newStuff = function() {
  console.log("It's full of (javascript) stars");
};
```

Code snippet is from basic-fin-plugin.txt

This initial example is imperfect, but it's the minimum needed to add a new function to jQuery. This pattern is enhanced and improved upon in the following pages.

Using $.extend()

In addition to JavaScript's prototypal inheritance pattern, jQuery also offers a utility method called `$.extend`, which can be used to enhance jQuery. As you learned in Chapter 3, at its most basic, `$.extend` is a method that merges two objects. When it's called with only a single argument, it merges the argument object *into* jQuery.

The following code extends jQuery with a method named `newStuff`:

```
jQuery.extend({
  newStuff: function() {
    console.log("It's full of (javascript) stars");
  }
});
```

Code snippet is from plugin-extend.txt

jQuery UI Widget Factory

The Widget Factory is a jQuery method that accepts two or three arguments: a `namespace`, an existing widget `prototype` to inherit from, and an optional object literal to become the new widget's prototype.

The Widget Factory is used behind the scenes on the jQuery UI project, and it's designed to create complex, stateful plugins with a consistent API.

The simplest possible implementation would be a single line, like this:

```
$.widget('namespace.newsStuff', {});
```

Code snippet is from simple-plugin-factory.txt

That's a call to `$.widget` with a namespace (`namespace.newStuff`) and an empty object as the prototype. It won't actually do much, of course, but it's a start.

You look at more features of the Widget Factory in "A Closer Look at the Widget Factory" later in this chapter.

Which to Use?

All of these methods are valid, and you're free to pick your preference depending on the needs of the plugin you're writing. Choosing patterns for plugin development is discussed in more detail later in the chapter. For beginning plugin developers, either of the first two might be a better place to start.

To simplify, most of the examples that follow use the more straightforward and JavaScript-centered `jQuery.fn` approach.

General Plugin Guidelines

Now that you've seen the basics of extending jQuery, it's time to look at some guidelines that will help keep your plugin development on track. From here, the basics of plugin development will, for the most part, be similar to developing jQuery applications, sites, or components. That said, you have some key differences and gotchas to keep in mind when writing plugins. This section outlines a few of those.

Remember the this Keyword

One error people commonly make when they move from basic to more advanced jQuery development is to forget where the `this` keyword points in the context of a plugin. In jQuery development, the `this` keyword commonly refers to the current DOM element being manipulated. In the immediate context of a plugin, `this` points to the current jQuery instance itself. So, instead of doing something like the following inside your plugin body:

```
$(this).toggle()
```

Code snippet is from extra-this.txt

you can actually just call:

```
this.toggle()
```

Code snippet is from simplified-this.txt

Inside the body of a plugin, wrapping `this` in `$()` is the equivalent of doing something like `$($("#element"))`.

The exception to that is when you're iterating over all the elements in the current jQuery collection. Inside the body of your `$.each` loop, the focus of `this` shifts to the current DOM element that's exposed in that particular iteration. The following code example shows this difference:

```
(function($){
// plugin definition
    $.fn.pinkify = function() {
//this refers to jQuery, each() is immediately available
      return this.each(function() {
//inside the loop this refers to the DOM element
        $( this ).css({
          "background" : "#fe57a1",
          "color" : "#fff",
          "text-shadow" : "none"
          })
      });
    };
})( jQuery );
```

Code snippet is from remember-this.txt

Always Ensure that $ Points to jQuery

One of the most important pieces of code to use when authoring jQuery plugins is also one of the simplest. Without fail, you should use an immediately executing function expression that binds $

to `jQuery`. It's always possible that some other library (commonly PrototypeJS) or other code has rewritten `$` to point some other value, so it's vital to protect against that eventuality.

The following code shows how to do this. A function expression is wrapped around the plugin definition. It accepts one argument, `$`, and because the function is immediately executed with `jQuery` as the single argument, `$` is guaranteed to be bound to `jQuery`.

```
(function($) {
  $.fn.newStuff = function() {
    /* $ is now jQuery, no matter what value
     * $ might have in the global namespace
     */
  };
})( jQuery );
```

Code snippet is from jquery-is-jquery.txt

Additionally, there's a common enhancement to this pattern that's worth taking a look at. It creates local references for `window` and `document` and ensures that `undefined` remains `undefined`. This pattern provides several benefits.

Having local references for `window` and `document` allows them to be minified inside the function body (every byte counts) and speeds up access to those objects inside the function body by shortening the lookup table.

Additionally, because `undefined` can be reassigned in older versions of the EcmaScript standard, it's a source of potential bugs if someone accidentally or maliciously redefines `undefined`. Defining it as an argument and then not defining it is a clever way to ensure that the value is as expected.

```
(function( $, window, document, undefined ) {
  $.fn.newStuff = function() {
    /* $ is now jQuery, no matter what value
     * $ might have in the global namespace
     */
  };
})( jQuery, window, document );
```

Code snippet is from window-document.-undefined.txt

Use Semicolons Properly

If you're lucky enough to have people use your plugin, it's important to remember that they'll probably end up concatenating and minifying your script along with other code. To that end, it's worth paying attention to proper semicolon usage.

If you follow good coding practice anyway, you should be fine, but it's especially important when your code is going to live on in unknown environments.

For reference, the *Google JavaScript Style Guide* (`http://google-styleguide.googlecode.com/svn/trunk/javascriptguide.xml#Semicolons`) says the following about semicolons:

"Relying on implicit insertion can cause subtle, hard to debug problems. Don't do it. You're better than that."

Translated — *semicolons are your friend.*

Additionally, it's a relatively common practice to include a leading semicolon in your plugin definition to ensure that your code will function properly in a minified and concatenated environment. It's possible (even likely) that other code will break when minified because of poor semicolon usage or other buggy statements. Inserting a semicolon at the beginning of your plugin definition ensures that any previous statements will be explicitly ended at that point.

Available for
download on
Wrox.com

```
; (function( $, window, document, undefined ) {
    $.fn.newStuff = function() {
    };
})( jQuery, window, document );
```

Code snippet is from leading-semicolon.txt

Return the jQuery Object Wherever Possible

jQuery is an example of a Fluent Interface, a software design pattern identified by Martin Fowler and Eric Evans and described by Fowler in 2005 (http://www.martinfowler.com/bliki/FluentInterface.html). The basic concept combines method chaining with an API that reads more like natural language to create a more natural, accessible API. In describing one implementation, Fowler said "The API is primarily designed to be readable and to flow." That description could apply equally well to jQuery.

With that in mind, it's clear that one of the key technical features of jQuery is the ability to chain methods. The concise, "Fluent" feel of the API provided by chaining was one of the features that really drew people into the library, and chaining remains a popular feature for jQuery and other JavaScript libraries, large and small.

This feature is enabled by the jQuery practice of, wherever possible, returning `this`, which points to the jQuery object. Because your plugin lives in that same environment, it's vital that your plugin also return the jQuery object wherever possible. Most of the time, then, your plugins will follow the pattern outlined in the following code example. It returns `this` in its immediate scope and maintains the full collection so that it can be passed along to other jQuery methods.

Available for
download on
Wrox.com

```
(function( $ ) {

  $.fn.pinkify = function() {
    return this.css({
      "background" : "#fe57a1",
      "color" : "#fff",
      "text-shadow" : "none"

    });
  };
})( jQuery );
```

Code snippet is from chaining.txt

Although this is a best practice and is preferred, sometimes it's not possible to return the jQuery object. That exception is valuable to note. Whereas you generally want to allow chaining, valid reasons exist to break the chain.

Types of methods that will break the chain are those that have to return a specific value. jQuery itself offers several examples. These can be a metric, like $.height (at least when it's called as a getter), a Boolean like $.inArray, or something else like $.type (which returns a String indicating the internal [[Class]] of a JavaScript object). The code that follows illustrates another exception. This plugin returns a Boolean indicating whether or not an element is larger than a set of provided dimensions:

```
(function($) {
  $.fn.isWider = function( width ) {
    return this.width() > width ;
  };
})( jQuery );
```

Code snippet is from iswider.txt

Iterating Over Objects

Oftentimes with plugin development, you're looping over all the objects in a collection and operating on each member. You will often need to do this with $.each. The following code illustrates this common pattern, returning the result of this.each:

```
function( $ ) {

  $.fn.randomText = function() {
    return this.each(function() {
      $( this ).text( Math.random * 1000 ).show()
    })
  };
})( jQuery );
```

Code snippet is from randomTxt.txt

Although this is common, it's important to note that in some cases, you don't need to use $.each. Look at the following example. The use of $.each there is redundant, because $.css will itself operate on every item in the collection.

```
function( $ ) {
  $.fn.pinkify = function() {
    return this.each(function() {
      $( this ).css({
        "background" : "#fe57a1",
        "color" : "#fff",
        "text-shadow" : "none"
      });
    });
  };
})( jQuery );
```

Code snippet is from extra-each.txt

The preceding code can be rewritten to look like this:

```
function($) {
  $.fn.pinkify = function() {
    return this.css({
      "background" : "#fe57a1",
      "color" : "#fff",
      "text-shadow" : "none"
    });
  };
})( jQuery );
```

Code snippet is from return-css.txt

Many jQuery methods will also return a full collection, so leverage that fact when authoring plugins. It's good to leverage what jQuery offers, especially when you're offering your code up to the community. Every little bit helps.

Applying Plugin Best Practices

The following section examines some plugin authoring best practices that the jQuery community has built up over the past few years. As with anything, not all of these will be applicable to every line of code you write, but it's good to understand these concepts for your own work and to understand the work of other plugin authors even better.

Applying the jQuery Plugin Pattern

In his post "A Plugin Development Pattern" (http://www.learningjquery.com/2007/10/a-plugin-development-pattern), Mike Alsup outlines a comprehensive set of best practices to follow when developing jQuery plugins. Although the post is several years old now, it still holds up and is cited as a vital resource for plugin developers. This section examines the pattern in some detail.

Claim Only a Single Name in the jQuery Namespace

Given the large number of plugins available and the common convergence of functionality and/or plugin focus, there exists a strong possibility that plugin names will collide. To limit this as much as possible, it's useful to claim only a single namespace for your plugin. For example, instead of offering up several related methods like this:

```
jQuery.fn.bestPluginEverInit = function() {
//init
};
jQuery.fn.bestPluginEverFlip = function() { {
//flip
};
jQuery.fn.bestPluginEverFlop = function() { {
//flop
};
```

```
jQuery.fn.bestPluginEverFly = function() { {
//fly
};
```

you could, instead, create a single entry point and expose additional functionality in a more unobtrusive way.

```
jQuery.fn.bestPluginEver = function() {
//single namespace
}
```

From that starting point, you could use a method lookup table to expose internal methods to the public endpoint. This pattern keeps a clean namespace by encapsulating all of your methods in the plugin's closure. They're then called by passing the string name of the method required, and then passing any additional parameters needed for the method as a second argument. This type of method encapsulation and architecture is a standard in the jQuery plugin community and it is used by countless plugins, including the plugins and widgets in jQuery UI. The basic pattern is illustrated in the following code:

```
(function( $ ){

  var methods = {
    init : function( options ) {
      // init
    },
    flip : function( howMany ) {
      // flip
    },
    flop: function( ) {
      // flop
    },
    fly  : function( ) {
      // fly
    }
  };

  $.fn.bestPluginEver = function( method ) {

    if ( methods[method] ) {
      return methods[ method ].apply( this,
        Array.prototype.slice.call( arguments, 1 ));
    } else if ( typeof method === 'object' || ! method ) {
      return methods.init.apply( this, arguments );
    } else {
      $.error( 'Method '
        +  method
        + ' does not exist in the bestPluginEver' );
```

```
    }
  };
})( jQuery );

// calls the init method
$( 'div' ).tooltip();

// calls the fly method
$( 'div' ).tooltip('fly');

// calls the flip method with an argument
$( 'div' ).tooltip('flip' , 'twice');
```

Code snippet is from single-namespace-pattern.txt

Additionally, Namespace Your Events and Data

In addition to claiming just a single name in the jQuery namespace, it's important to be frugal with your plugin events and data as well. With events and data, the issues are under the hood and are therefore less obvious. That doesn't mean that it's not important to play nice.

To that end, when setting events, take advantage of the ability to add event namespaces to the bound events. This simple technique enables you to safely unbind events without the danger of unbinding events bound to the same elements by code outside of the scope of your plugin.

You accomplish this by appending .namespace to the end of the bound event name. The following code illustrates this pattern by setting a namespaced resize event on the window:

Available for
download on
Wrox.com

```
(function( $ ){

  var methods = {
    init : function( options ) {
      $( window ).bind( 'resize.bestFunctionEver', methods.flop );
    },
    destroy : function( ) {
        $( window ).unbind( 'resize.bestFunctionEver' );
    },    flip : function( howMany ) {
      // flip
    },
    flop: function( ) {
      // flop
    },
    fly  : function(  ) {
      // fly
    }
  };

  $.fn.bestPluginEver = function( method ) {
   // method calling code
  };
})( jQuery );
```

Code snippet is from event-namespace.txt

Similarly, if your plugin needs to store data, it's best to store it under a single $.data entry. If you need to store multiple pieces of data, you should do so with an object literal containing all of the necessary data in that single $.data entry.

The following code example shows the use of an object literal with $.data:

```
var data = this.data('bestPluginEver');
if (!data) {
    this.data('bestPluginEver',{
        "color" : "blue",
        "title" : "my dashboard",
        "width" : "960px"
    });
}
        }
```

Code snippet is from namespaced-data.txt

If you follow these simple guidelines, the danger of a namespace collision is significantly reduced. This will save someone, somewhere down the road a mess of trouble.

Accept an Options Argument to Control Plugin Behavior

There's nothing more frustrating as a developer than trying to remember the order of arguments in a function or method call — *"Does the code to execute come before or after the number of milliseconds in setTimeout?"* One or two are okay but anything more than that and you're likely to have to go to the documentation to figure out what argument goes where.

Additionally, in the case where you have multiple, *optional* arguments, you can run into confusing function calls strewn with empty arguments, like this:

```
soManyOptions("#myDiv", ,  , 14 , "#ff0000" );
```

Code snippet is from empty-arguments.txt

No one wants to deal with code like that. It's confusing (*"Am I on the fifth argument or the fourth"*) and, honestly, ugly.

To alleviate that, it's recommended that you accept an object as an options argument that can extend the default settings when the plugin is invoked. The following code illustrates accepting an options argument and using $.extend to merge it with the plugin defaults.

This is the preferred way to provide complex configuration options.

```
(function( $ ){

$.fn.bestPluginEver = function( options ) {

    var settings = $.extend( {
        "color" : "blue",
        "title" : "my dashboard",
        "width" : "960px"
```

```
    }, options);

    return this.each(function() {

      // best.plugin.ever
    });
  };
})( jQuery );

$('div').bestPluginEver({
  'color' : 'AliceBlue'
});
```

Code snippet is from configuration-object.txt

Provide Public Access to Default Plugin Settings

Building on the previous example, it's also beneficial to expose the default plugin settings directly. That way, you can set plugin defaults without having to call the plugin. This feature makes it easy for plugin users to customize the plugin across their implementation with minimal code. The following code example illustrates this. It similarly extends the default options with $.extend, but also directly exposes the $.fn.bestPluginEver.defaults object. As you'll remember from earlier in the chapter, $.fn is an alias for jQuery.prototype, which is a live link. That means any changes to $.fn.bestPluginEver.defaults will affect any instance of the plugin created before or after the change is made to the defaults object. This is in contrast to the scope of the options argument, which affects only that specific instantiation.

One interesting thing to note is the use of an empty object passed as the first argument to $.extend. This ensures that the prototypal defaults object remains intact when the options argument is invoked. This pattern allows both for single instances to be updated with extend as well as retaining the ability to set global plugin defaults by overriding the prototypal default.

```
(function( $ ){

  $.fn.bestPluginEver = function( options ) {

    var settings = $.extend( {}, $.fn.bestPluginEver.defaults, options );
    return this.each(function() {

      // best.plugin.ever
    });
  };
  $.fn.bestPluginEver.defaults = {
      "color" : "blue",
      "title" : "my dashboard",
      "width" : "960px"
  };

})( jQuery );


//set global default by overwriting the prototypal property
$.fn.bestPluginEver.width = "768px";

/* call the plugin with an options
```

```
*   argument to override the new default in a single instance
*/

$("div").bestPluginEver( {"width" : "960px" });
```

Code snippet is from public-settings-access.txt

Provide Public Access to Secondary Functions (As Applicable)

This technique is a direct parallel to the technique outlined in the previous section. The key difference is, instead of exposing just settings to the outside world, individual methods are available to alter and extend.

In the following example, a basic `sort` function is defined in the plugin body. Because it's designed to be rewriteable, it's easy to drop in a different sorting algorithm.

```
(function($) {
  $.fn.dataCruncher = function( options ) {
    var data = $.fn.dataCruncher.sort( data );
    return this.each(function() {
      // do stuff with data
    });
  };
  $.fn.dataCruncher.sort = function(data) {
    for ( var j = 1 test = data.length; j < test; j++ ) {
      var key = data[j],
      i = j - 1;
      while ( i >= 0 && data[ i ] > key) {
        data[ i + 1 ] = data[ i ];
        i = i - 1;
      }
      data[i + 1] = key;
      return data;
    }
  };

})( jQuery );

//offer a new sorting option
$.fn.dataCruncher.sort = function( data ) {
  var len = data.length;
  for ( var i = 0; i < len; i++ ) {
  var index = i;
  for ( k = i + 1; k < len; k++ ) {
    if ( data[k] < data[index] ) {
      index = k;
    }
  }
  var temp = data[ i ];
  data[ i ] = data[ index ];
  data[ index ] = temp;
}
```

Code snippet is from public-methods.txt

Keep Private Functions Private

The flipside to exposing pieces of your plugin to outside enhancement is that it can cause unpredictable results if you're not careful with identifying which pieces should be accessible and which shouldn't. If it's important to the function of your plugin and won't offer any real benefit by being exposed to plugin users, it's probably best to keep that function private. To do that, simply define the function inside the body of your function, but outside of the return object.

```
(function($) {

  $.fn.dataCruncher = function(options) {
    //inaccessible outside the plugin
    function privateSort( data ){
      //private method
    }
    return this.each(function() {
      var data = privateSort( data );
    });
  };
};
```

Code snippet is from private-functions-private.txt

Support the Metadata Plugin

Of all of the original recommendations, this is one that isn't as relevant as it once was. The Metadata plugin itself has been deprecated in favor of similar functionality provided by $.data(). Still, it's worth looking at in case you find yourself working with an older version of jQuery either refactoring old code or working in an environment where the core library hasn't been updated in some time.

The Metadata plugin extracts data from a DOM element and returns it as an object. It provides a convenient, markup-based method for customizing plugins. One example of where this can be extremely handy is if you need to extract data for use in a plugin out of a CMS. Imagine allowing CMS authors to update slideshow options by clicking a couple of checkboxes and then exposing their choices with metadata.

Support for the Metadata plugin is easy to add, so it can be a handy addition to your plugin configuration options.

The following code sample illustrates support for Metadata. It tests for the presence of $.metadata, and if the plugin is there, it merges any data found with the settings and options object that drives the style passed into CSS.

```
<html>
<head>
<script src="http://code.jquery.com/jquery-1.7.1.js" ></script>
<script  srcs="jquery.metadata.js"></script>
<script>
(function($) {
  // plugin definition
  var settings = {
    "background" : "#fe57a1",
```

```
      "color" : "#fff",
      "text-shadow" : "none"
    };
    $.fn.pinkify = function( options ) {
      return this.each(function() {
        var style = $.extend( settings, options ),
        $this = $( this );
        style = $.metadata ? $.extend( style, $this.metadata() ) : style;
        $this.css( style );
      });
    }
  })( jQuery );


  $( document ).ready(function() {
    $('.pinkify').pinkify()
  });
  </script>
  </head>
  <body>
  <ul>
      <li class="pinkify"> Hot pink </li>
      <li class="pinkify { color : '#000' }">
        Black and Pink. Very hip.
      </li>
      <li class="pinkify { color : 'green' }">
        Not so sure about this one.
      </li>
  </ul>
  </body>
  </html>
```

Code snippet is from metadata.txt

UTILIZE AND LEARN FROM EXISTING PLUGIN PATTERNS

Once you have the basics of plugin development down and want to expand your horizons to include some very advanced options for plugin development, another, more recent, resource to look at is Addy Osmani's article "Essential jQuery Plugin Patterns" (http://coding.smashingmagazine .com/2011/10/11/essential-jquery-plugin-patterns/) and the associated Github repository (https://github.com/addyosmani/jquery-plugin-patterns). In it, Addy presents a well-researched series of starting points for plugin development. The options range from a simple example (shown in the next code sample) that will already look pretty familiar to you, to advanced options supporting module patterns like RequireJS, Asynchronous Module Definition (AMD), and CommonJS.

As both a simple starting point for your own plugin code and as a learning resource, the article and associated repository are essential reading. The following code example from https:// github.com/addyosmani/jquery-plugin-patterns/blob/master/jquery.basic.plugin-boilerplate.js shows one such piece of boilerplate code along with the associated comments. As you can see, a lot of thought went into the pattern itself and each line is given a careful explanation. Some of the options may be too advanced for you right at the beginning of your exploration of plugin development, but for medium to advanced plugin developers, it's an extraordinary resource.

```
/*!
 * jQuery lightweight plugin boilerplate
 * Original author: @ajpiano
 * Further changes, comments: @addyosmani
 * Licensed under the MIT license
 */

// the semicolon before the function invocation is a safety
// net against concatenated scripts and/or other plugins
// that are not closed properly.
;(function ( $, window, document, undefined ) {

    // undefined is used here as the undefined global
    // variable in ECMAScript 3 and is mutable (i.e. it can
    // be changed by someone else). undefined isn't really
    // being passed in so we can ensure that its value is
    // truly undefined. In ES5, undefined can no longer be
    // modified.

    // window and document are passed through as local
    // variables rather than as globals, because this (slightly)
    // quickens the resolution process and can be more
    // efficiently minified (especially when both are
    // regularly referenced in your plugin).

    // Create the defaults once
    var pluginName = 'defaultPluginName',
        defaults = {
            propertyName: "value"
        };

    // The actual plugin constructor
    function Plugin( element, options ) {
        this.element = element;

        // jQuery has an extend method that merges the
        // contents of two or more objects, storing the
        // result in the first object. The first object
        // is generally empty because we don't want to alter
        // the default options for future instances of the plugin
        this.options = $.extend( {}, defaults, options) ;

        this._defaults = defaults;
        this._name = pluginName;

        this.init();
    }

    Plugin.prototype.init = function () {
        // Place initialization logic here
        // You already have access to the DOM element and
        // the options via the instance, e.g. this.element
        // and this.options
    };

    // A really lightweight plugin wrapper around the constructor,
    // preventing against multiple instantiations
    $.fn[pluginName] = function ( options ) {
        return this.each(function () {
```

```
            if (!$.data(this, 'plugin_' + pluginName)) {
                $.data(this, 'plugin_' + pluginName,
                new Plugin( this, options ));
            }
        });
    }

})( jQuery, window, document );
```

Code snippet is from jquery.basic.plugin-boilerplate.js

As you can see, this boilerplate code encapsulates many of the best practices illustrated in this chapter and adds a couple of important enhancements, such as preventing multiple plugin instantiations looking for the presence of the plugin in `$.data`.

You can't go wrong starting with such a solid foundation, and because the project is on Github, it will benefit from the ongoing eyes and tweaking offered up by the larger jQuery community.

A CLOSER LOOK AT THE WIDGET FACTORY

It was touched on briefly, but the Widget Factory provides an alternative, powerful path to jQuery plugin development. It's a slightly more advanced option, but it offers several features that might be beneficial depending on the style of plugin you're looking to write. The following list outlines some of the useful features that come along automatically once you buy into the Widget Factory method of plugin creation. You'll notice that many of these were touched on in previous sections. They come along for the ride with the Widget Factory.

➤ Prevention of multiple instances of the plugin on the same object.

➤ Methods to enable, disable, or destroy the widget.

➤ Widgets are stateful, so destroying the instance returns the DOM element to its original state.

➤ Namespace and prototype creation.

    ➤ A pseudoselector is also generated from the namespace and name.

➤ The ability to override default settings with new options.

    ➤ Default values are exposed to set plugin defaults.

➤ Methods for setting and responding to changes in plugin options.

➤ Plugin instance accessible via the object's stored `data`.

➤ Automatic method lookup table.

Although the earlier example you saw was a one-liner, truly getting up and running with the Widget Factory is significantly more involved than a one-liner.

The following code shows the minimum needed to get a `$.widget` plugin going. You pass it a `namespace` to run under and then an object literal to serve as the prototype of your widget. The object literal should include an `options` object; a `_create` function, which will automatically run the first time the widget is called; a `_destroy` (or `destroy`, if you're using 1.8) function, which destroys an instantiated plugin and cleans up the DOM; `_setOption`, which responds to option changes; and then your plugin methods.

```
;(function ( $, window, document, undefined ) {

  $.widget( "best.widget" , {
    options: {
      hashtag: "#hotpink"
    },
    _create: function () {
      //create
    },

    _destroy: function () {
      //destroy
    },
    _setOption: function( key, value ) {
      /* In jQuery UI 1.8, you have to manually invoke
       * the _setOption method from the base widget
       */
       $.Widget.prototype._setOption.apply( this, arguments );
      // In jQuery UI 1.9 and above, you use the _super method instead
      this._super( "_setOption", key, value );
    },
    pluginMethod : function(){
    //plugin functionality
    }
  });
})( jQuery, window, document );
```

Code snippet is from widget-factory.txt

AN EXAMPLE PLUGIN IMPLEMENTATION

As you can probably tell from the breadth of options presented in this chapter, you have a lot of ways to approach jQuery plugin development. There's no *one true way.*

That means you need to choose patterns and options to follow depending on the goals of your plugin.

As the following code sample shows, the plugin takes a DOM element and, based on several of the lengthy available options, creates an HTML Canvas element in the same position and containing the same text as the target element. In this case, it's pointed at all of the H1s on a page.

This simple example plugin uses Ben Alman's *Globally and Per-Call Overridable Options (Best Options Pattern)* (as it's called in the "Essential jQuery Plugin Patterns" article) to expose a hefty configuration object to both global and per-call configuration. Because it's so heavily skewed toward the style of the Canvas element the plugin creates, the plugin needs to offer full-featured configuration. Because it could operate on many elements on a page, it made sense to allow for default configuration override as well as per-call configuration.

Even in this small plugin, you'll see a variety of the techniques discussed earlier in this chapter:

➤   A semicolon leading into an immediately executing function expression

➤ $, window, document, and undefined passed in as variables to ensure that $ is always jQuery, undefined is always undefined, and to shorten lookups to document and window

➤ Configuration via an `options` object and the jQuery method `$.extend`

➤ Returning `this` to allow chaining of the method

➤ Exposing the default options for global configuration

```
;(function ( $, window, document, undefined ) {

  $.fn.canvasizr = function ( options ) {
    options = $.extend( {}, $.fn.canvasizr.options, options );

      return this.each(function () {
        var $this = $( this ),
        pos = $this.position(),
        width = $this.outerWidth(),
        height = $this.outerHeight()
           + parseInt( $this.css( "margin-top" ) )
           + parseInt( $this.css( "margin-bottom" ) ),
        canvas = document.createElement( "canvas" ),
        $canvas = $( canvas ),
        ctx = canvas.getContext( "2d" );
        $.extend( ctx,options );
        canvas.width = width;
        canvas.height = height;
        ctx.fillRect( 0, 0, parseInt( width ), parseInt( height ));
        if( options.border){
          ctx.strokeRect( 0, 0, parseInt( width ), parseInt( height ) );
        }
        ctx.fillStyle = ctx.textColor;
        ctx.fillText( $this.text(), 8, parseInt( height )/2 );
        $canvas.css({
          "position" : "absolute",
          "left" : pos.left +"px",
          "top" : pos.top +"px",
          "z-index":1
        });
        $( "body" ).append( $canvas );
      });
    };


  $.fn.canvasizr.options = {
    textColor : "#ffffff",
    fillColor:  "#ff0000",
    strokeStyle : "#000",
    border: false,
    font : "20px sans-serif",
    lineCap : "butt",
    lineJoin : "miter",
    lineWidth :  1,
    miterLimit :  10,
    shadowBlur :  0,
    shadowColor : "rgba(0, 0, 0, 0)",
    shadowOffsetX :  0,
    shadowOffsetY :  0,
    textAlign :  "start",
```

```
        textBaseline : "alphabetic"
    };

})( jQuery, window, document );
```

Code snippet is from canvasizr.txt

The following code sample shows the plugin in action. Initially, a default fill style is set for all instances of the plugin. Following that, the plugin is called twice, once on #special and once on a collection of three elements: #first, #second, and #third". Different options are specified each time the plugin is called to produce different results. The output of this code can be seen in Figure 12-1.

```
$.fn.canvasizr.options.fillStyle = "#fe57a1";
$( "#special" ).canvasizr({
    font : "30px Consolas,'Lucida Console',monospace"
});
$( "#first, #second, #third" ).canvasizr({
    textColor : "#ffffff",
    fillStyle:  "#ff0000",
    font : "40px sans-serif",
    border:true
});
```

Code snippet is from canvasizr-called.txt

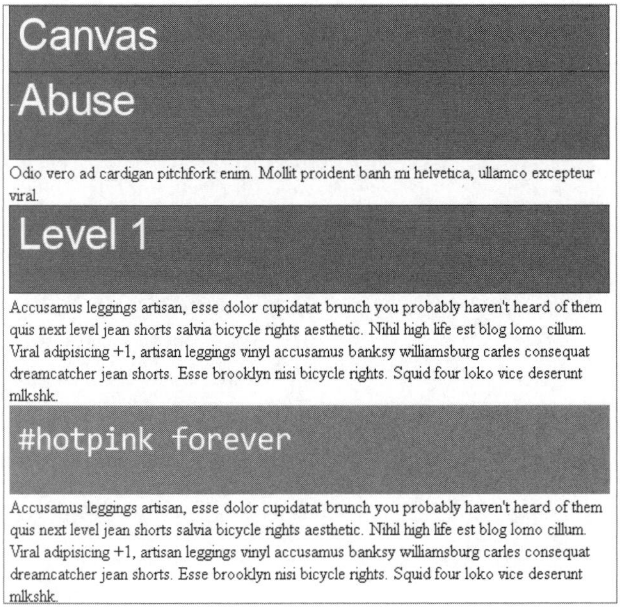

Canvas
Abuse

Odio vero ad cardigan pitchfork enim. Mollit proident banh mi helvetica, ullamco excepteur viral.

Level 1

Accusamus leggings artisan, esse dolor cupidatat brunch you probably haven't heard of them quis next level jean shorts salvia bicycle rights aesthetic. Nihil high life est blog lomo cillum. Viral adipisicing +1, artisan leggings vinyl accusamus banksy williamsburg carles consequat dreamcatcher jean shorts. Esse brooklyn nisi bicycle rights. Squid four loko vice deserunt mlkshk.

#hotpink forever

Accusamus leggings artisan, esse dolor cupidatat brunch you probably haven't heard of them quis next level jean shorts salvia bicycle rights aesthetic. Nihil high life est blog lomo cillum. Viral adipisicing +1, artisan leggings vinyl accusamus banksy williamsburg carles consequat dreamcatcher jean shorts. Esse brooklyn nisi bicycle rights. Squid four loko vice deserunt mlkshk.

FIGURE 12-1

SUMMARY

You should now have solid foundation on the ins and outs of jQuery plugin development. With a thorough look at the basics and an examination of more advanced options, you should be able to create your own powerful, configurable plugins that will play nicely with others. You should know how to extend jQuery, how to expose a variety of configuration and enhancement options, and how to fit your plugin into the existing jQuery ecosystem by providing common features, by practicing good code style, and by keeping your plugin footprint to a minimum.

You also now have several resources available to further explore jQuery plugin development.

13

Advanced Asynchronous Programming with jQuery Deferred

WHAT'S IN THIS CHAPTER?

➤   The Promises/A Proposal

➤   The jQuery Deferred Object

In this chapter, you learn about the jQuery Deferred object. `$.Deferred`, introduced in version 1.5, is a chainable utility object that provides fine-tuned control over the way callback functions are handled. For example, instead of merely having a single success method for your `$.ajax` calls, you can now define multiple callbacks that can be combined with precision and flexibility.

This chapter also introduces the CommonJS Promises/A proposal that fed the design of `$.Deferred`. Following that foundation, you learn about the jQuery implementation in detail.

Leveraging the power of `$.Deferred` will make some unpleasant coding patterns disappear. Monolithic success blocks, chock full of application logic, will be a thing of the past. Awkward timing with asynchronous requests and unmaintainable function calls buried at the end of other function calls can be put to bed with `$.Deferred`. `$.Deferred` pulls all of that logic up a level and gives it a clear structure that's more maintainable, more flexible, and is, as is often the case with jQuery, a fun pattern to use.

BUILDING BLOCKS

`$.Deferred` is built on existing work and concepts from sources outside the jQuery project. To understand the feature in the fullest, it's useful to look at those sources directly. This section will outline the origin of the pattern, which will ease you into an understanding of jQuery's specific implementation.

Promises

Basically defined, a *promise* is a proxy for the result of an action that will happen at an unspecified time in the future.

Although they're relatively new to jQuery, software promises have been around for a good while. The name and concept of promises dates back to a paper written in 1976 by Daniel P. Friedman and David Wise. Though language implementations are generally more academic than practical, library implementations exist for Java, Scala, Ruby, Perl, Python, and Common Lisp. Closer to home, a major JavaScript implementation has been in place in the dojo framework from version 0.9.

Because they're so easily asynchronous, they're particularly suited to web programming, so it was inevitable that they'd land in jQuery.

The Promises/A Proposal

jQuery's specific implementation is based on the Promises/A proposal from CommonJS.

CommonJS is a group centered on interoperability in JavaScript and the growth of a healthy JavaScript ecosystem similar to the ones that have developed around other languages like Python, Ruby, and Java. The group's main focus is on the question of modules, which the Common JS Modules API addresses directly, but they've worked on several other language features. One is promises. The CommonJS wiki lists several proposals for the Promises pattern. Promises/A proposal is from Kris Zyp. It's defined as follows:

> *A promise represents the eventual value returned from the single completion of an operation. A promise may be in one of the three states, unfulfilled, fulfilled, and failed. The promise may only move from unfulfilled to fulfilled, or unfulfilled to failed. Once a promise is fulfilled or failed, the promise's value MUST not be changed The immutable characteristic of promises are important for avoiding side-effects from listeners that can create unanticipated changes in behavior and allows promises to be passed to other functions without affecting the caller, in same way that primitives can be passed to functions without any concern that the caller's variable will be modified by the callee.*
>
> *A promise is defined as an object that has a function as the value for the property 'then'.*

```
http://wiki.commonjs.org/wiki/Promises/A
```

The following code sample presents a simplified look at the concepts presented in the Promises/A proposal.

Assuming that `ajaxPromise` returns a promise that can be in one of three states (unfulfilled, fulfilled, or failed), the following illustrates the general principle:

```
var promise = ajaxPromise() {
    //XHR request
    //state is set to fulfilled, unfulfilled, or failed
    //depending on the result of the request
    return state
};

function unfulfilled(){
```

```
    //handle negative result
  }
  function fulfilled() {
    //handle successful result
  }
  function failed(){
    //Error!
  }

  promise.then(
    unfulfilled,
    fulfilled,
    failed
  );
```

Code snippet is from pseudocode.txt

In English, `ajaxPromise` goes off, gets some data with an `XMLHttpRequest`, and when the request finishes, it returns a promise in one of the three states. The `then()` method routes the result to one of three functions designed to handle that state. None of that logic is bound to `ajaxPromise` itself. It's all handled outside the function, which allows `ajaxPromise` to remain much more generic because less application logic is bound to it directly.

Now that you've got some history on the concept, in the next section, you look at the power of jQuery's Deferred implementation.

THE JQUERY DEFERRED OBJECT

jQuery's implementation adds onto the basic premise of the promise with several useful enhancements. Importantly, it also integrates directly with one of the core features of the library, `$.ajax`, so Deferred opens up a world of possibilities once you've got your head wrapped around them.

As is the jQuery way, the format of the implementation is heavy on the ability to chain methods in a convenient way. It's also written in a friendly, human-readable style.

This section looks at jQuery's basic implementation and walks through some of the more advanced features available.

$.when, Deferred.done, and Deferred.fail

When working with Deferreds, you'll find that a lot of activity flows through the new jQuery method `$.when`. `$.when` accepts either one or more Deferred objects (which importantly include `$.ajax` calls) or a plain object.

If a Deferred is passed to `$.when`, its promise object is returned by the method. You see more about how to manage jQuery's promises in a later section, but additional methods are then available to chain and structure callbacks.

The first two methods are `Deferred.done` and `Deferred.fail`.

`Deferred.done` accepts a single function or array of functions to fire when a promise is resolved successfully.

`Deferred.fail` also accepts a function or array of functions. It fires when a promise is rejected.

As a note, if an argument is passed to `$.when` and it is not a Deferred, it is treated as a resolved Deferred. If no other Deferred objects are passed to `$.when`, then `Deferred.done` fires.

The following code presents a bare-bones jQuery Deferred example using `$.when`, `Deferred.done`, and `Deferred.fail`.

The example starts off by defining three functions. The function `fib` does some math and then displays an unordered list with the results of that calculation. Two other functions are then defined, `success` and `failure`. These are simple functions that change the messaging in an `h1` depending on the result of the first function. The interesting piece is that one or the other will fire depending on whether the promise is resolved or rejected.

```html
<!doctype html>
<html>
<head>
<meta charset="utf-8">
</head>
<body>
<div id="main">
  <h1></h1>
  <ul id="numbers">
  </ul>
</div>
<script src="http://code.jquery.com/jquery-1.7.1.min.js"></script>
<script>
function fib() {
  var int1 = 0,
  int2 = 1,
  int3,
  sequence = "<li>0</li><li>1</li>";
  for ( var i = 3; i <= 100; i++ ) {
    int3 = int1 + int2;
    int1 = int2;
    int2 = int3;
    sequence += "<li>"+int3+"</li>"
  }
  $( "#numbers" ).append( sequence ).show( 500 );
}
function success() {
  $( "h1" ).text( "Fibonacci!" );
}
function failure() {
  $ ("h1" ).text( "No numbers?" );
}
$(function(){
  $.when( fib() )
```

```
    .done( success )
    .fail( failure );
});
</script>
</body>
</html>
```

Code snippet is from basic-deferred.txt

If you've been paying attention, you'll remember that if a function is passed to `$.when` and it isn't a Deferred object, it's treated as a resolved Deferred and the `Deferred.done` method is called. In this case, the `Deferred.fail` method will never fire.

So, although it's valid, and will work basically as expected and illustrates the basic pattern, it's missing the star of the show. The next code sample shows `fib` redefined to leverage the Deferred object. The function now returns `Deferred.promise`. The logic of the previous `fib` function is passed into `$.Deferred` as an argument.

It's important to note the resolution of the promise as a callback to `$.show`. This is an important pattern discussed in depth in the next section.

```
<!doctype html>
<html>
<head>
<meta charset="utf-8">
</head>
<body>
<div id="main">
  <h1></h1>
  <ul id="numbers">
  </ul>
</div>
<script src="http://code.jquery.com/jquery-1.7.1.min.js"></script>
<script>
function fib() {
  return $.Deferred(function() {
    var int1 = 0,
    int2 = 1,
    int3, sequence = "<li>0</li><li>1</li>";
    for (var i = 3; i <= 100; i++) {
      int3 = int1 + int2;
      int1 = int2;
      int2 = int3;
      sequence += "<li>" + int3 + "</li>"
    }
    $("#numbers")
      .append(sequence)
      .show(1000, this.resolve);
  }).promise();
}

function success() {
  $( "h1" ).text( "Fibonacci!" );
```

```
}
function failure() {
  $ ("h1" ).text( "No numbers?" );
}
$(function(){
  $.when( fib() )
    .done( success )
    .fail( failure );
});
</script>
</body>
</html>
```

Code snippet is from proper-deferred.txt

Although this is a simple example, it illustrates the power of the Deferred pattern. Callbacks in jQuery are a common source of tight coupling. They're often defined in place, as anonymous functions with too little attention paid to abstraction.

The following animation example presents a clear illustration of how Deferred can untangle your program logic, allowing for greater code reuse and a cleaner overall architecture. Without Deferreds, callback logic for animations is tied directly to the animation call as an optional `complete` argument. `complete` is defined as a function that will be fired when the animation ends. An example of the traditional manner of doing this is shown in this first code sample:

Available for
download on
Wrox.com

```
<!doctype html>
<html>
<head>
<meta charset="utf-8">
</head>
<body>
<div id="main">
 <div id="statusbar" style="display:none">
 </div>
</div>
<script src="http://code.jquery.com/jquery-1.7.1.min.js"></script>
<script>
function updateStatus() {
  var $update = $("<ul />"),
  $statusbar = $("#statusbar"),
  html = []; // text buffer
  for ( var i = 0, test = 20; i < test; i++ ) {
    html.push( "<li>status update</li>");
  }
  html = html.join("\n"); // buffer -> string
  $update.append(html);
  $statusbar.append($update);
  $statusbar.slideDown(5000, function() {
    console.log("animation is done! On to the next operation");
  });
}

$(function(){
```

```
      updateStatus();
    });
    </script>
    </body>
    </html>
```

Code snippet is from tight-callbacks.txt

Though there's a simple `console.log` in the `complete` argument in this example, far more complicated application data is commonly packed into similar `complete` callbacks.

This might be acceptable if `updateStatus` will *only* ever be used with the anonymous callback function. If it needs to be matched with other functions, it's a different story. Pulling the logic from a callback function buried deep inside `updateStatus` allows for more flexibility in terms of code reuse.

Alternatively, to solve this, you could add a `callback` function as an argument to `updateStatus`, but using Deferred and returning a resolved promise is far more flexible. The following code sample shows how `updateStatus` could be rewritten to leverage Deferreds:

```
function updateStatus() {
  return $.Deferred(function() {
    var $update = $("<ul />"),
    $statusbar = $("#statusbar"),
    html = []; // text buffer
    for ( var i = 0, test = 20; i < test; i++ ) {
      html.push( "<li>status update</li>");
    }
    html = html.join("\n"); // buffer -> string
    $update.append(html);
    $statusbar.append($update);
    $statusbar.slideDown(1000, this.resolve);
  }).promise()
}
```

Code snippet is from decoupling.txt

With just the simple application of a Deferred, `updateStatus` is now much more flexible. Instead of being tied to a single callback, you can now use that same piece of code in several different flows. The upcoming code block shows several ways in which it could be used to take advantage of Deferreds.

The example contains three callback functions. The first is equivalent to the original anonymous functions passed in as a callback in the first example. The second, `alternativeCallback`, represents a different path to follow after the animation completes. If the same animation is running on a second page, a different piece of markup will have to be updated. The third, `happyBirthday`, represents a function to be called in a special case where a specific UI update would be required, a "HAPPY BIRTHDAY" message indicator, for example. Three uses of `$.when` follow. The first replicates the original case with a single callback function. The second shows the alternative callback. The third shows multiple callbacks.

```
function callback(){
  console.log("The animation is done. On to the next operation");
}
function alternativeCallback(){
  console.log("The animation is done. Let's follow a different path.");
}
function specialCase(){
  console.log("This is a special case. Let's do a special UI update.");
}

$.when( updateStatus() )
  .done( callback );

//an alternative callback

$.when( updateStatus() )
  .done( alternativeCallback );

//multiple callbacks

$.when( updateStatus() )
  .done(
    [ callback,
      specialCase ]
  );
```

Code snippet is from decoupled-callbacks.txt

As you can see, the code nicely decoupled the callback logic from the animation buried in the function body. This allows for greater code reuse and presents a much clearer pattern for any other developers on the project to grasp. No one even needs to read `updateStatus` to know how the application flows. It's all laid out in (nearly) plain English.

Deferred.then Syntactic Sugar for Deferred.fail and Deferred.done

As with aliases for `$.ajax` like `$.get` and `$.post`, jQuery provides a convenient alias for the core Deferred objects: `Deferred.then`. `Deferred.then` accepts two arguments, one for resolved promises and the other for rejected promises. Like the functions it maps to, `Deferred.done` and `Deferred.fail`, the arguments for `Deferred.then` can either be individual functions or an array of functions.

The following code sample shows the original Deferred example from earlier in the chapter rewritten to use `Deferred.then`.

```
<!doctype html>
<html>
<head>
<meta charset="utf-8">
</head>
<body>
<div id="main">
  <h1></h1>
  <ul id="numbers">
```

```
      </ul>
    </div>
    <script src="http://code.jquery.com/jquery-1.7.1.min.js"></script>
    <script>
    function fib() {
      return $.Deferred(function() {
        var int1 = 0,
        int2 = 1,
        int3, sequence = "<li>0</li><li>1</li>";
        for (var i = 3; i <= 100; i++) {
          int3 = int1 + int2;
          int1 = int2;
          int2 = int3;
          sequence += "<li>" + int3 + "</li>"
        }
        $("#numbers")
          .append(sequence)
          .show(1000, this.resolve);
      }).promise();
    }

    function success() {
      $( "h1" ).text( "Fibonacci!" );
    }
    function failure() {
      $ ("h1" ).text( "No numbers?" );
    }
    $(function(){
      $.when( fib() )
        .then( success, failure );
    });
    </script>
  </body>
</html>
```

Code snippet is from deferred-then.txt

Because Deferred methods are chainable, `Deferred.then` can be combined with `Deferred.done`, `Deferred.fail`, or even additional `Deferred.then` calls.

Using the Deferred Aspects of $.ajax

As was previously mentioned, `$.ajax` is a Deferred object and the `success`, `error`, and `complete` callback methods are analogous to `Deferred.done`, `Deferred.fail`, and `Deferred.always`, respectively. The following code shows a typical `$.get` request:

```
$.get("/status/json/",
  function( data ) {
    var $update = $( "<ul />" ),
    $statusbar = $( "#statusbar" ),
    html = "",
    statusMessages = data.statusMessages;
    for ( var i = 0, test = statusMessages.length; i < test; i++ ) {
```

```
      html += "<li>" + status[i] + "</li>";
    }
    $update.append(html);
    $statusbar.append($update);
    $statusbar.slideDown(1000);
  }
);
```

The next code block shows the same Ajax request, written using Deferreds. It's important to note that the arguments passed to updateStatus are the same that would be passed to the callback function of a typical Ajax request. It includes the data, a text string indicating the status of the request, and the jQuery XMLHttpRequest (jqXHR) object. Also introduced in jQuery 1.5 as part of the $.ajax rewrite, the jqXHR object is an enhanced version of the standard XMLHttpRequest object. It comes complete with all of the Deferred methods, which means anything that you learn about the standard Deferred object is similarly available on all $.ajax requests.

```
function getStatus() {
  return $.ajax({
    url : "/status/json/",
    dataType : "json"
  })
}

function updateStatus( data ) {
  var $update = $( "<ul />" ),
  $statusbar = $( "#statusbar" ),
  html = "",
  statusMessages = data.statusMessages;
  for ( var i = 0, test = statusMessages.length; i < test; i++ ) {
    html += "<li>" + statusMessages[i] + "</li>";
  }
  $update.append( html );
  $statusbar.append( $update );
  $statusbar.slideDown( 1000 );
}
$.when( getStatus() )
    .done( updateStatus );
```

On the surface, the preceding code may not seem like much of an improvement over the traditional callback method. It's a little bit longer and it's a little less free-flowing than the traditional inline callback used in jQuery Ajax requests. Beyond the surface, it's useful to note that once again, the callback logic is decoupled from the specific Ajax request. This immediately makes that getStatus function more flexible. Additionally, as with any Deferred object, multiple $.ajax requests can be passed into $.when and multiple callbacks can be chained to respond to changes in the promise status, so the possibilities are greatly expanded. The next example presents an exaggerated, but hopefully illustrative example.

```
$.when(
   $.post("/echo/json",
     function() {
        console.log("1")
      }
   ),
    $.post("/echo/json",
       function() {
          console.log("2")
       }
   ),
    $.post("/echo/json",
       function() {
          console.log("3")
       }
    )
).then([
   function() {
      console.log("4")
   },
   function() {
      console.log("5")
   },
   function() {
      console.log("6")
   }
]).then([
   function() {
      console.log("7")
   },
   function() {
      console.log("8")
   },
   function() {
      console.log("9")}
]).then([
   function() {
      console.log("10")
   },
   function() {
      console.log("11")
   },
   function() {
      console.log("12")}
]).done(
   function() {
      console.log("Electric Company!")
   }
);
```

Code snippet is from multiple-callbacks.txt

Execute a Function No Matter What the Promise Resolution Is with Deferred.always

Oftentimes, you want a function to be called no matter what the promise resolution is. This is analogous to the `complete` callback, which fires on any resolution of an `$.ajax` request. In the world of Deferred, the method to use is `Deferred.always`. Like the rest of the Deferred methods, `Deferred.always` takes a single function or an array of functions to fire whenever a promise is resolved or rejected. The following code shows a simplified example that changes the "last updated" indicator in a mail application.

```
$.when(
    $.ajax( "/get/mail/" )
).done(
    newMessages,
    updateMessageList,
     updateUnreadIndicator
).fail(
    noMessages
).always(
    function() {
      var date = new Date();
      $( "#lastUpdated" ).html( "<strong>Folder Updated</strong>: "
        + date.toDateString()
        + " at "
        + date.toTimeString()
      );
    }
)
```

Code snippet is from always.txt

Chaining and Filtering Deferreds with Deferred.pipe

`Deferred.pipe`, introduced in jQuery 1.6, provides a method to filter and further chain Deferreds. A common use case utilizes the ability to chain Deferreds to create an animation queue. The following code shows a simplified example that uses a chained animation used to manage the build out of the components of a web application. Once the animation queue is complete, the promise is automatically resolved and the done method is fired.

```
function buildpage() {
    return $.Deferred(function( dfd ) {
        dfd.pipe(function() {
            return $( 'header' ).fadeIn();
        })
        .pipe(function() {
            return $( '#main' ).fadeIn();
        })
        .pipe(function() {
            return $( 'footer' ).fadeIn();
        })
    }).resolve();
```

```
    }
$.when( buildpage() )
  .done(function() {
    console.log('done')
  }
);
```

Code snippet is from deferred-pipe-animation.txt

`Deferred.pipe` allows for more than just convenient chaining; it provides a very handy way to filter Deferreds based on secondary criteria. `Deferred.pipe` accepts three arguments: a `doneFilter`, a `failFilter`, and a `progressFilter`. The concept of progress is covered in a later section. For now, you focus on filtering standard Deferred objects.

The following code shows an example of filtering an `$.ajax` response based on component data. This example expands on the skeleton mail update application you saw previously. In this example, assume the mail service always returns a successful HTTP response in the 200 range, even when there's no mail. Therefore, the `$.ajax` success function always runs. With `Deferred.pipe`, you can examine the data provided by the service and test whether or not there are messages in the data object. If there are messages, the response is accepted as a valid, successful response and the data is passed along to the `Deferred.done` methods. If there are no messages, you reject the promise with `Deferred.reject`. This sets off the `Deferred.fail` methods.

```
$.when(
  $.ajax( "/get/mail/" )
).pipe(
  function( data ) {
    if ( data.messages.length > 0 ) {
      return data
    } else {
      return $.Deferred().reject();
    }
  }
).done(
  newMessages,
  updateMessageList,
  updateUnreadIndicator
).fail(
  noMessages
).always(
  function() {
    var date = new Date();
      $("#lastUpdated").html("<strong>Folder Updated</strong>: "
        + date.toDateString()
        + " at "
        + date.toTimeString()
      );
  }
);
```

Code snippet is from advanced-pipe.txt

Resolving and Rejecting Promises

As you've seen in passing throughout this chapter, you occasionally need to manually resolve or reject promises. You've already encountered the two most common methods to do this: `Deferred.resolve` and `Deferred.reject`. What you haven't seen is the optional `args` argument in use. Both of these methods accept an optional argument that will, in turn, be passed to the `Deferred.done` or `Deferred.fail` methods depending on the resolution of the promise.

The following example shows a simplified illustration of these optional arguments. Returning to the mail example, the code snippet creates an updated date string to represent the time of the mail update. This string is passed along to the `Deferred.fail` and `Deferred.done` methods. Additionally, the number of messages is passed to `Deferred.done` to update the `#message` paragraph with the current number of new messages retrieved.

```
function newMessages( obj ) {
  $( "#message" ).text("you updated at "
    + obj.date
    + "  and have "
    + obj.number
    + " new messages"
    )
}
function noMessages( obj ) {
  $( "#message" ).text("you updated at "
      + obj.date
      + " and have no new messages"
    )
}
$.when(
  $.ajax( "/get/mail/" )
).pipe(
  function( data ) {
    var date = new Date();
    date = date.toDateString() + " at " + date.toTimeString();
    if ( data.messages.length > 0 ) {
      return $.Deferred().resolve({
        date: date,
        number: data.messages.length
      });
    } else {
      return $.Deferred().reject({
        date: date
      });
    }
  }
).done(
  newMessages
).fail(
  noMessages
);
```

Code snippet is from resolving-and-rejecting.txt

Additionally, the related methods `Deferred.rejectWith()` and `Deferred.resolveWith()` are available to allow you to set a specified `this` context as the first argument when resolving or rejecting a Deferred.

Tracking Progress with Deferred.progress and Deferred.notify

Added in jQuery 1.7, the `Deferred.progress` and `Deferred.notify` methods combine to allow for in-process updating of long-running functions.

The basic setup is simple. At different points in your application, you set `notify` methods that are designed to fire at specific points in an application or in a long-running method. `Deferred.notify` accepts an optional argument, which will be passed along to the `Deferred.progress` callback. The related function `Deferred.notifyWith` accepts a context argument indicating the desired `this` context for the `Deferred.progress` callback. The `Deferred.progress` callback method is added to the chain. This callback method should be designed to handle whatever message was sent along via `Deferred.notify` or `Deferred.notifyWith`.

In the simple example that follows, the function `longRunning` is a Deferred that uses `setTimeout` to take `5000ms` to resolve its promise. Before the timer is started, there's a string notification sent out. The `progress` function accepts that argument and inserts the update text into the DOM. After the process is finished, you notify again that the process is complete and then manually resolve the promise.

In theory, the text update could have been handled by the `Deferred.done` callback, leaving the progress callback to handle just the original notification. There's just a nice symmetry to using `Deferred.notify` at both ends of the process. Also, there's always a case to be made for keeping repetition of code down to a minimum. So it just makes sense to keep all of the notifications bound to progress.

```javascript
var longRunning = function() {
  return $.Deferred(function(dfd) {
    dfd.notify( "operation started" )
    var callback = function() {
      dfd.notify( "operation finished" );
      dfd.resolve();
    }
    setTimeout( callback, 5000 );
  }).promise();
}
longRunning().progress(
  function( notification ) {
    $( "#notifier" ).text( notification ).fadeIn( 500 );
}).done(function() {
  $( "#notifier" ).css({
    "color" : "green",
    "font-weight" : "bold"
  })
});
```

Code snippet is from deferred-progress.txt

Debugging with Deferred.state

If you ever find the need to debug Deferred resolution (and you will if you ever get deep into using Deferreds), you'll be taking advantage of Deferred.state.

A simple utility function, Deferred.state returns a string value representing the current state of a Deferred. The three return values are "pending," "resolved," and "rejected."

Table 13-1 defines the three states.

TABLE 13-1 Potential Deferred States

STATE	DEFINITION
pending	The Deferred object is not yet in a completed state.
resolved	The Deferred object is in the resolved state, meaning that the deferred.resolve() method has been called and the Deferred's done callback methods have fired.
rejected	The Deferred object is in the resolved state, meaning that the deferred.reject() method has been called and the Deferred's fail callback methods have fired.

The following example shows Deferred.state calls sprinkled throughout a short Deferred chain based on the long-running function example from the previous section.

Available for
download on
Wrox.com

```
var longRunning = function() {
  return $.Deferred(function( dfd ) {
    dfd.notify( "operation started" );
    console.log( dfd.state );
    var callback = function() {
      dfd.notify( "operation finished" );
      dfd.resolve();
    }
    setTimeout( callback, 5000 );
  }).promise();
}


longRunning().progress(
  function( notification ) {
    console.log( dfd.state );
    $( "#notifier" ).text( notification ).fadeIn(500);
}).done(function() {
  console.log( dfd.state );
  $( "#notifier" ).css({
    "color" : "green",
    "font-weight" : "bold"
  })
});
```

Code snippet is from deferred-state.txt

SUMMARY

You should now have a solid understanding of the possibilities and power of jQuery's Deferred object and its many available methods.

Throughout the chapter, you've seen examples of Deferred being used to pull application logic outside of function bodies and into the more maintainable, flexible structure provided by methods like `Deferred.when`, `Deferred.then`, and `Deferred.done`.

You also learned about creating, resolving, and rejecting promises manually, a vital piece in unlocking the power of Deferred.

Additionally, you had some exposure to more obscure options like the ability to notify on the progress of a Deferred and the ins and outs of debugging with `Deferred.state`.

Once your head is truly wrapped around Deferreds, you'll start looking at your current and past codebases with the goal of refactoring that old code to leverage the power and structure provided by Deferred. The flexibility and clarity it brings to your application code makes it one of the most important recent features added to the library.

14

Unit Testing with QUnit

In this chapter, you learn about the benefits of *unit testing* and about the specific unit testing framework created and used by the jQuery project itself, QUnit. You learn how to write your own tests and how to integrate QUnit with your own projects to increase code quality, maintainability, and overall confidence.

AN INTRODUCTION TO UNIT TESTING

If you're coming to jQuery and JavaScript engineering from some other programming discipline, the concept of unit testing is likely familiar to you. If that's the case, or you're among the minority of front-end engineers already doing unit testing, feel free to skip ahead to the sections that deal specifically with unit testing with QUnit. Otherwise, read on and learn about the benefits of a development approach centered on a structured, atomic testing framework.

As a note, this is an area of front-end engineering where there's an opportunity to get ahead of the curve. As the DailyJS *JavaScript Developer Survey 2011 Results* (http://dailyjs .com/2011/12/15/javascript-survey-results/) show, only 42 percent of JavaScript engineers are unit testing their code. That number is up from 2010, but it still shows that there's a gap between the tools commonly used in other programming disciplines and the ones used in the average JavaScript project.

As you'll soon see, the benefits are potentially significant, so ramping up to include unit testing in your development toolbox is a worthwhile effort.

WHAT IS UNIT TESTING?

Unit testing is a software practice where individual pieces of code (called units) are tested to determine their viability for a specific task. Units should be as small as possible, have one or a few inputs, and a single output.

Unit tests are generally automated, either as part of a build process, or as a pre-commit hook for check-ins or some other step of the software life cycle. Each test returns a binary pass/fail result.

Unit testing is a vital partner of a style of testing much more familiar to JavaScript developers: *functional testing*. Functional testing, what most people think of as "QA" or, more formally, acceptance testing, tests the site or application from the end user's perspective, after it's complete. Unit tests flip that model on its head. Unit tests are written alongside the code they're meant to test and are, most importantly, written from the developer's perspective.

Instead of testing the result, an end user will see unit tests analyze the expected result, from a software perspective, of a piece of code.

Benefits of Unit Testing

Some of the benefits of unit testing should be obvious. Testing code early and often improves code quality by uncovering issues that might be glossed over with simple, unstructured developer tests. Better code quality means fewer bugs during functional testing or, worse, in production.

"Fewer bugs" should make everyone involved with your project happy, including your users.

Beyond producing better code at the start of a project, one other key use of unit testing is *automated regression testing*. This is one of the most important uses of unit testing in the jQuery project itself. Using automated unit tests ensures that new features and/or bug fixes don't introduce other errors. This is a key to ensuring the stability of the library.

Rick Waldron's line in the *jQuery Bug Fixing Guide* (http://weblog.bocoup.com/javascript-jquery-bug-fixing-guide) bellows (in all caps) the importance of this with the admonition "ALWAYS RUN THE FULL SUITE BEFORE COMMITTING AND PUSHING A PATCH!!!" *That's clarity.*

Running the full test suite and ensuring all tests still pass means you've added to, but not subtracted from, the library as a whole.

The unit testing structure allows for easier *refactoring*. Because you know exactly what tests a particular piece of code needs to pass, you can more confidently refactor that code without the nagging fear that you're missing some dependency or other. No developer wants to feel the fear that the code she or he has rewritten will bring the whole application crashing down. Passing existing unit tests alleviates that fear significantly.

Additionally, because good unit testing relies on testing standalone modules, coding for unit testing forces developers to write *more loosely coupled code*. You want to avoid writing tests that spread across more than one module, so you're forced to write more abstract interfaces for inputs and outputs that can more easily be mocked up in a testing framework.

Coding for standalone unit tests also means that code can be tested and verified well before other, dependent systems are complete. With a well-documented interface and well-written unit tests, modules can be coded confidently even if other modules are to be created later on in the process. This can be especially beneficial with large teams spread across different organizations. A consultant can come in, create a module for which he's specifically suited, and if his code is well tested and works properly with the agreed-upon interface, he could theoretically move on to his next gig, well before the rest of the organization catches up to his progress. This doesn't negate the need for integration tests (tests to ensure that the actual systems involved function as expected when coupled together), but it should alleviate many of the surprises that can pop up with a less structured approach to development.

Test-Driven Development

Unit testing is the foundation of an advanced software methodology called Test-Driven Development (TDD). TDD encourages extremely short development cycles by centering the development life cycle on small unit tests. A developer will start by writing a failing unit test. He'll then write the minimum amount of code to pass that failing test. Finally, he'll move on to the next feature and/or refactor the code for better quality. Although this chapter doesn't go into specific TDD practices, TDD is often mentioned alongside unit testing, so the relationship is important to point out.

Basically, though you can't do TDD without unit tests, you *can* unit test without signing up to practice the full spectrum of TDD.

Understanding What Makes a Good Unit Test

Now that you know about the basics of unit testing, it's important to get a sense of how to create a quality unit test.

There are several hallmarks of a good unit test. The following list outlines some tenets to follow. In general, unit tests should be:

➤ **Automated:** Getting developers to do anything is hard enough as it is. Testing has to be as easy as possible or else there won't be buy-in from the front lines.

➤ **Fast:** Anything else and developers are going to be less likely to get with the testing program.

➤ **Focused:** They should test as narrow a component as is possible to cut down on ambiguity.

➤ **Independent:** This can be approached from two different angles. Both are important:

  ➤ **Self-contained:** Tests need to be atomic. This means that you may need to use some code to stand in for external inputs/outputs. This code is known in testing circles as "mocks" or "stubs." You see more about mocks later in the chapter.

  ➤ **Standalone:** In addition to having no external dependencies, unit tests should be able to be run in any order, without having sequential dependencies on any other test.

➤ **Consistent:** Tests should always return the same results.

➤ **Readable:** Tests should be clear in intent and focus so that the developers that follow you onto a project will be able to pick up on the purpose of your tests without so much ramp-up time.

➤ **Maintainable:** Unit tests will live with your project, so they should be maintainable. Having out-of-date tests is better than having no tests at all, but out-of-date tests will cause their own problems.

➤ **Trustworthy:** Developers should have complete confidence in the result of a unit test.

Now that you've got a handle on unit testing in general, it's time to take a look at the star of the show, QUnit.

GETTING STARTED WITH QUNIT

QUnit was born May 2008, out of the jQuery project's own testrunner. As it evolved, it was spun off as a separate project, gaining a name, documentation, and eventually being completely decoupled from jQuery.

If you're comfortable with the concepts of unit testing in general, getting up and running with QUnit is relatively straightforward. The following section outlines the key structure of QUnit testing and illustrates the basic assertions you'll use to test your code.

The QUnit Hello World Using equal

The following file shows a bare-bones QUnit test. It contains a copy of jQuery, a copy of the QUnit script file, a copy of the QUnit CSS file, and some script and markup that make up the body of the test itself.

The script block uses the QUnit method `test`. `test` does what the name implies — it sets up a test to run. Here it accepts a pair of arguments, a name, "Hello World," and a function that actually represents the test. The function argument itself uses the QUnit function `equal`. In unit testing terminology, `equal` is referred to as an *assertion*. An assertion indicates what you expect the code to do. As the name implies, `equal` tests equivalence. It accepts three arguments: an `actual` variable to be tested, the asserted `expected` value, and a `message` to display alongside the assertion.

The markup contains several QUnit-specific HTML elements:

`#qunit-header` contains the name of the test suite.

`#qunit-banner` shows up red with a failing test and green if all tests pass.

`#qunit-userAgent` displays the `navigator.userAgent` property.

`#qunit-tests` is a container for the test results.

#qunit-fixture is where you place and manipulate your test markup. You learn more about #qunit-fixture in a later section.

```html
<!DOCTYPE html>
<html>
<head>
<script
src="http://code.jquery.com/jquery-1.7.1.js">
</script>
<link rel="stylesheet"
  href="http://code.jquery.com/qunit/git/qunit.css"
  type="text/css"
  media="screen" />
<script
src="http://code.jquery.com/qunit/git/qunit.js"></script>
<script>
$( function(){
  test("Hello World", function() {
    var message = "hello world";
    equal( message,
      "hello world",
      "We expect the message to match"
    );
  });
});</script>
</head>
<body>
  <h1 id="qunit-header">QUnit example</h1>
  <h2 id="qunit-banner"></h2>
  <div id="qunit-testrunner-toolbar"></div>
    <h2 id="qunit-userAgent"></h2>
    <ol id="qunit-tests">
    </ol>
  <div id="qunit-fixture">Test Markup</div>
</body>
</html>
```

Code snippet is from simple-test.html

Running that single test produces the output shown in Figure 14-1.

FIGURE 14-1

If you see that for all of your tests, it's time to go to lunch. *You've earned it.*

The Differences between xUnit and QUnit

Although the name might imply otherwise, it should be noted that QUnit isn't part of the xUnit family.

xUnit is the name given to a family of testing frameworks that trace their roots back to a design by Kent Beck, outlined in the paper "Simple Smalltalk Testing: With Patterns" (http://www .xprogramming.com/testfram.htm). Originally implemented for Smalltalk as SUnit, this design has gone on to be ported to several other languages including Java (JUnit), C++ (CppUnit), and .NET (NUnit).

Though QUnit shares basic concepts like assertions, significant differences exist between the xUnit design and QUnit. For example, in the previous example, you saw two arguments for `equal:actual` and `expected`. In the xUnit design, the order of those arguments is reversed.

Say xUnit and QUnit also have completely different assertion names. Looking again at the previous example, `equal` is analogous to the xUnit assertion `assertEquals`. They serve the same purpose, just with slightly different syntax. Another difference is that some assertions included in xUnit are missing from QUnit.

None of this will matter if you're not familiar with the xUnit family, of course. If you are, it is worth keeping your eye on the differences so you don't get tripped up moving forward.

Now that you've gotten that potential gotcha out of the way, you can continue your examination of QUnit.

A Failing QUnit Test

You've seen a passing test; now it's time to look at a failing test. With the same markup as the previous example, you can run the following `test` with an `equal` assertion:

```
test("Hello World", function() {
    var message = "Goodbye cruel world";
    equal( message, "hello world", We expect the message to match " );
});
```

Code snippet is from failing-test.html

As you can see in Figure 14-2, a failing test provides much more interesting information than a passing test. For starters, the message defined as the third `test` argument is displayed alongside the `expected` and `actual` values of the variable being tested, in this case "hello world" and "Goodbye cruel world," respectively. Additionally, it does a diff of the variables and a pointer to the line that generated the error.

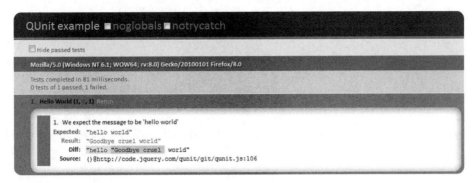

FIGURE 14-2

Testing for Truthiness with ok

In some ways, this would have made a better "Hello World" example, because it's the most basic assertion. ok accepts two arguments: a Boolean state to test and a message to display in the case of a failing test. It passes if the state is truthy. The following code example shows ok in action. It tests whether the return value of a function is an array using the jQuery method $.isArray.

Available for
download on
Wrox.com

```
test("Truthiness is golden", function() {
  var val = function(){
    var arr = [1,2,3,4,5]
    //dostuff
    return arr;
  }
  ok( $.isArray(val()), "We're expecting an array as a return value" );

});
```

Code snippet is from ok.html

Setting Expectations

One good habit to get into is to set expectations for your tests. Basically, you tell QUnit, "Expect to see *x* assertions." If QUnit doesn't see exactly *x* assertions, the whole test will fail. This is true even if the assertions that did run all passed.

Tests might not run for a variety of reasons, from something as simple as a typo to more complicated issues relating to application flow. You see the prime example of why expect is important when you learn about asynchronous testing in a later section.

You set expectations in QUnit in two ways. The first is by calling the expect method within the test body. The following example shows expect in use. Two assertions are expected but only one is present, so the whole test fails.

```
test("Hello World", function() {
    expect(2)
    var message = "hello world";
    equal( message, "hello world", " We expect the message to match." );
});
```

Code snippet is from expect.html

Figure 14-3 illustrates the result of this test. The test fails even though all of the assertions that did run passed.

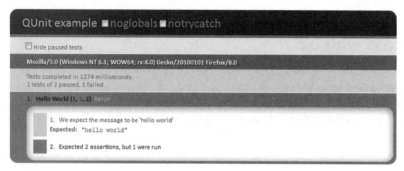

FIGURE 14-3

In addition to the `expect` method, it's possible to set expectations with an optional second argument to the `test` method:

```
test("Hello World", 2, function() {
    var message = "hello world";
    equal( message, "hello world", "We expect the message to match" );
});
```

Code snippet is from expect.html

While both are valid options, and you'll see both in use in large test suites, the explicit call to `expect` within the test body is much cleaner and easier to read. I prefer it over the second argument to `test`.

Additional Assertions

Table 14-1 lists all available assertions in QUnit. For the most part, they all have the same straightforward syntax you've already seen with the other assertions in this section. They either provide negative assertions like `notEqual` (the opposite of `equal`) or offer more/different levels of precision like `deepEqual` and `strictEqual`. Familiarize yourself with this list; it will help when you're writing your own tests and need that extra bit of precision.

TABLE 14-1: QUnit Assertions

ASSERTION	ARGUMENTS	DESCRIPTION
Ok	state, message	A Boolean assertion. Passes if state is truthy.
Equal	actual, expected, message	A comparison assertion. Compares actual and expected. Passes if actual and expected are leniently (==) equals.
notEqual	actual, expected, message	A comparison assertion. Compares actual and expected. Passes if actual and expected are leniently unequal.
deepEqual	actual, expected, message	A deep recursive comparison assertion. Recursively compares objects. Fails if some property isn't equal.
notDeepEqual	actual, expected, message	A deep recursive comparison assertion. Recursively compares objects. The inverse of deepEqual. Passes if some property isn't equal.
strictEqual	actual, expected, message	A comparison assertion. Compares actual and expected. Passes if actual and expected are strictly (===) equal.
notStrictEqual	actual, expected, message	A comparison assertion. Compares actual and expected. Passes if actual and expected are strictly unequal.
Raises	block, expected, message	This assertion tests if code throws an error.

Testing DOM Elements

If you're doing any DOM manipulations (and because you're reading a jQuery book, you probably are), you'll want to be able to test the output. QUnit provides an interface to do just that. To test DOM elements, simply set your markup in #qunit-fixture, make your DOM magic, and then use assertions to test the state of the DOM. QUnit will reset qunit-fixture after each test.

A simple example is shown in the following code:

```
<!DOCTYPE html>
<html>
<head>
<script src="http://code.jquery.com/jquery-1.7.1.js"></script>
<link rel="stylesheet" href="http://code.jquery.com/qunit/git/qunit.css" />
<script type="text/javascript" src="http://code.jquery.com/qunit/git/qunit.js"></script>
<script>
$(function(){
```

```
test("DOM", function() {
  expect(3);
  $test = $("#dom-test");
  $test.css("width","200px").text("Testing the DOM").show();

  equal( $test.css("width"), "200px", "200px!" );
  equal( $test.text(), "Testing the DOM", "We're testing the DOM" );
  equal( $test.css("display"), "block", "display:block" );
  });
});
</script>
</head>
<body>
  <h1 id="qunit-header">QUnit example</h1>
  <h2 id="qunit-banner"></h2>
  <div id="qunit-testrunner-toolbar"></div>
  <h2 id="qunit-userAgent"></h2>
  <ol id="qunit-tests">
  </ol>
  <div id="qunit-fixture"><div id="dom-test" style="display:none"></div></div>
</body>
</html>
```

Code snippet is from dom-test.html

The jQuery project contains many more examples. With the amount of DOM manipulation that goes on with jQuery, the project needs to ensure that it's performing reliably. Therefore, hundreds of assertions exist to test the state of the DOM.

Using noglobals and notrycatch

Two additional options to note have been staring you in the face throughout all the examples you've seen so far. They appear as options on every test as two checkboxes, `noglobals` and `notrycatch`, as shown in Figure 14-4.

FIGURE 14-4

Both set file-level flags on the test that will change the behavior of all tests performed on the page.

The `noglobals` flag will fail a test if a new global variable is introduced by the running code. If you're coding in ES5 strict mode or are running a code linter like JSHint (http://www.jshint .com/), this shouldn't be a problem for you. It's still a useful check to have for those situations where globals might sneak through to the testing phase.

This simple example shows a test that will trigger the `noglobals` flag and the ensuing error message in the testrunner, as shown in Figure 14-5:

```
test("Hello World", function() {
  message = "hello world";
  equal( message, "hello world", "We expect the message to be 'hello world'");
});
```

FIGURE 14-5

Setting notrycatch will run QUnit without a surrounding try-catch block. This will actually stop the testrunner in its tracks but will allow for deeper debugging of an issue. The following example shows this option in action:

```
test("No Try-Catch", function() {
// $$ will cause an exception
  var test = $$(this).isGonnaExplode();

  equal( test , "Return Value of Doom", "We're looking for a cool return value" );
});
```

Figure 14-6 shows the exception in Firebug. Without notrycatch, the Firebug console would be empty and the error would be logged in the testrunner.

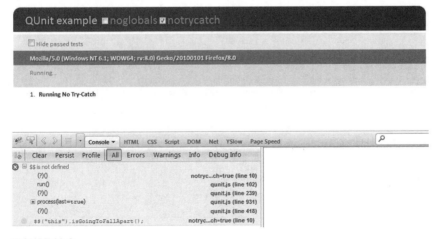

FIGURE 14-6

In addition to running these tests by checking some checkboxes, you can also run them by appending a querystring parameter to the URL. To run tests with `noglobals`, for example, you would run this test list:

```
http://example.com/tests/tests.html?noglobals=true
```

This is a handy feature if you're running multiple tests on a large application.

Organizing Tests into Modules

One key feature of QUnit is the ability to organize tests into modules. Just like the code you're testing, the ability to organize code into separate modules allows for greater flexibility when running tests.

Grouping multiple tests that target a specific method or feature is a prime example of module usage. Looking at the test suite for the jQuery core in Figure 14-7, you can see that the project is broken into 17 separate modules.

⏱ Latest commit to the **master** branch			
Reformat jshint errors to be readable; make post-compile.js write dir...			
rwldrn authored December 15, 2011			commit `f724bc6c92`
→| **timmywil** committed December 15, 2011			

jquery / test / unit

name	age	message	history
ajax.js	December 06, 2011	Fix #10466. jQuery.param() should treat object-wrapped primitives as ... [rwldrn]	
attributes.js	December 06, 2011	Fix #5571. Setters should treat `undefined` as a no-op and be chainable. [gibson042]	
callbacks.js	November 06, 2011	Fix #10691. Remove all instances of equals() and same(), as these are... [mikesherov]	
core.js	December 06, 2011	Refine the jQuery.isWindow check. [rafBM]	
css.js	December 12, 2011	When the width/height computed unit is not pixels, return that instea... [timmywil]	
data.js	December 06, 2011	Fix #5571. Setters should treat `undefined` as a no-op and be chainable. [gibson042]	
deferred.js	November 08, 2011	Have Deferred.always return the object onto which it is currently att... [jaubourg]	
dimensions.js	December 06, 2011	Fix #5571. Setters should treat `undefined` as a no-op and be chainable. [gibson042]	
effects.js	December 08, 2011	Fix #8498. Add cssHooks[prop].expand for use by animate(). [mikesherov]	
event.js	December 13, 2011	Fix #11021. There should be no mangling of the "hover" namespace. [dmethvin]	
exports.js	November 14, 2011	Landing pull request 586. Create exports.js for exporting jQuery to w... [jrburke]	
manipulation.js	December 06, 2011	Fix #5571. Setters should treat `undefined` as a no-op and be chainable. [gibson042]	
offset.js	December 06, 2011	Fix #5571. Setters should treat `undefined` as a no-op and be chainable. [gibson042]	
queue.js	December 06, 2011	Fix #5571. Setters should treat `undefined` as a no-op and be chainable. [gibson042]	
selector.js	October 13, 2011	Update sizzle; Add sizzle cache collision iframe test. Fixes #8539. [timmywil]	
support.js	November 18, 2011	No global vars allowed. Declare 'body' in support. [timmywil]	
traversing.js	December 12, 2011	Use Sizzle.Expr.match.globalPOS for identifying POS selectors in trav... [timmywil]	

FIGURE 14-7

Additionally, you can filter modules at run time (more on that in a second) and set up specific environment variables for the module's test to run under.

The following code shows a simplified module, complete with two additional new features that empower the custom environment: `setup` and `teardown`. These are methods that are run before and after the tests in the module, and allow for great flexibility in terms of setting up the test environment for similar methods.

The following example sets up a variable to test throughout the module, `arr` (an array). It also stores a value in a variable, `control`, to test against later, on the off chance that something crazy happens to `arr` during the test. Inside the module itself are two `tests`. One contains two `ok` assertions and the other contains `deepEqual`. These are all testing different pieces of the Array.

```
module("fun with arrays", {
  setup: function() {
    this.arr = [1,2,3,4,5];
    this.control = this.arr.length;
  },
  teardown: function() {
    equal(this.arr.length, this.control, "Just Checking to see if it's still
an Array");
  }
});
test("Truthiness is golden", function() {
  expect(3);
  var bool = $.isArray(this.arr);

  ok( bool, "We're expecting an array" );

  bool = this.arr.indexOf(5);
  ok(bool, "We expect 5 to be in the Array");

});
test("Getting Deep", function() {
  expect(2);
  deepEqual(this.arr, [1,2,3,4,5]);
});
```

Code snippet is from module.html

Running these tests produces the output shown in Figure 14-8. As you can see, the tests are nested under the "fun with arrays" module name.

FIGURE 14-8

This organizational approach allows you to test specific site sections or features without having to run an entire test suite. This is a useful feature if you're on a large project with many associated tests.

Filtering Tests with URL Parameters

Similar to the way you can set the `noglobals` and `notrycatch` flags with query parameters, you can also filter tests. Simply add `?filter=filtername` to the URL and QUnit will only run tests whose names contain `filtername`. This can be based on module names or test names and allows you to easily target specific features when doing tests.

The use of this feature is made apparent when bug fixing the jQuery core. Although you're required to run the full test suite before issuing a pull request, you *don't* want to test the entire library when you're testing against your feature-specific fix.

With filtering, you can only test against the pertinent areas while doing development and then you only need to run the full test once, before you send off your (presumably heroic) bug fix.

ASYNCHRONOUS TESTING

Sometimes, you need to be able to control the flow of a test. An obvious example is an Ajax request. Looking at the following code sample, you see an Ajax request that is part of the `test`. Inside the callback are two assertions, `ok` and `equal`.

Available for
download on
Wrox.com

```
test("stops & starts", function() {
expect(2);

var url = "/data/json/";

$.getJSON(url, {name: "Testing"}, function(data) {
ok(data, "data is returned from the server");
equal(data.name, "Testing", "We're Testing");
});
});
```

Code snippet is from broken-ajax-test.html

Running the test generates the result shown in Figure 14-9.

FIGURE 14-9

This is an unexpected result.

Because the Ajax request is asynchronous, neither of the tests is run. You're not going to catch many errors that way. Thankfully, QUnit provides a pair of methods to control this flow: `start` and `stop`. Rewriting the previous test to work as expected, the test is paused with `stop()` before the Ajax request, and then the test is restarted with `start()` at the end of the callback.

```
test("asynch", function() {
    expect(2);

    stop();
    $.getJSON("/data/json/", function(data) {
        ok( data, "We expect to get data from the server");
        equal(data.name, "Testing", "We expect the name property to match);
        start();
    });

});
```

Code snippet is from start-stop.html

Running this code produces the desired result. As you see in Figure 14-10, both expected tests are run and both pass.

FIGURE 14-10

Using asyncTest

Like the convenience methods available with `$.Ajax`, QUnit has a convenience method for the common pattern of starting a `test`, and then stopping it for an asynchronous action.

The following code sample shows the previous example rewritten with that convenience method, `asyncTest`:

```
asyncTest("asynch", function() {
    expect(2);

    $.getJSON("/data/json/", function(data) {

        ok( data, "We expect to get data from the server");
```

```
    equal(data.name, "Testing", "We expect the name to match);

    start();
  });

});
```

Code snippet is from asynctest.html

This is a definitely a recommended option. It guarantees your asynchronous tests will be set up correctly and will allow you to differentiate between regular and asynchronous tests. Doing so will make your tests more readable. Other developers will know, without reading any of the assertions or other logic within the `test` body, that this is an asynchronous test.

Mocking Ajax Requests

Though it's possible to test Ajax requests with live data, it's not recommended. As you'll remember from earlier in the chapter, one of the fundamentals of unit testing is that tests be self-contained. To that end, it's a best practice to mock your Ajax requests.

Thankfully, there's a plugin already available to do just that in QUnit. Mockjax from the fine folks at appendto (`https://github.com/appendto/jquery-mockjax`) allows you to set up URLs that will be captured by the Mockjax plugin. Doing so means they'll be intercepted before they hit the traditional Ajax method and the response will be handled by Mockjax. Mockjax allows you to craft a testable response and customize it with headers of your own design.

Rewriting the previous example to better follow testing best practices, the following example shows a way to wire up a proper, testable Ajax request with Mockjax.

In this example, the Mockjax plugin takes three arguments: the `url` to be captured and mapped to Mockjax, the `responseTime`, used to simulate latency, and the `responseText`, which, in this case, will be converted to the JSON `data` passed into any successful Ajax callback methods.

With Mockjax, the test is now self-contained.

Available for
download on
Wrox.com

```
test("asynch", function() {
expect(2)
  $.mockjax({
  url: '/data/json/',
  responseTime: 100,
  responseText: {
    status: 'success',
    name: 'Testing'
  }
});
  stop();
  $.getJSON("/data/json/", function(data) {
    ok( data, "We expect to get data from the server");
      equal( data.name, "Testing", "We expect the name match");
```

```
        start();
    });

});
```

Code snippet is from mockjax.html

Even without an Internet connection or a completed data service, the test will pass. This allows you to test *your* code without worrying about the state of other parts of the system. If you're working in a large team, this ability to write and *test* to an interface without the interface existing is invaluable. Figure 14-11 shows a completed test using mockjax.

FIGURE 14-11

Additional Mockjax Features

Because modern web application development needs to handle more than just a simple, successful JSON request, you'll be glad to know that Mockjax has enough features to handle most Ajax situations. It's worth exploring them in full because you never know what you might have to accommodate in testing, but the two that follow are worth looking at right off the bat.

Using a Mockjax Data Proxy

One especially nice feature is the ability to create a data proxy. Listing out a couple of data elements when setting up a simple test is convenient, but if you're trying to test a full interface, it can be awkward to wrap a large data structure inside the plugin setup call. To fix this, Mockjax has an option to set a data proxy, which will point to a static file to serve as the data source for your Ajax request. All it takes, other than having the file itself, is to add an optional `proxy` parameter when the plugin is set up. The simplest possible example would look like this:

```
$.mockjax({
  url: '/data/json',
  proxy: '/mock/data.json'
});
```

Do that and you can use complicated data structures without worrying about embedding them directly in your testing framework. Note that you do need to have access to `JSON.stringify`, which may require the use of `json2.js` (`https://github.com/douglascrockford/JSON-js`) if you're going to be testing in legacy browsers.

Adding Additional HTTP Headers

Mockjax also allows you to set additional HTTP headers. For advanced Ajax programming, this is vital. Some standard ones, like HTTP status and contentType are available directly from the Mockjax setup object. Others can be set using an optional headers property, which can contain a series of name/value pairs representing the desired HTTP headers. The following example shows all three of these headers:

```
$.mockjax({
  url: '/data/json',
//file not found!
  status: 40,
  contentType: 'text/json',
  headers: {
    secretSauce: 'shhh'
  }
});
```

PUTTING IT ALL TOGETHER IN A TEST SUITE

Once again, the jQuery test suite is going to offer some lessons on how to organize QUnit tests. There's really no better place to look for practical QUnit implementation hints because it's the largest, most mature set of QUnit tests available.

As you saw earlier, the jQuery test suite is broken out into 17 modules representing more granular sections of the library, like data, css, and deferred. Within those modules are multiple tests, each containing multiple assertions. To get a sense of how those modules are organized in a real project, take a look at this heavily edited version of the Core test module presented in the following code sample. Many tests have been dropped and almost all of the assertions have been commented out, but the lessons on structure, granularity, and the way tests evolve can still be seen throughout.

Specific features are tested individually with multiple assertions per test. Also, note the presence of bug report numbers as in jQuery.merge() and jQuery('html', context). These issues were reported, test cases were created, and the code was fixed. The test cases remain, providing confidence that the bug remains fixed even months or years later. Additionally, a simple reminder that QUnit is JavaScript and that tests can be dynamically created can be seen in the jQuery .camelCase() test, which uses an Array of test subjects and then jQuery.each to loop through them, testing each of the seven expected assertions.

```
module("core", { teardown: moduleTeardown });

test("Basic requirements", function() {
    expect(7);
  ok( Array.prototype.push, "Array.push()" );
  ok( Function.prototype.apply, "Function.apply()" );
  ok( document.getElementById, "getElementById" );
  ok( document.getElementsByTagName, "getElementsByTagName" );
  ok( RegExp, "RegExp" );
  ok( jQuery, "jQuery" );
```

```
  ok( $, "$" );
});

test("jQuery()", function() {
  expect(29);
//29 assertions
});

test("selector state", function() {
  expect(31);
//31 assertions
});
test("jQuery('html')", function() {
  expect(18);
//18 assertions
});

test("jQuery('html', context)", function() {
  expect(1);

  var $div = jQuery("<div/>")[0];
  var $span = jQuery("<span/>", $div);
  equal($span.length, 1, "Verify a span created with a div context works,
#1763");
});

test("first()/last()", function() {
  expect(4);

  var $links = jQuery("#ap a"), $none = jQuery("asdf");

  deepEqual( $links.first().get(), q("google"), "first()" );
  deepEqual( $links.last().get(), q("mark"), "last()" );

  deepEqual( $none.first().get(), [], "first() none" );
  deepEqual( $none.last().get(), [], "last() none" );
});

test("map()", function() {
  expect(8);
//8 assertions
});

test("jQuery.merge()", function() {
  expect(8);

  var parse = jQuery.merge;

  deepEqual( parse([],[]), [], "Empty arrays" );

  deepEqual( parse([1],[2]), [1,2], "Basic" );
  deepEqual( parse([1,2],[3,4]), [1,2,3,4], "Basic" );

  deepEqual( parse([1,2],[]), [1,2], "Second empty" );
```

```
  deepEqual( parse([],[1,2]), [1,2], "First empty" );

    // Fixed at [5998], #3641
    deepEqual( parse([-2,-1], [0,1,2]), [-2,-1,0,1,2],
    "Second array including a zero (falsy)");

    // After fixing #5527
    deepEqual( parse([], [null, undefined]), [null, undefined],
    "Second array including null and undefined values");
    deepEqual( parse({length:0}, [1,2]), {length:2, 0:1, 1:2},
    "First array like");
});

test("jQuery.extend(Object, Object)", function() {
  expect(28);
  //28 assertions
});

test("jQuery.each(Object,Function)", function() {
  expect(14);
//14 assertions
});

test("jQuery.sub() - Static Methods", function(){
    expect(18);
//18 assertions
});

test("jQuery.sub() - .fn Methods", function(){
  expect(378);
//378 assertions

});

test("jQuery.camelCase()", function() {

  var tests = {
    "foo-bar": "fooBar",
    "foo-bar-baz": "fooBarBaz",
    "girl-u-want": "girlUWant",
    "the-4th-dimension": "the4thDimension",
    "-o-tannenbaum": "OTannenbaum",
    "-moz-illa": "MozIlla",
    "-ms-take": "msTake"
  };

  expect(7);

  jQuery.each( tests, function( key, val ) {
    equal( jQuery.camelCase( key ), val, "Converts: " + key + " => " + val );
  });
});
```

Code snippet is from jquery-suite.html

SUMMARY

You've now been introduced to the fundamental concepts of unit testing. You've also been introduced to everything you need to write your own unit tests with QUnit. From the assertions you'll use to the methods you'll use to test DOM manipulations and Ajax interactions, you have a full toolset at your disposal to start testing your own applications.

This chapter also marks the end of the book. At this point, you've gone in-depth through much of what jQuery has to offer. From the core concepts covered in the first half of the book to the more advanced topics covered in the later chapters, you should be a confident, capable jQuery programmer. Moving beyond simple DOM manipulations, canned animations, and implementing plugins, you should be ready to go toe to toe with the ninjas and pirates of the JavaScript world. Maybe you're going to dive in and do some plugin development of your own, enhancing and extending core jQuery functionality into new and useful areas, or maybe you're going to dive in and add some rigor to your JavaScript practice with a formal testing framework using QUnit. Whatever lessons you take away from this book, the biggest one should be that any library or tool is only as valuable as you make it. Diving into the subject with the depth you have in this book will empower you to make jQuery very valuable indeed.

We can't wait to see what you do with that power.

Plugins Used in this Book

Firebug Firebug is a Firefox plugin that provides multiple web development tools to edit, debug, and monitor CSS, HTML, and JavaScript.

```
http://getfirebug.com/
```

FireQuery FireQuery is a Firebug extension for jQuery development.

```
http://firequery.binaryage.com/
```

Modernizr Modernizr is a small JavaScript library that helps you take advantage of the new HTML5 and CSS3 capabilities by providing feature detection, utilities, and element normalization in legacy versions of Internet Explorer.

```
http://www.modernizr.com/
```

QUnit QUnit is a powerful, easy-to-use, JavaScript test suite used by the jQuery project to test its code and plugins.

```
http://docs.jquery.com/QUnit
```

Data Link Plugin The Data Link plugin links objects together, allowing for each object's properties to update when one or more properties change.

```
https://github.com/jquery/jquery-datalink
```

Globalization Plugin The Globalization plugin enables complex culture-aware number and date parsing and formatting. This includes the raw culture information for hundreds of different languages and countries, as well as an extensible system for localization.

```
https://github.com/jquery/globalize
```

HTML5-Form Plugin This plugin adds HTML5-specific form validation to all versions of Internet Explorer and Firefox.

```
http://www.matiasmancini.com.ar/jquery-plugin-ajax-form-validation-html5.html
```

Easing Plugin The Easing plugin is a jQuery plugin that gives advanced easing options for animations.

```
http://gsgd.co.uk/sandbox/jquery/easing/
```

Metadata Plugin Metadata plugin extracts metadata from classes, child elements, and attributes including HTML5 data attributes.

```
http://archive.plugins.jquery.com/project/metadata
```

JsViews JsViews is a plugin that provides data-driven views, built on top of JsRender templates.

```
https://github.com/BorisMoore/jsviews
```

JsRender JsRender provides high-performance, pure string-based JavaScript template rendering without DOM or jQuery dependency.

```
https://github.com/BorisMoore/jsrender
```

jQuery Templates Plugin This plugin integrates with jQuery to provide templating to data objects or arrays to be rendered in the HTML DOM.

```
http://api.jquery.com/category/plugins/templates/
```

Mockjax Plugin This plugin provides Ajax mocking for requests/responses within the standard behavior flow.

```
https://github.com/appendto/jquery-mockjax
```

JsFiddle This plugin provides a web-based testing environment for HTML, CSS, and JavaScript programs. This is a good way to test out the code samples in this book.

```
http://jsfiddle.net
```

INDEX